TEN THOUSAND EYES

Richard Collier

TEN
THOUSAND
EYES

THE LYONS PRESS

940. 54 COL
8-29-11

To the Men and Women
—living and dead—who broke down
' The Wall '

FOREWORD

THIS IS a true story about a group of civilians, a stretch of coast-line, and a Wall made up of guns and concrete and steel. On one day in history—6th June, 1944—all the war shrank to this stretch of coastline, and to break down this Wall was the most important task on earth.

That we succeeded was due to many factors—not the least being the valour of those civilians. " Securing the blue print of the German Atlantic Wall," General Omar Bradley, who led the First U.S. Army on D-Day, said later, " was an incredible and brilliant feat—so valuable that the landing operation succeeded with a minimum loss of men and material." Those who made it possible are the heroes and heroines of my story, having worked two years for this day, though many died before the day had dawned.

The fantastic conception of a network of amateur spies formed to crack Hitler's Atlantic Wall was only the beginning of it all. Some of that has been told before in the *Souvenirs of Colonel Passy* and Colonel Rémy's *Memoirs of a Secret Agent of Free France,* and I am grateful to M. André Dewavrin (" Colonel Passy ") and M. Gilbert Renault (" Colonel Rémy ") for permission to draw on these, as well as for the patient hours they spent answering my questions in Paris and Lisbon.

My special gratitude is due to General Charles de Gaulle and the members of his Cabinet, particularly to M. Olivier Guichard, Colonel de Bonneval, and M. Jacques Foccart; to M. Marcel Girard, Colonel and Madame Corbasson, M. Robert Thomas, M. and Mme. Léonard Gille and M. André Heintz for countless hours of testimony; to them and to many other officials for the opportunity to study papers and maps in the archives of the Ministère de la Guerre, Comité des Anciens Chefs de Réseau des F.F.C., and the Ministère de la Défense Nationale. Capitaine de Vaisseau Yves Delpeuc'h put at my disposal his brilliant unpublished study of the Atlantic Wall; M. Daniel Lomenech generously supplied photographs; M. Denizet and Professor Cras of the Service Historique de la Marine, M. Yecompte de Lisle, Municipal Archivist of Caen, and M. Henri Michel, Comité d'Histoire de la Deuxième Guerre Mondiale, found time to guide me through a mass of material, published and unpublished. There were others, too, more than can be mentioned here, but none of them are forgotten.

Lastly, to my wife, who encouraged me to write it, researched it with me, kept me up to it and typed every word of it, I owe a debt which a lifetime of writing could never translate into words.

Kingswood,   R. C.
August, 1957

CONTENTS

CONTENTS

ILLUSTRATIONS

Chapter One

A PLAN IS DEVISED

ON THE day that France fell, Captain André Dewavrin boarded the S.S. *Meknes*, the last troopship in a convoy escaping from Brest, shortly before midnight.

Later, as the ship slid silently across the harbour, he stood alone in the bows and took his last view of France: the white flashes of the German guns, trembling like summer lightning above Saint Thégonnec. For a moment Dewavrin felt frightened and alone, thinking that now he belonged nowhere at all.

Dewavrin did not look like a man who was going to play much part in the war. At twenty-eight his fair wispy hair was fast receding above a domed scholar's forehead; the brooding almost puzzled look that pouted his full gentle lips and creased the smooth pink and white skin lent colour to this impression. Many people who baulked his purpose during the next four years were deceived by this, failing to note that the steady blue eyes could glow with cold implacability, or the stubborn almost sculptured line of the jaw, the most striking clues of his refusal to be cheated of his destiny.

Most of that night, 19th June, he spent in the bows, still sweating in the thick polar kit that only five days back he had worn as a captain of engineers at Narvik, and thinking about North Africa, where he believed that his regiment was routed. Absorbed in the future he could thus press back the shame of a past still only twelve hours old: the street barricades ripped to matchwood by white-faced men scared of reprisals, rifles stacked ingloriously outside bistros, their owners sprawled drunkenly in the sour-smelling twilight, the fishermen's wives, in their rusty black, like mourning, weeping openly on the

13

quays. Petain had revealed his country's destiny, and the word had flashed like wireless from house to house: " It's over . . . it's *over* . . . the old man's said so. . . ."

One thought had shaped itself in Dewavrin's mind as the poison of defeat did its work: what could he, a regular soldier, do above and beyond the call of duty to wipe out this shame? The thought stayed with him for a long time and through much heartbreak before the resolve was triumphantly discharged, shaped and adjusted by the changing needs of war. None of the almost incredible events for which he was responsible formed part of a predictable pattern. There was no one moment in which André Dewavrin saw both the magnitude of the target which only the shock-wave of six million men could crumble, and the means by which each of the target's individual features could be known and assembled months in advance. War is seldom so dramatic or so obligingly cut-and-dried. The most he could foresee then was that of the 1000 Frenchman aboard the *Meknes* many would one day storm ashore on the coast of France, and if there was any justice in the world, he would survive to help them.

At dawn on 21st June someone shouted land, and they all tumbled up from their cabins, some in black silk shoulder capes, some in riding-boots and white leggings, some in shirt-sleeves, shivering in the pre-dawn chill. In the milky light from the east they could see the calm grey stretch of water merging into smoke stacks and customs sheds and what looked like miles of slate roofs.

" *Nom de Dieu*," someone groaned. " This isn't Africa. It's England. . . ."

It began to rain.

Dewavrin took a long purposeful look at Southampton Water, then went below to finish dressing. His plan remained the same. It was now a question of adjusting the details.

A warrant officer led them through drizzling streets to Trentham Park, and there for eight days they stayed under canvas, lamenting the shame that had befallen their country. Only gradually did news filter through to them of an unknown

French General who had taken virtually the same stand as Churchill. Isolated by the Norway campaign, they did not know that this man, de Gaulle, had been recently appointed French Under Secretary of State for War, but the general impression of the newcomer—" Big Charley," the men called him —was that he meant business. Though his refusal to surrender was treason in the eyes of Vichy, there was no doubt that de Gaulle was a Frenchman who loved his country with a love fiercely proud and tenderly compassionate. The only honourable course, he told officers and men, was to do as he had done, disavow Petain and fight on from England. For Dewavrin, who had been away from camp during his visit, a few recalled his ringing climax: " France has lost a battle—but she has not lost a war! Every Frenchman who can must rally under one banner, so that through them France can take its rightful place in this struggle. . . ."

Dewavrin would have hated the idea of being dubbed a romantic, yet despite the decision of his fellow-officers to continue their war from French soil, he was secretly attracted by de Gaulle's lonely stand. Twenty-four hours of heartsearching followed, before his decision had crystallised, but at dawn on 1st July while his regiment was en route to Casablanca, Dewavrin had already arrived in London in search of de Gaulle.

The General's headquarters were at St. Stephen's House, Westminster, and the young regular's first glimpse of this drab red-brick commercial building was not inspiring. A man in worn blue livery took him three flights in a creaking lift to join a queue of officers and civilians, many of them weary and unshaven with bloodshot eyes. Through an open doorway he saw a long thin lieutenant of cavalry skipping like a ballet dancer round a battery of shrilling telephones, pencil poised in one hand as he fumbled for the mouthpiece.

By mid-morning it was Dewavrin's turn. He followed the lieutenant into a long well-lit room overlooking the Thames, and there was de Gaulle behind a vast executive desk, cold grey eyes boring into him. As the General uncoiled his six feet three inches and shook hands formally, Dewavrin noticed he was

15

smoking heavily, and later he came to know this as a sign that de Gaulle was under pressure.

Dewavrin saluted smartly, gave his name and rank. Then, before he could gather breath, came the questions:

" Regular or temporary? "

" Regular, *mon Général*."

" Any decorations? " Fast and staccato, like carbine fire.

" None, *mon Général*." (Though the M.C. and the Croix de Guerre for his work at Narvik came through a bit later.)

" Speak English? "

" Fluently, *mon Général*."

" Done any fighting yet? "

" I was at Narvik, *mon Général*."

A second's pause. Then: " All right, *you* can start my Intelligence Service—the Deuxième Bureau. Lieutenant de Boislambert, outside, will find you an office."

Dewavrin drew himself up and saluted crisply. Furiously absorbed in papers again, the General did not even see him. Dewavrin found himself outside, breathing a little faster than when he had gone in, then glanced at his watch. De Gaulle had taken exactly one minute twenty-five seconds to chart his destiny.

An orderly led him to a small meagrely-furnished room smelling of dust and ink. Sitting down, Dewavrin stared from the window at the tugs fussing on the grey river, and tried to collect his thoughts. He, André Dewavrin, was in charge of the Free French Intelligence Service. As of this moment, without recruits, he *was* the Free French Intelligence Service. It was unthinkable, yet it was true.

André Charles Lucien Dewavrin, the shy former Assistant Professor of Fortifications at Saint-Cyr, the Sandhurst of France, who knew pages of Plessis and Legrand's Standard Manual of Fortifications by heart, and could tell you all the structural weaknesses of the famous Hindenburg Line, knew nothing whatsoever about military Intelligence, or what it set out to achieve, and had, moreover, no conception of what made up a Deuxième Bureau, let alone how it operated. Dewavrin was certain of only one thing: his new chief would want quick results.

Hour by hour, day by day, he racked his brains trying to achieve an end. One of the first problems was staff. Assuming that he had a free hand to recruit his own, Dewavrin sounded two of his friends, fellow-officers who had served with him in Norway, and both were willing to have a try. The elder, Maurice Duclos, a tall handsome ex-stockbroker from Paris, who loved good food, fine wine and beautiful women, was a striking contrast to Alex Beresnikoff, a lean serious youngster whose passion for fresh air (and wide-open windows) was considered by his colleagues a disgustingly English trait.

It seemed to Dewavrin in the first days that only faith and a sense of humour kept the three of them going. In the bare little office, from nine to five, they worked hard—at making work. Their one consolation was that the founding of this Free French Intelligence Service, however amateurish and makeshift, was a proof of France's will to fight. It was the measure of their faith that they cut their expenses to the bone. Between them they had less than £100 in personal savings, and already bed and breakfast at 69 Cromwell Road, Kensington, was costing them each two pounds a week. As yet they received no regular salary and dinner became a one-and-sixpenny feast of baked beans and coffee at a Kensington milk-bar. They thought of nothing but their newly-created Intelligence Service. And because they believed their task was so far from normal, they at once invested it with fantasy. They thought in terms of truth drugs, ravishing blondes and disguises to simulate a club foot. Thus nourished on the food of fiction, they went to such extremes as they later blushed to recall.

Each morning about that time a battered blue London taxi cab stood on the rank outside 69 Cromwell Road; most of the inhabitants of the Royal Borough had left for the country and other taxis rarely joined it. Since the three young men were often late in the morning they got into the habit of piling into it, and asking to be driven to Westminster, and economising on lunch. The fourth time they arrived at St. Stephen's House, the driver, a weathered old Cockney, shook his head.

17

" 'S all right," he told Dewavrin gruffly. " Nothing to pay."
" Nothing to pay? " Dewavrin was baffled.

" That's what I said, guv'nor. You're General de Gaulle's
young men, aren't you? " Taking their stunned silence for
assent, he went on, " I like the French, see, guv'nor—I was
in the last lot myself—so this is on the 'ouse, as we say."

Three secret agents preserved a frozen calm until they had
reached the top secrecy of the Deuxième Bureau. Then, in a
strangled voice, Dewavrin asked, " Can you, under any circumstances, imagine a Parisian taxi-driver doing that? " And,
feelingly, as they shook their heads: " No more can I. It
means one of two things—either he's a British Intelligence agent
checking up on us or he's a German spy."

When, in the course of the next few days, the taxi-driver
disappeared, their worst suspicions were confirmed. " It's our
uniform," Dewavrin said. " A French uniform is too con-
spicuous. The sooner we get into ordinary civilian clothes and
fool them the better." The others agreed solemnly; the idea
that the taxi-driver had gone in search of a more lucrative rank
only occurred to them later.

Duclos, who loved disguises, said it was well known that all
Englishmen dressed like diplomats, so the three pooled a
portion of their savings and went to Moss Bros. in Covent
Garden in search of protective coloration. An hour later when
they emerged the transformation was complete: black coats,
stiff white collars and striped trousers, each man impeccably
bowler-hatted and carrying a stick. After some days it dawned
on them they were so correctly dressed that each passer-by
now gave them a long reflective look. Reluctantly they wrote
the outfits off to experience and compromised with lounge
suits.

Cover-names, however, seemed a better idea. All of them
had families in France, and they suspected the sober truth that
if German Intelligence ever discovered their identities, it might
go badly for those they had left behind. Duclos, always the
man-about-town, suggested they should pick their names from
stations on the Paris Metro system, and thus, after due delibera-
tion, Duclos became St. Jacques and Beresnikoff Corvisart,

18

while Dewavrin became Colonel Passy, after a station near the Bois de Boulogne. (When these names eventually reached the German *Abwehr* (counter-espionage) in Paris, the experts were puzzled. It was as if British or American secret agents had suddenly adopted pseudonyms like Lieutenant Holborn or Captain Columbus Circle.)

One thing was clear to Dewavrin from the start: there could be no Free French Intelligence Service without the British. The British, he knew, had an Intelligence Service with long experience in such matters, with all the factors that an agent would need to function across the Channel—money, speed-boats, printers to manufacture false identity papers, correspondents in the neutral cities, Lisbon, Stockholm and Berne.

Dewavrin wondered about his own countrymen. What could they offer? Well, agents would have to cross the Channel, so men for a start—men who had known one stretch of country-side all their lives, who had swum in the Loire or the Seine as boys and courted by those same rivers on summer nights, who had harvested their corn and raised their children within the compass of remembered acres. Men whose blood and bones were of the soil, who could be as inconspicuous in their own terrain as a leaf on a poplar tree.

That was the ideal—but both men and money were in short supply. To pay the 2000 men who had rallied to his banner, de Gaulle had brought to England only 100,000 francs (about £500) entrusted to him by President Reynaud. Then should they wait until more men had filtered back to England, through Spain, from Switzerland, in little leaking fishing boats from the Channel ports? Clearly that meant taking time, and, also quite clearly, there was not going to be much time. Out of the present chaos a good agent might seize the initiative, taking up the threads of life where he had left off without attracting attention.

" For God's sake," Dewavrin challenged his fellow-musketeers, after hours of this, " doesn't anyone have any ideas? "

Bnt all of them were groping in the dark, trying to formulate a working basis for something in which they had no training. And Dewavrin became moody, withdrawn.

There *must* be a way. Because there *had* to be.

His logical scholarly brain began to work overtime, sifting basic principles. Familiarity with a given region was essential. The first agents must know each stick and stone of their territory like the men on the spot, the men who had never left the district for the space of a night.

Men on the spot. . . . Now there *was* a new idea.

Dewavrin got out the map, locating the arteries that stemmed from the beating heart of Paris all over France. Roads! At least 25,000 miles of national highways of first strategic importance. The scarlet ribbon of Route Nationale 13, that hugged the saw-tooth Normandy coastline from Cherbourg almost to Caen, then swung sharply inland to the capital. A labourer set by the Council to repair a stretch of that road might see much of the military traffic that passed along it—if he were taught what to look for.

Railways! Another 25,000 miles of iron life-lines between ports and cities. Who would know better the war material flowing from north to south—tungsten, copper, coal—than the shunters in the marshalling yards en route?

And not only economic information, but defence. Supposing the Germans *didn't* invade England? Pill-boxes and tank-traps bulking in green lanes and city streets suggested that the English were ready, but supposing the Germans dug in, fortifying the Channel coast to rule out reprisals? One day the Allies would have to attack—but to attack they would first have to plumb the secrets of defence. Aerial photography, he supposed, would play the major part in determining the strong-points, but from 40,000 feet a lot of that would have to be carefully reconstructed guesswork.

Even a farmer's wife, picking up eggs round the hayricks, could be trained to observe some of those factors—providing she went about her daily task as she had always done. That was it! Agents who looked normal because they *were* normal. People who on the surface were preoccupied only with the hopes and the needs of their own small cosmos.

That would mean a network of men and women in each area, patiently gathering information. Government officials, technicians, farmers, bank clerks—virtually unknown to one another, but working to the same end in each area under one man's direction.

And for greater security even this man, their chief, would know only a few of his agents, and would receive his directions from de Gaulle through yet another source.

It was a beautiful plan, but you would need thousands of volunteers to stand a chance of success.

Well, all right then—thousands of civilians, of little people, all working in different networks, organised from and bound to London by a thin indestructible bond of courage and faith.

That was the start of it. It seemed cold logic to Dewavrin, but it was against the precedent of any Intelligence Service in the world.

Chapter Two

—AND THWARTED

A FEW days later, out of the blue, came what seemed like the perfect stroke of luck. One morning, as Dewavrin was busy perfecting details of his scheme, a tall man with a Roman nose and alert brown eyes entered his office, wearing the uniform of a Commander in the Royal Navy. He introduced himself as director of the French Section of British Intelligence, and since he is still very much alive and active in other spheres he must, until more fraternal days, be known merely as " the Commander."

The Commander said that he had called on General de Gaulle to ask whether the Free French could furnish secret agents for a special mission and the General had suggested he contact the Deuxième Bureau. The Prime Minister, he explained, wanted immediate information about Hitler's intentions along the French coast, particularly in Normandy and Brittany.

Aerial reconnaissance, he stressed, already showed marked activity in the region of Quimper and Douarnenez, and on the Normandy beaches between Courseulles and Ouistreham. But only an agent on the spot, noting the troop dispositions and shipping concentrations, could build up the complete picture of Hitler's invasion plans.

Dewavrin felt a strange shaft of excitement at the feeling that his plans were approaching a tangible reality. He ventured the suggestion that before an agent returned to France to settle down for an unspecified period he would need a lot of briefing.

It was then that the Commander dropped his bombshell.

" They'll only have to be in the field for five days," he said. " Time enough to find the answers to a questionnaire which we shall give them."

Dewavrin was appalled. " Five *days*? "

The Commander explained that each man's area would only consist of about twenty square miles. They would be well briefed on what to look for, and how to recognise it.

For a moment Dewavrin felt quite sick. Then he said, " I think I can find you the men you want, but I've also worked out a scheme for employing agents over a rather longer period."

" Oh, yes? " said the Commander politely, glancing at his hat. " What's that? "

Dewavrin launched as best he could into a résumé of his scheme, trying to convince himself as much as the other that he had been influenced more by logic than by patriotism. When he had finished, the Commander nodded equivocally. He didn't, of course, deny that there were interesting factors in the scheme, but at the present moment . . .

It was evident that he saw the project as a shade far-fetched, and Dewavrin, with force, suggested as much. The Commander hedged a little. Not far-fetched, but hardly on classic lines, and in any event, definitely a long-term project.

" It may be a long war," said Dewavrin rather sulkily.

" I'm not turning the idea down," the Commander assured him. " In any case, that's not my job. I'll pass it on to the right people and let you know."

The two principal reactions to Dewavrin's scheme for turning French civilians into secret agents were (*a*) polite scepticism, (*b*) lukewarm interest. The War Cabinet were understandably suspicious of a scheme which, from the security angle, placed all too much reliance on the human element, and there was little evidence to suggest that Frenchmen in France would embrace the cause of de Gaulle rather than that of Pétain.

One man understood Dewavrin's ideas and did his best to console him: Sir Claude Dansey, a quiet intensely sympathetic man in his late sixties, who was at that time Deputy Director of M.I.6. With thirty years of practical experience " Uncle Claude," as his staff called him, wisely counselled patience, though he received Dewavrin's willing co-operation in the screening of all who volunteered as agents at the former Royal Patriotic School for Girls, Battersea.

Meantime Dewavrin was working with the Commander on the first leg of the Churchill mission: the landing of an agent to bring back urgent information from the Brittany peninsula. Dewavrin's first choice, an intense fair-haired youngster of twenty-seven, named Jacques Mansion, was accepted without a quibble, and once Mansion had boarded a motor fishing boat at Plymouth on 17th July, the Commander was anxious to get the Normandy agents under way as soon as possible. But here he came up against a seemingly insoluble problem—no agents.

The target date was approaching and Dewavrin was in despair, when the irrepressible Duclos said, " Well, why not send *me* to Normandy? I've got a week-end châlet at Langrune, on the coast, and I know all that coastal area round Ouistreham like the back of my hand. That's where I learned to sail a boat as a kid. I could found permanent networks in each department of Normandy—Calvados, the Eure, the Manche. And what's more, *mon ami*, my father's stockbroking agency is in Paris; if I can only get that far, I could establish my central control there. If anyone can start a network along the Atlantic coast, given a little time, it is I, Maurice Duclos."

It's now or never, Dewavrin thought; if they turn this down, then they turn me down, and de Gaulle can find someone else to run his Intelligence Service, because I'm off to a combatant unit. The establishing of a permanent network on the Normandy coastline now seemed the crucial test by which his theories stood or fell. There was an agonising period of waiting while Churchill examined the proposals, but in two days they had their answer: Duclos could go, but someone else must go with him to bring back a synthesis of the most urgent information immediately. That only left Beresnikoff, who was to return within five days. They would also have to send back daily reports by carrier pigeon.

The nicest part came in the form of a rider. Duclos had official sanction to do his best on permanent contacts within the time-limit of a month.

24

It was all Dewavrin could do to stop himself from singing. The Prime Minister of Britain agreed with his idea—well, *half*-agreed, anyway.

After that Dewavrin saw little of Duclos and Beresnikoff. Both of them had been taken in tow by British Intelligence to learn such mystifying skills as the care of carrier pigeons and how to make invisible ink. Most evenings the young engineer spent alone in Lyons' tea shops, his dinner growing cold on the marble-topped table as he dreamed of a vast network of small anonymous citizens scattered all over France.

The greatest problem, and this he had to face squarely, was finding the agents who could act as spark-plugs. Volunteers were still few and far between, and those that did come forward proved, for a multitude of reasons, unsuitable.

Then, one afternoon in the last week of July, someone knocked at the door of the Deuxième Bureau. Dewavrin called, " Come in," and a short, broad-shouldered man, bald and square-jawed, was smiling at him round the door. Dewavrin's first instinct was that he had come to the wrong office, but the newcomer only blinked at him gently, announced that his name was Gilbert Renault, and that he had been told to see " Colonel Passy " with a view to employment on a secret mission.

" Well, I'm Colonel Passy," Dewavrin agreed, reaching for a scratch-pad. " Can I have your rank, m'sieu? "

" I have no rank," Renault had to confess. " I'm a civilian."

Dewavrin grunted. " Your profession in civil life then? "

Renault smiled apologetically passing over his papers. " I was financing films."

" Films? Well, I don't really see . . . In any case, it says here that you worked for the Eagle Star Insurance Company in Paris."

" Well, yes, I did. Sometimes they invested in film production and I looked after the financial side of it."

Dewavrin felt that he was losing his grip on the situation. A little stiffly, he asked how all this was relevant and at once

Renault began to talk. He explained that he had been so frequently to Spain that he thought he could easily get a fresh transit visa from the Consulate in London. Once in Spain it would be easy to cross the frontier into Vichy France, at Pau, and from there into the occupied zone. His friend, the French Consul in Madrid, would surely help.

Dewavrin was interested despite himself. The Unoccupied Zone then covered all the southern area of France, from the Lake of Geneva to S. Jean Pied de Port on the Spanish frontier, and this was the means of entry that he had envisaged. " Just a moment," he said, trying to stem the flood. " Were you doing Intelligence work in Spain? "

Renault shook his head. " Not at all, I was making a film about Christopher Columbus. But let me explain my idea."

He talked deliberately, methodically, always half-smiling, for half an hour. He talked so much that Dewavrin could not get a word in edgeways. His monologue embraced civilian contacts over the length and breadth of France. He laid great stress on the fact that one of his closest friends was a lawyer in Nantes. Because of his business a country lawyer could cover a wide terrain without attracting attention.

Dewavrin listened thoughtfully, taking in the salient points. Financing films, he thought, scripts about Christopher Columbus. . . . It didn't sound very professional, yet by a different line of reasoning, Renault had arrived at an analogous conclusion to his own. He was not seeing France's war in cloak-and-dagger terms at all. He was seeing it in terms of the man-in-the-street, the simple faithful immemorial people of France.

He coaxed Renault from his office finally, assuring him that he would get in touch with him as soon as Renault had been formally screened by the British. If volubility was an asset, he thought, Renault could surely talk his way out of anything.

In the lift going down, Renault felt the first pangs of conscience. His first impression of Dewavrin had been of a youngster pretending to be very sure of himself but who knew almost nothing about espionage. Even the pencilled half-sheet of notepaper tacked to his door " Colonel Passy. Deuxième Bureau " had an amateur flavour. He was aware that he had traded on this, talking so glibly and persuasively that he had half-persuaded Dewavrin to take him on.

Renault was sincere enough in his desire to join de Gaulle. On 19th June at Lorient, he had, for no other reason, boarded the *Lista*, a 12,000-ton Norwegian cargo boat bound for Falmouth. But while Dewavrin's one problem had been to get his theories accepted, Renault's motives were more complex. Mingled with his grief for his country's capitulation was the pain of separation from those he loved more than his life.

It was bad enough, he thought, that his mother and five sisters should have been left behind in France. They still awaited news of him in the old shuttered house in the rue Carnot, at Vannes, where he had been born thirty-six years ago, the son of a chief insurance inspector. But in their care Renault had left Edith, his wife, and their three children.

He walked slowly up the stone canyon of Whitehall in the fierce sunlight, past the Ministries, heavily-sandbagged, and the steel-helmeted sentinels, a small worried man in an alien city. He could see the faces of his children too clearly to need to refer to the facsimiles housed in his old leather wallet. Catherine, his elder daughter, with the proud chin and steady grey eyes, was now ten years old. Jean-Claude, his son, was a year older, shy and fair-haired. At eight Cécile already had her mother's warm smile and generously impulsive nature.

And Edith. Slim, blonde, fine-boned, with something of a Madonna's serenity of face. Renault had loved her ever since he had first seen her, standing on the stairs of her apartment in Paris, greeting her guests at a " surprise party " to which someone had inveigled him. Before he had even spoken to her he had decided to make her his wife. That had been twelve years ago, and since then they had grown closer. Even life on the fringe of the too smart, too hectic Paris film world—four cocktail parties a night dutifully attended from a choice of twenty, an elaborate expense-account dinner with clients, a *boîte de nuit* as hot and noisy as a zoo—had only strengthened

27

their feelings for one another. Edith had always understood, and they had always been able to laugh at the worst of it.

She had not even tried to stop him when he left his mother's house just after breakfast on 18th June to find his way to the coast. As always when he had gone on a journey she had merely slipped a note into his pocket for him to find and open later. This time it had said, " I believe in you, and I'll wait as long as it takes."

Renault thought with a twinge of shame of how he had bluffed the interviewing officers at St. Stephen's House into directing him to Dewavrin's office. It was true that he had many contacts, but he had no notion of the work a secret agent must do, no real conception of how to collect vital information. That afternoon he had improvised to Dewavrin with the conviction of desperation. To see Edith and the children again, he was prepared to risk his life. If there were stranger or less orthodox reasons for becoming a secret agent, Renault did not know of them.

For a moment, typically, he wondered whether he was not being selfish. Supposing de Gaulle had greater need of him elsewhere? No matter how much a man loved his wife and children, surely his country had first priority when the Germans had all Europe? Yet he knew that if Dewavrin did send him back to France, he would count himself the luckiest Frenchman alive, and he would not let his chief down. He would not only be an agent, somehow he would learn to be a good one.

Meantime he must wait patiently at the Buckinghamshire cottage of his friend, George Gunn, the film producer, who had vouched for him, rescued him from the transit camp and given him a room. He caught the late afternoon train from Marylebone to Gerrard's Cross. Being Renault he had decided that the least he could do to repay such kindness was to mow the lawn.

Chapter Three

PAVING THE WAY

Through the stifling eternity of 4th August, when the thermo-meter quivered in the eighties, Dewavrin clung to his office without even a break for meals, sweating and worrying. He awaited some crumb of news from Intelligence that the mission of Duclos and Beresnikoff, the first official attempt to establish a permanent network on the Normandy coastline, had been successfully launched. But no news came.

He had no way of knowing the problems that faced his friends across the Channel but they were considerable.

A little before 4 a.m. that morning, Duclos and Beresnikoff had transferred from a naval speed-boat to a rubber dinghy three miles off the coast at St. Aubin. Then, with a coughing roar, the launch turned for the open sea. With chilled hands, the two agents began to paddle. Abruptly a searchlight came on, a white finger probing uncertainly on the dark water. The sound of the speed-boat's engines had been heard on land. Presently, failing to find any objective, the searchlight blotted out.

But the coastal patrols were taking no chances. Somewhere along the coast a German speed-boat started up. Duclos breathed a silent prayer because the morning mist, rising thickly from the sea, now cut off all visibility for more than twenty yards. Suddenly a great wash from the bows of the speed-boat set their dinghy rocking violently; the German patrol passed within fifty yards of them, then the engine noise died away.

They worked fast now, saving words. Rowing the dinghy in near the small harbour of St. Aubin they beached it at the foot of the cliffs before deflating and sinking it. Now, carrying the pannier of pigeons and cheap fibre attaché-cases, they began

29

to ascend the track which climbed 200 feet to the bluffs above. The cold graveyard smell of the fog stung their nostrils. Suddenly they stopped. In the pre-dawn chill they had heard a sentry cough.

From the sound they judged that he was directly above them. It was obvious now that they would have to detour, and just as obvious that carrying a basket of pigeons on a game of hide-and-seek in the mist was asking for trouble. Hiding their pannier in the crevice with a supply of grain they detoured and reached the bluff at another point. Passing within a hundred yards of two other sentries, they reached Duclos's deserted châlet at Langrune three miles away, by doubling like fugitives along ditches under cover of the fog.

From an academic standpoint, their work was not unsatisfactory. Taking three days, Duclos indulged his passion for disguise, passing himself off as a peasant (" an odd peasant," a colleague said later, " wearing overalls and dark sun-glasses ") tramping the coastal roads and mapping in his mind the whole region from Arromanches to Le Havre. Every harbour and tidal river seemed choked with the unwieldy convoys of converted barges massed for Hitler's " Operation Sea-Lion," and in cafés the land-loving soldiers of the *Wehrmacht* talked uneasily of the choppy Channel crossing, taking comfort from their officially-issued " morale maps " which showed England as only ten minutes' sailing time away.

Now it only remained to recover the pigeons, but though Beresnikoff, hiding out in the châlet, had tried three times he could never reach them. The whole coast was alive with sentries. Armed with precious information about Hitler's invasion plans, the two agents were powerless to transmit it. The area was so closely guarded that even the idea of contacting friends and trying to start a network now seemed farcical. Escape became their only concern.

But even escape proved to be out of the question. Four times in the next three weeks, the naval speed-boat was back as arranged, the crew ready to launch a dinghy as soon as they saw the guiding signals. And four times Duclos and Beresnikoff, chilled to the bone on the beach below St. Aubin, almost wept with rage, knowing that once again the fog which had at first saved them had masked the signals from their torches.

On 1st September they parted company. Duclos was heading for Paris, to try to establish a network among his former commercial contacts. Beresnikoff left for Vichy to get himself demobilised, and obtain an up-to-date sample of identity papers.

A network on the coast of Normandy looked like being a tall order.

By mid-September Dewavrin had given both Duclos and Beresnikoff up for lost. Mansion had returned from Brittany a fortnight earlier, loaded with information and even reporting friends who were willing to hold a watching brief, but in his grief and bitterness that his friends had died for his idea, Dewavrin was inconsolable. Twice he begged for a transfer to a combat unit, but each time de Gaulle persuaded him to stay on until things were better organised.

But it was all so *infuriating*! Dewavrin had a copy of the 7th August, 1940, agreement between Churchill and de Gaulle in his desk, and it was there, in black and white, all he had wanted and fought for, with Britain agreeing to become financially responsible for his, Dewavrin's organisation, Free France to make repayment by supplying up-to-date military intelligence from the other side of the Channel. True, the building up of permanent networks was to take second place to the swift infiltration and exfiltration of professional agents, but it was a beginning.

The trouble was that agents were still not forthcoming, and as yet, despite Dewavrin's many impassioned meetings with Sir Claude Dansey and the Commander, no one in Intelligence knew enough about what papers you needed to live and circulate freely in France to take the risk. To Dewavrin, who knew that " Operation Sea-Lion " was off, possibly for ever, it was a bitter blow. What, he wanted to know, was going to happen along the Atlantic coast now?

The determined young chief of de Gaulle's Intelligence Service was not, any more than the members of the War

31

Cabinet, gifted with second sight. His main concern, like any good Intelligence chief, was to establish a reliable network along the now thinly-defended coastline, in the event of it one day becoming of first strategic importance. Fate, not Dewavrin, was re ponsible for the happier coincidences.

The last person from whom he expected any information on the subject was Renault. The little man had duly passed the Commander's screening and left for Lisbon on a Sunderland flying boat in the second week of August. Several preliminary dispatches came in the next few weeks, as he explored ways and means; all were duly coded, written in invisible ink, and sent as trade correspondence from the French Consulate in Madrid via Gibraltar in the way that had been agreed. In one of them, which raised Dewavrin's eyebrows, Renault mentioned a long rapturous reunion he had enjoyed with his wife and children, who were safely with him in Madrid. (It was the first Dewavrin had heard of a wife *or* children.) But after that, silence.

It was not broken until 1st December, when a thick sheaf of coded flimsies arrived on Dewavrin's desk. He remembers now that he was " pretty excited," sensing that it was something big, and when it had been decoded he lost no time in calling the Commander.

Together they went eagerly and methodically through the dispatch marked RZ 1—the " R " was for Renault, " Z " meaning correspondence—which was dated from Perpignan in the last week of November. In it Renault informed them that he had now been in the Occupied Zone in France three weeks. Already, in the guise of an insurance inspector, he was in touch with specialists on the spot. At Bordeaux, old Papa Fleuret, the pilot of the port, was going to furnish him with all the comings and goings of the great German battleships, the *Scharnhorst* and the *Gneisenau*. Gauthier, the technical director of the dockyard, would keep them posted on the construction of new ships. There were scale maps showing oil refineries and airfields. Much the same sort of coverage for Brest, Quiberon, Lorient, La Pallice and Merignac.

" This man," said the Commander as he riffled through the

32

blue flimsies, " is good." And Dewavrin, who lost no opportunity for putting over propaganda, answered spiritedly, " These *men* . . . because here we have the beginnings of the networks."

Months passed after that, but despite Renault's promising start, Dewavrin's scheme remained obstinately in embryo. By the beginning of 1941, when both Duclos and Beresnikoff had returned by devious routes to London, all Dewavrin's obstinacy had come to the fore. He determined that Duclos should parachute back, armed with a transmitter, and start again in Normandy.

On the night of 14th February Duclos was dropped from a Halifax near Bugue, in the Dordogne; the Unoccupied Zone was less closely guarded than the flat Normandy plains. This time a radio operator and a transmitter, a clumsy 60-lb affair in a varnished black box, went with him, and, from the beginning, everything went disastrously wrong. Twenty feet from the ground, Duclos's parachute harness snagged on a pine tree; he fell heavily and sideways and when he tried to pick himself up he knew from the searing white-hot pain that his ankle was broken. The transmitter, too, was useless, its condensers mangled beyond repair.

Eventually, with the help of some friendly farmers, Duclos was lucky enough to reach Paris, adopting his crutches as a new disguise, to carry on the network that he had built around his father's stockbroking agency. Through their aid he was able to make important contacts in Le Havre and Dunkirk, but the hopes of building a network in Normandy with central control from Paris, were as far away as they had ever been.

Dewavrin would not give up.

Supposing, he thought, Renault could extend his coverage to take in the whole coast. By late autumn, when the idea had crystallised, Renault's networks were already covering the coast from Biarritz to St. Malo, a hundred agents dotted strategically along 500 miles of coastline. Since London had put six transmitters at their disposal, supervised by a technical adviser, Captain Guy Julitte, not one morsel of information concerning the movements of the U-boat pack, or the *Scharnhorst*, the

Gneisenau or the *Prinz Eugen* eluded them. Their expenses, travelling, hotels, the bare necessities of life, ran to 150,000 francs a month. But between St. Malo and Le Havre, a coastal sector of 200 miles in length, Dewavrin's coverage was non-existent and even the Commander's independent sources were comparatively few.

Renault, like Duclos, now made his headquarters in Paris. There he might find contacts in outlying provinces like Normandy which could not be tracked down in the province itself.

It was only one of many factors emerging during these months that called for urgent discussion. To Dewavrin it was strangely unreal; Renault above all the others had helped to create the networks, working from nothing but the will of men to fight, to triumph, to expunge their shame, yet he and Renault had met, at the most, half a dozen times. Dewavrin knew that Renault was now well established in Paris, but he could not visualise very clearly the extent of the risks he ran in the cold, sad city, how his networks functioned, how he kept in touch with his family. Now, urgently, he wanted to see Renault, and to hear these details from his own lips.

On 27th February, 1942, after many signals and postponements because of weather, Renault and Guy Julitte flew through the night, travelling by Lysander from a landing-ground code-named " Guardian Angel," near Rouen, to Tangmere airfield, Sussex, and the British officer who met them asked, in amazement, what they could possibly have brought in three sacks weighing more than 100 lb.

" Dispatches," said Renault anxiously, as if he had offended against some canon. " Only dispatches from my networks."

He had not come any too soon. In this month also, along the coastline of Normandy, moving eastwards from Cherbourg through Arromanches, through Courseulles, through Ouistreham to Le Havre, a stocky eagle-nosed regular soldier, *General-feldmarschall* Erwin von Witzleben, commanding Army Group D, which held France, was on the last leg of a tour of inspection. His terms of reference were stark and simple: " The Fortification of the West."

The war against the Wall was beginning.

34

Chapter Four

A TARGET IS KNOWN

ON THE first day of March, Renault was blissfully unaware of this. What was striking him most forcibly was the gratifying —if bewildering—contrast between August, 1940, and the present. Then everyone had been friendly but cautious; now even imperturbable intelligence officers went out of their way to wring him by the hand. Dispatch RZ 39—which included plans of the submarine base at St. Nazaire—was received with rhapsodies, and the modest Renault learned with horror that for his work in founding the networks he had been awarded the D.S.O. He has refused to discuss it ever since.

Even de Gaulle's Intelligence Service had outgrown its shoe-string beginnings. Now known as the Bureau de Contre Espionnage, Renseignements et d'Action (B.C.R.A.) it was that week moving into a twenty-seven-room suite in a gleaming white office block at No. 10 Duke Street, behind Selfridge's. In this week, too, Dewavrin—newly promoted " Commandant Passy "—noted in his journal: " Thanks to Renault and to RZ 39, my conception of the networks is at last taken seriously."

Neither he nor Renault had any premonition that a bigger target lay ahead. Renault's first concern was to put in a detailed report of his networks; for security reasons he had never been able to send details from Paris. At the week-end he sat down in a quiet mews off Baker Street and began.

Dictating, he was always conscious of the small cell at the back of his mind that enjoined caution. Describe the head-quarters building in general terms, but never let slip, even to Dewavrin, the address or the camouflage: a furniture manufacturer's business at 72 Avenue des Champs-Elysées, above the Ermitage Cinema. You could say that you employed a staff of ten on these premises, with another twenty-four deployed in dusty hole-in-corner offices throughout the city; you could detail how each man or woman had his or her own department dealing with reports on airfields, harbours or factories. But you could give only their cover-names—Jim, Bob, Roger—even if, as was unlikely, you knew their real identity. For one who knew Renault's true identity there were ten who knew him by other cover-names—Monsieur Raymond, Monsieur Watteau, Monsieur Morin, Monsieur Jean-Luc, or the name by which he was to become famous, Colonel Rémy.

Renault felt a sudden revulsion against the agent's schizoid life: you were a trusted agent, but the real reasons you were asked to study a target were withheld in case you cracked or sold out. You trusted London to send planes and funds and radios but by agreement you held back many personal details of your own organisation. Only by shutting his mind to the implications could Renault, a man of sterling principles who loathed intrigue, carry on.

Two nights later, dining at the Waldorf with Dewavrin and his deputy, a bald laughing man like a genial monk named André Manuel, some of what he felt came crowding to the surface. But though he begged earnestly that London office should take the networks more fully into its confidence, Dewavrin shook his head.

" The more the war progresses," he said decidedly, " the less you or any of your *braves garçons* will know. The less *I* shall know. If one of you does get some information that's useful on a long-term basis, you won't hear a word of praise or even interest out of anybody." Then, compassionately, seeing Renault's face: " I know how you must feel about it—but think of the risk if everyone in the networks knew the full strategic implication of what they were doing."

" It isn't that," said Renault, distressed. " It's—well, it's the others. I'm their only contact with London—they only see France. Is it any wonder they sometimes ask themselves whether London makes any use of the information they get,

36

or whether they're even interested." He ended bitterly, " Or whether they just risk their lives for nothing."

After a pause Dewavrin said, " And yet, in spite of that, you know, they'll have to go on—and they *will* go on. The only thing I know is that when we do return, there won't be enough gold in France to repay their faith." And he and Manuel were silent, thinking of their Paris, with sunlight on the boulevards and tourists drinking *demi-blonds* outside the Café de la Paix, and Renault's Paris, sustained by the faith of the few.

To Dewavrin and Manuel and all the others Renault remained an enigma: How had he done it? They could never quite understand his talent for self-effacement, his deprecating modesty, and nothing in his appearance suggested the leader, the man-of-action. To look at, he was the man the poll-takers light on when they seek out the man in the street; the harassed father of a family, always overloaded with parcels, struggling into the Metro in the six o'clock rush. Only in retrospect was it apparent that he was unselfish to the point of saintliness, which was why many men died rather than betray him, and that his ruses against the Germans worked because he saw this war as a holy crusade, and in ordinary life lacked any guile at all. Even his great central transmission agency in Paris, which he had placed under the protection of Our Lady of Victories, was code-named the Confrérie de Notre Dame, the Brotherhood of Our Lady. Yet there were contradictions. He was careless of discomfort but revelled in luxury. He had a banker's taste in fine cigars, and sharp sauces, but talked with moving simplicity of Michel, his baby son, born a year ago in Madrid.

" One day," he confided to Dewavrin after one conference, " it may be necessary to get my family out of France in a hurry."

" How are they? "

" Oh, as well as you can expect. I've got them at Baud, in Brittany, at the moment, but it's a wretched life for my wife —moving house six times in the last eighteen months. But little Michel—you ought to see that baby. I swear he'll be walking really well soon."

37

" We *could* arrange a pick up," suggested Dewavrin, marvelling, and Renault, as if they were discussing a jaunt to the seaside, answered: " Oh, Edith wouldn't fly—not with the baby. It'll have to be a sea operation."

Dewavrin took him to lunch with de Gaulle in his suite at the Connaught Hotel and the General, after reading his report, asked many questions, staring at him sombrely like an Old Testament prophet, before smiling and wishing him good luck. Afterwards, back at Duke Street, Dewavrin returned to his old love. His finger travelled eloquently along a map of the French coastline; pin-pointing the 200-mile gap that still existed between St. Malo and Le Havre. Renault had no ideas as to where he might found a permanent network in that area, but he promised to look into it as soon as he got back.

Dewavrin considered. " You might try Cherbourg," and yes, Renault rather thought he would. Cherbourg was a port and a submarine base and seemed the obvious centre to lay the foundations of a network.

The conversation switched to last-minute instructions. Then, suddenly, " What about those six radio operators? You do keep them separate from your main headquarters, don't you? " Both men knew that the radio operator's job, chained to his bulky set, presented the biggest hazards of all—to the Paris office as well as themselves.

Renault assured him that none of his operators even knew where head office was. They were located in a chain of villas in the Paris suburbs, and the coded groups were fed to them by messengers who carried them in easily-destructible containers —newspapers or match-boxes. Each man was instructed to switch to a fresh post after two transmissions.

He spent his last morning, the morning of 28th March, doing some last-minute shopping for his agents: soap, cigarettes, chocolates. Then, loaded with parcels, he made his way to Duke Street, taking the lift to the third floor.

He could feel the silence as he entered Dewavrin's office. It was almost as if they had been discussing him. Dewavrin was at his desk, looking white and strained. Manuel and Julitte, the technical adviser, a thick-set good-looking fellow, were there, too. Without speaking Manuel handed him a message. It was from Robert Delattre, Renault's personal radio officer, who was responsible for air liaison, and had just been decoded:

FIVE RADIO OPERATORS ARRESTED STOP AM READY FOR OPERATION THIS EVENING CEILING TEN KILOMETRES STOP BOB

For a moment it was like being kicked in the stomach. Then, " What are you going to do? " Dewavrin blurted out.

Renault took time replying, and at last, trying to make his voice sound reasonable, he said, " Well, I don't know yet. Until I get there and find out what's happened, I can't know."

" You'll go in spite of this? " Dewavrin was genuinely staggered.

" Of course." He wasn't indulging in any mock-heroics. Edith and the children were expecting him. So was his staff at head office, all of them. He had to go.

In grim silence they lunched at the Waldorf. *Why?* Renault tortured himself, all though the meal. *Why?* How could it have happened? The thought was still with him as he said good-bye to Dewavrin, and all through the long drive back to Tangmere with the British conducting officer, until at last at ten o'clock, the Lysander was slithering along the runway, rising into the night; an hour of cold swooping darkness (still wondering) until far below the warning " T " sprang up on " Guardian Angel." Then the question faded as they dropped, buffeted by head winds, down, down, then rocking over the coarse grass, taxi-ing gently anti-clockwise as the Lysander turned for a fresh take-off, the breathless scramble to reach the ground and off-load the parcels. Faces gleamed pale in the darkness, another sack of dispatches tumbled aboard, thinking vaguely, that's RZ 40, a hand gripping his, François Faure, his No. 2, going with it. There were waves, shouts, then the engine blared into life, and as the Lysander climbed the question came back like a remembered fear: *Why?*

Next morning, in his apartment in the Square Henri Paté, on the southern fringe of the Bois de Boulogne, listening in silence while Delattre told him the worst news yet, he knew why. The operator Julitte had appointed as his successor before returning to England, a thin, self-satisfied man named Subsol, had disregarded instructions, transmitting several days from a villa in the suburb of Chatou. In this week the Gestapo had put a fleet of thirty-six radio-detector vans into operation in the streets of Paris. Peugeot vans covered with grey tarpaulin which moved very slowly along the gutter, no faster than a man walking. These mobile listening-posts, constantly on the alert, could report at once to the Gestapo's central control-point at 525, Rue de Saussaies. Delattre, a hatchet-faced, unemotional man, not given to hyperbole, said that they were capable of arriving at an operator's door within twenty minutes of his beginning transmission.

Thus the Gestapo had found Subsol—and in his pocket unforgivably was a notebook with the cover names and addresses of his operators. Five radio operators, five transmitters—and how many contacts when the Gestapo tightened the thumb-screw?

Dear God, Renault thought, there's no answer to that one. Or rather there was, and he didn't like it: more radios, more operators, shorter transmissions. Bigger, more suicidal risks. The link with London, which he and Dewavrin had worked so hard to implement, hung by the thread of one radio. Supply drops, Lysander pick-ups, even the delivery of dispatches— everything hinged on the one radio left to them. With one radio he had to found a network in Normandy.

Afterwards it seemed ironic that what Dewavrin had tried spasmodically to establish for almost two years should have been accomplished in a matter of days. He gave quick orders. The Bordeaux cell must be contacted to send a relief transmitter. London must parachute in more transmitters to help them carry on. And all day, shuttling by subway from the left bank to Sacré-Coeur and back to the Opéra, checking with his agents in offices and cafés, he asked about Normandy until someone —he never remembered who—suggested he might contact Pierre Brossolette.

Renault, whose politics were well right of centre, bristled.

" You mean the journalist who wrote articles for that Socialist daily *Le Populaire*. Surely he's a bit of a firebrand? "

Later that day, with a characteristic pang of shame, he relented. After all, what had politics to do with it? If France was ever to achieve greatness, it would be through the unity of all creeds and colours and classes. A meeting was fixed, and Renault went to a small newsagent's shop in the rue de la Pompe, poised high on a hill above the Seine and the Eiffel Tower.

The meeting was a surprise.

He had expected a big embittered Radical, dogmatic and slovenly, but behind the counter of the shop he found a neat intense bird-like man, slightly built and with darting brown eyes. Thick hair as black as washed coal was swept carelessly back from a handsome sardonic face, streaked by a forelock as white as a jay's.

The two men retired to warm themselves by the stove in a small smoky basement. Brossolette explained that this was his headquarters; the shop, which sold crayons and exercise books to the pupils of the Lycée Janson-Sailly, was the cover for a small Resistance organisation specialising in propaganda. Renault liked him at once, finding him restless and vital, and promised to get him to London to see de Gaulle. Now what about Normandy? " I know just the people for you," Brossolette said.

Next morning they met on the Champ de Mars, the long cypress grove below the steel skirts of the Eiffel Tower, and Brossolette had another man with him. A small dapper man of precise gestures, moustached, with gold-rimmed glasses, named Marcel Berthelot. Cover-name Lavoisier. Profession, ex-diplomat, with a useful background of peacetime intelligence work.

" Berthelot can help you," Brossolette said. " He works for another organisation. He will tell you about it."

They walked up and down in the mist, under the dripping trees. This was nothing new to Renault. In this way he had built fourteen other networks. In a crowded café on the boulevards you met a contact. You drank too much bad coffee with him, you smoked too many cigarettes, but he gave you an introduction. Another café: more coffee, the butts piling thicker in the ashtray. Or the setting could vary: Renault had interviewed potential agents in small sour bars, in chemists' shops, in family kitchens over great copper tureens of soup, once on a deserted racecourse.

But not the procedure—that never varied. Unhurried, you watched, you listened, you exchanged small jokes. If the man opposite seemed anxious to leave quickly, that was a bad sign, betraying nerves, and almost ruled him out from the first. Like a psycho-analyst, you tried to diagnose gestures and speech-forms of which he was unaware, probing his strength, his loyalty. And one fine morning you met a man who lived on the spot, a man with the fire of Verdun in his blood, gay, fearless and incorruptible, and this was your man.

Now he had two good allies in the struggle, Brossolette and Berthelot. But both were Parisians; neither was *the* man.

" To-morrow morning," Berthelot was explaining, " you will meet my chief. He has many agents in northern France. At about ten o'clock walk along the bridle-path that runs beside the Avenue Henri-Martin. You will see a tall man, looking like a cavalry officer, exercising a small brown dog. He will be expecting you."

Thus it was that a little after ten the following morning Renault found himself in the Bois de Boulogne, shaking hands with a powerfully-built man who until then had been very busy exercising a stumpy brown basset hound. Colonel Alfred Touny, the dog-owner, was tall and distinguished, like an actor from the Comédie Française, his hair silvered and well kept. His eyes were deep and penetrating, the nose large and drawn like a scimitar, the mouth compassionate, with a wry humour. He led Renault to his fine apartment on the rue du Général Langlois, and Renault admired the modern blond wood and the silken curtains, while they drank tea from Sèvres china, Alphonse, the basset hound, sitting on his master's knee, while the Colonel explained the origins of his Resistance movement, sometimes breaking off the conversation to murmur " *Tais toi, mon petit,*" and feed Alphonse some biscuit soaked in tea.

At first, when Touny claimed that his movement, called the Organisation Civile et Militaire (O.C.M.) had 5,000 supporters in Normandy and Brittany, Renault was inclined to be sceptical. Scores of small Resistance organisations, mostly of political origin, had mushroomed all over France in the last two years, but lack of funds or radio contact with London, had quickly put paid to most of them. But Touny's O.C.M., founded by a Colonel Heurteaux, who had been arrested in 1941, had at least kept going, and with refreshingly practical aims. With shock-troops already organised for the day of liberation, they had specialised in gleaning military intelligence for their use, and what they badly needed now was a link with de Gaulle. Their funds, Touny explained, were non-existent, but they had valuable contacts among the French railways and postal services.

Renault came to a decision. At any one time his agent, Verrière, the manager of the Boulevard Haussmann branch of the Credit du Nord, held 2,000,000 francs of de Gaullist funds. " I have authority from my chief to finance any organisation that will work under orders from London," he said. " To-morrow I can make it possible for you to have 200,000 francs. Now I must explain what I want along the coast. . . ."

When he had finished, Touny said, " I have a good agent for you, though he doesn't operate from Cherbourg. But he can get you anything you want from Caen. . . ."

" Caen? " The old Norman city was eighty miles from Cherbourg and Renault did not hide his disappointment. " Of course that would be of help to us, but——"

Touny cut in, " I think you will find he can help you with Cherbourg, too. He travels constantly." Renault hesitated a moment, then said finally: " Well, all right—but I must see him urgently."

" To-morrow afternoon at three o'clock," Touny told him, " go to 77 rue Caulaincourt. The right-hand apartment on the second floor. My assistant whom you met yesterday will be there too," and Renault noted with approval that the suave-spoken Colonel had not mentioned the unknown's name and had left him to memorise the address. Renault's work had already suffered enough from the imprudence of Subsol, the radio operator.

" I am sure," Touny said in parting, " that my man will be able to procure you up-to-date information on everything that the Germans are building along the coast."

" Building? " This was a new one to Renault. " What are they building? "

" He can tell you better than I," Touny confessed. " But there is something going on along that coast . . . that I know."

A hundred miles north and west of Paris, along the sloping sandy Normandy coastline, something was indeed going on. A dream was in the process of becoming hard reality. The Germans were building a wall.

The idea had been conceived, rather later than Dewavrin had anticipated, in September, 1941—just a year after the conception of the networks. Generalfeldmarschall von Witzleben, who seems always to have feared an Allied invasion, had proposed that the Army begin work on permanent coastal defences. The only sizeable fortifications on the French mainland, he pointed out, were seven heavy coastal batteries between Boulogne and Calais. The famous Todt Organisation which had built the Siegfried Line, were busy constructing bombproof U-Boat pens, and had neither labour nor materials to spare, but von Witzleben was no man to give up easily. At the time when Renault was returning to England, after reconnoitring defence sites along the coast, he began construction.

Then, on 23rd March, 1942, Hitler issued his famous Directive No. 40. Pearl Harbour, coupled with the setbacks of the Russian campaign, now made Allied invasion more than a possibility. Hitler's directive was designed to take care of this. Coastal defences backed by troops must ensure that an invasion could be smashed right on the beaches where it started. Field Marshal von Rundstedt took over all coastal defences between Antwerp and the Spanish frontier, and none too soon; five days later, when the British sailed the old U.S. destroyer Campbeltown *up the Loire at St. Nazaire, the splintering crash of the Joubert dock gates reverberated as far away as Berchtesgaden. To defend the French mainland to the death became priority.*

In Normandy, as elsewhere, von Rundstedt allotted first priority to the tidal rivers which thread inland like silver ribbons from the coastline

44

to the wooded rich pasture towards Alençon and Mayenne. At Cabourg commanding the mouth of the Dives, at Honfleur on the Claire, there were to be heavily defended strongpoints. Beaches where only small surprise landings were possible, were to be covered by strongpoints tied in, where possible, with coastal batteries. The rest of the coast was to be patrolled; every position defended to the last man.

In the spring of 1942 this megalomaniac scheme for encasing all Europe in a solid girdle of concrete had one overall title : Atlantic Wall.

On the afternoon of Wednesday, 1st April, a powerfully built man with a lion's mane of greying hair named Marcel Girard was walking north between grey cliffs of office blocks towards Montmartre and the Rue Caulaincourt. He walked quickly, with a rolling gait like a sailor, his executive-sized bulk feeling the pull of the steep-winding streets; once when his leg began to hurt again he had to pause for breath.

A front-line soldier of World War I, Girard had come through bloody conflicts like " First Ypres " without a scratch, but in this war, only two years old, he had been less lucky. At Dunkirk, as Captain of Artillery, a hail of machine-gun bullets had almost severed his right leg at the knee, and there had followed six long months in a military hospital at Brussels before the Germans repatriated him in January, 1941. Not long after, chance had brought him in contact with Colonel Touny, and on Touny's behalf, using the cover name Moreau, he had organised an impressive group of patriots in his home town, Caen. His papers identified him as a busy cement salesman dividing his time between Paris and Caen. He was thick-set, heavily jowled, with a look of scowling purpose that made people listen when he talked. Aged forty-one, but already looking older.

A warm afternoon hush lay over the old white plastered houses of the Rue Caulaincourt. On the second floor of No. 77 Girard rang a bell, and was relieved to see Berthelot answer the door. The room seemed shadowed, dim, full of solid mahogany furniture and silver-framed sepia portraits. From an overstuffed leather chair, Renault rose to shake hands.

Neither Girard nor Renault inquired who owned the flat

and, in fact, never knew. Each organisation had a rota of safe apartments, where meetings could be held; the average " danger money " paid for the loan of the keys was 600 francs a month.

Soon they were deep in a lively discussion on various aspects of Resistance, and Renault decided that he liked Girard immensely. Carelessly dressed in an old sports jacket, shapeless pullover and flannel trousers, he gave the impression of a man only interested in essentials. As he listened the attention showed in his heavy impassive face; his soft brown eyes rarely left Renault's face, the strong bear-like hands clasped his knees. Renault was explaining, " Up to now London has always urged me to concentrate on the area between Biarritz and Mont St. Michel. All our attempts to establish a network on the coast of Normandy have failed. Now it has become important to bridge the gap. My suggestion is that under Berthelot's supervision you should take charge of all the area between St. Malo and Le Havre. It is up to you to say whether that is practicable."

" Practicable enough." Girard's booming voice, thickened with a strong local accent, seemed to shake the room. He went on to explain the ostensible schedule of his weekly movements. His old firm, *Société des Ciments Français*, were making a good play of working with the Germans, which gave him free passage between Paris and Caen as well as an occasional *laisser-passer* to Cherbourg, Le Mans and Argentan. Only the head of the firm and a few others knew that Girard had not sold one ounce of cement since demobilisation, using the job as a useful cover for full-time Resistance.

When he had finished, Renault went on: " Don't ask me exactly what London has in mind, because I don't know either. But I've heard so much about a network in Normandy that I must get results. For example, you must give priority to guns."

Girard said: " I understand. You want to know exactly where they're sited and when. Now if I can find people to work along the coast, which should not be insuperable "— as he smiled the brown eyes lit up, there was a great flash of white teeth, and Renault felt a tremendous sense of reassurance —" exactly what details would you want? " Guns, eh? Girard

46

was thinking. And casemates, too, he didn't doubt, and machine-gun nests. He knew a man named Meslin who knew every inch of that coast. Renault was still talking.

" Whoever you get, brief them to get *every* detail. London's complained that some of my agents have been selecting their own details, which is fatal, because neither you nor I nor anyone know exactly what's significant to London. So when there are guns, let us know what calibre they are, and their range. How far apart they are, and how many men are manning the battery. If there are mines, then let's know what kind *they* are—anti-tank or just booby trap. How far do they stretch? Are the perimeters of the minefields patrolled, and if so at what hours? My people in London have given me a standard questionnaire and I'll let you have a copy to take away with you."

By the time he had finished he had talked for more than an hour and his throat was dry. (Proof that his briefing was succinct; among his friends Girard was famous for brushing aside long-winded arguments and driving home his own point.) But Renault, not knowing that, felt only a secret glow of triumph. This was *the* man. Strong, incorruptible, a born leader. Of all the agents he had briefed he had never felt more confident that a man would get results.

" One more thing," he said. " To us, in Paris, you will have a different cover-name. We shall call you Malherbe." He remembered that the great seventeenth-century man of letters had been born at Caen.

Girard took this in his stride, but said, as he rose to go, " One more thing, m'sieu. If, as you say, your radio network has been having difficulties, how do you propose to keep me in touch with London? "

" Don't worry," Renault said. " We'll find a way." Afterwards he thought that only his unwavering faith in the protection of Our Lady could have made him speak with such certainty.

Chapter Five

A NETWORK IS BORN

ON THE Saturday following his interview with Renault, Girard was back in Caen[1]. In peacetime, like most other townsmen, he would have spent that morning fishing for trout on the banks of the River Orne, whose brown waters neatly bisected the city. To-day he had business to do—Dewavrin's business.

Caen was much like Girard himself—shrewd, solid, undemonstrative. It was a farmer's city. The narrow cobbled streets ran between steep-pitched red-tiled houses, and the cologne of these streets was wood-smoke and farm manure. Red dairy cattle, geese and pigs plashed in the dirt roads that formed its perimeter. The drink of the region was calvados, a potent greenish-yellow applejack, and no Tripe à la Mode de Caen, the brown glutinous stew designed for hungry farmers, was complete without a jiggerful. And when hungry farmers sat down to table, no meal was complete without the *trou Normand*, the Norman hole, a calvados taken midway through a ten-course meal to make room for the rest.

The people were short, square and stocky, great hunters and great fighters, who had fought the English for a hundred years, and would have fought them, if need be, for a hundred more. In peacetime the tourists had come with Baedekers to the " City of a Hundred Spires," snapped the fine eleventh-century churches which everywhere pierced the skyline, then moved on to Paris for fun. For them Caen reserved the

[1] For the chain of command between the network and London *via* Caen, Paris and the Atlantic ports see back endpaper.

For a list of all the principal characters in the story with their functions and cover names, see Appendix.

For map of the region Cherbourg—Le Havre see front endpaper.

Norman look—cynical, kindly, humorous, argumentative. They had never had too much time for tourists. Their life was encompassed by the Wednesday and Saturday markets, when big shaggy Percherons brought the cartloads of rich Isigny butter and fine ripe Camemberts rumbling on to the cobbles of the Place Saint-Sauveur. To them this life among the damp apple orchards and forests, where the greybeards still remembered wolves, alone made clean uncomplicated sense.

Girard, the son of a local vet., had been one of them for forty years. He knew some men who would die to set it free.

Still walking, he came to the docks. Swedish and German freighters, flags stencilled on their trim white sides, were tied up in the basin. Girard walked until he came to the Pont de la Fonderie, spanning the canal. Beside the bridge was a mellow red-brick house with stone-sashed windows, ringed peacefully by a semi-circle of five chestnut trees. Inside, a notice on the wall of the tiled corridor said " Department of Highways and Bridges." Girard stumped along it, turning right and climbed creaking wooden stairs to a pitch-pine door labelled " Eugène Meslin, Chief Engineer of Roads and Bridges."

Meslin was a handsome blond man in his fifties, tall and broad-shouldered. *Ciments Français* had a factory near Caen, and he and Girard had done business many times in the years before the war. Since then inevitably the two men had grown mutually indignant over other things than the rising price of cement.

When Meslin had dismissed his secretary, Girard said briskly, " Well, I've made contact with London, at last. We can start work."

He gave Meslin brief details of his meeting with Renault and went on to explain that the network would be divided into cells—perhaps half a dozen. Meslin would take charge of the Caen cell. In time Girard had hopes of establishing other cells in Cherbourg, Bayeux, St. Lô and Le Havre, as well as in inland industrial centres like Alençon and Rouen.

Meslin, tugging his blond moustache, was impressed, with reason. The territory involved was roughly 18,000 square

49

miles—a little more than half the size of Ireland. " You'll want a lot of men," he suggested.

Girard's big bear-like paw thumped the table. " That's just what we *don't* want! The more men we have, the greater the danger—too many people know too many other people. Someone talks and . . ." He blew out his cheeks in a rude but expressive noise. " Limit your cell to fifty men at the most—that way there is less risk."

" All right," said Meslin peaceably. " What's our principal objective? "

" The Atlantic Wall," Girard told him, and was conscious of the sensation he had created.

As the Government engineer responsible for all non-military maintenance, Meslin had freedom to travel almost eighty miles of the Normandy coastline. Now in his quiet methodical fashion, never once raising his voice, he told Girard what he knew of the beginnings of the Atlantic Wall in Normandy. Since March *Oberbauleitung* (Construction Sector) *Normandie*, the Todt Organisation H.Q. at St. Malo, had almost trebled its strength in the area. Dotted across the dairy pastures and orchards that lay between Caen and the sea were camps holding 4,000 men—Dutch and Belgian deportees as well as French labour. On the instructions of the chief engineer, the infamous *Oberbauleiter* (Todt Lt.-Colonel) Bürger, more than 600 men and women whose only crime had been to live on the coast had been deported. Already at Vierville, Colleville and St. Laurent-sur-Mer the bulldozers had moved in to crush their pretty white beach-houses to powder.

In some areas, Meslin said, the *zone interdite* (forbidden zone) extended twelve miles inland from the seashore, as far as Route Nationale 13, the Paris-Cherbourg highway. But on many secondary roads black-and-white striped barriers, manned by sentries, had sprung up between the green hedges, and what the Germans were planning beyond those barriers no man could say with certainty.

The engineer added that it was practically impossible to get beyond these check-points. Lynx-eyed sentries rechecked passes every few miles.

Girard gave the impatient sweep of his fist with which he brushed aside argument. Words flowed from him in a torrent. "Absolutely ridiculous—nothing is impossible if we set our minds to it. . . . *You* can go there for a start."

"I'm only one man," said Meslin incontrovertibly, "and there are certain zones where *I* can't go."

"But there are others. They use local labour on the fortifications, for a start. And they haven't evacuated the farms, they like our eggs and butter and cattle too well. So we can get farm workers or people who have business on the farms. Those people can move around, doing their ordinary jobs and using their eyes."

"All right," Meslin assured him. "I'll get busy."

A few days later, when Girard returned to Caen, Meslin reported progress. "Things are moving," he said. "Most that we know are willing to come in with us, and they're meeting to-night at the Café des Touristes. I thought you would want to talk to them personally. Incidentally"—a smile twitched his lips—"do you play dominoes?"

Girard looked puzzled. "Indifferently. Why?"

A game was a good excuse for a café meeting, Meslin explained, and a café was a safer place for regular meetings than a house. Girard approved. The key to success, as Dewavrin had told Renault to stress to all network chiefs, was to keep everything normal.

A little before six that evening ex-Captain of Artillery Marcel Girard, now chief organiser of "X" Network, arrived at the Café des Touristes to meet the nucleus of his network. The café stood at No. 73 Boulevard des Alliés, one of Caen's many cobbled streets (the Allies referred to had fought in a long-forgotten war in 1914) and at first glance there was no one detail to distinguish it from a thousand other French cafés. Outside, discreet gilt lettering on the glass windows announced merely "Paul. Vins. Tabacs."; inside, marble-topped tables, red leather benches backed by brass rails running alongside mirrored walls, a coffee machine bubbling on the zinc bar, the sour smell of wine mingling with the bitter-rough haze of

51

caporal tobacco. The café's chief claims to distinction were its *patron* and its *chauffage*—the central heating apparatus. Paul Berthelot, who ran the café (no kin to Girard's chief), was a staunch Resistant, and the broken boiler in his basement had been agreed on as the network's first " letter-box," where agents could deposit daily hand-written titbits of information.

" Scrupulously hygienic fellows, these Germans," said Meslin dryly. " I don't think it will occur to them that we're keeping top-secret information in such a filthy place." And despite all their later disasters and triumphs, time and events were to prove him right.

Sitting at a marble-topped table, sipping a cognac, Girard watched as Meslin's chosen few drifted in and shook hands formally, in France a courtesy observed even before such grimly purposeful discussions as this. " *Alors, mon vieux, ça va?* " " *Ça va bien—et vous?* " Most were ordering apéritifs at the *zinc* and chaffing Paul, before drifting over to join Girard and Meslin at the tables. Most of the group Girard knew by sight if not personally; though Caen's population numbered over 57,000, solid country loyalties bound its people closer than most. The bulk of those gathered to-night were small-town tradesmen, sporting old-fashioned watch-chains and drawing thoughtfully on blackened pipes, but fighters to a man. It would have done Dewavrin's heart good to see them.

Léon Dumis, for example, the garage proprietor, small and dapper with his trim toothbrush moustache and thoughtful blue eyes, now joining them with a Cinzano in his hand. He was hardly seated before the patron's wife appeared and Dumis, all in one movement, jumped up, snatched off his beret and tucked it under his arm to reveal a head as bald and polished as an egg. But this grave courtesy, as Girard knew, stopped short at providing a German truck with so much as a litre of gasoline. Dumis had closed his garage on the day war broke out and since demobilisation had made do on his dwindling savings.

Girard was glad to see Jean Chateau, the electricity board inspector, there. A big, placid man, with carefully brushed-back hair, Chateau had been one of Normandy's first Resistants, along with Roger Deschambres, the melancholy red-haired plumber, who lived a few streets away. Alongside them, not talking much, was a shy fair-haired young man of thirty, Robert Thomas, looking more English than French, who now had a job in the potato controller's office on the rue des Carmelites. Younger than the rest, with slender sensitive fingers like a flute-player's, Thomas at first seemed always on the defensive, but it was the background of two years' resistance that Girard read in the wary grey eyes, an endless chain of houses " safe " and " blown," and hit-and-run transmissions in Brest and Alençon.

Such men were discreet and Girard was glad to have them, but now, to hold watchful daily vigil over the talkative ones, the vast reassuring shadow of Wilfrid Torres loomed over the meeting. As a close friend of Captain Gaubert, head of the Caen gendarmerie, Torres would be forewarned on Gestapo *coups* and inevitably had drawn a job as the network's security officer.

Nom de Dieu, thought Girard, there is a man who thinks quickly. Always the Germans were pressing Torres to work for them and always he regretted infinitely—no equipment. In June, 1940, when the Germans entered Lorient, they had found Torres, harbour works contractor, busy constructing piers for the French Navy. The Germans had decided that Torres and his two wagon-loads of pile drivers could be of use to them at Brest, helping the Todt Organisation construct the U-Boat pens which Renault's networks had repurted. Torres had asked for eight days' grace to settle his affairs and was given four. The Germans had loaded his wagons on to freight trucks, labelled them " Brest " and left them in a siding at the Gare Maritime. Torres had used his four days' grace to enlist the aid of a sympathetic shunter, change the labels to " Caen " and then tactfully disappear. Back in Caen he had supervised the unloading of the wagons and had the contents stored in a disused warehouse near his house. Now, with skeleton equipment, Torres had to subsist on such minor repairs as Meslin could find for him, but at least there were eight tons of pile-driving and dredging equipment that would never work for the Germans.

The last and most picturesque member of the group had, as always, arrived late. Looking at him, Girard felt an odd blend of affection and impatience, of irritation and respect. No man, meeting René Duchez, the house painter, ever failed to react to him. You loved him or you thought him the biggest fool on earth, you despised him or believed him the cleverest secret agent Dewavrin ever had. Duchez was just forty, with bold blue eyes, always twinkling with devilry, and a long humorous upper lip. The painter's pleasure was to make light of everything, especially danger, and it was his boast that he had nerve enough to fool the smartest German born. Girard could hear him now: " *C'est le sang-froid, mon ami—c'est toujours le sang-froid.*"

No one had ever estimated—or challenged—Duchez's capacity with the calvados, but this could be deceptive. At the very moment you thought him fuddled he would say something so much to the point, so full of horse sense, that you knew his high rather bony head was functioning clear as a bell. Then, at the thought of how he had fooled you, the painter would shake with silent laughter for minutes on end, for Duchez had a child's simple acceptance of life as it came. Of all the agents it was probably only he who did what he did for the sheer hell of it.

On the surface their meeting was as innocent as could be. At two adjoining tables, four men—Girard, Meslin, Chateau, Duchez—were absorbed in two separate games of dominoes. Four others, grouped round them, were providing a protective wall with their backs, plus as much advice, chaff and good-humoured insult as the players would tolerate. The rest of the café was reflected by the mirrors facing them.

Once the games were under way, Girard began talking very quietly, his voice a low rumble in his throat. He said " Our friend here . . ."—referring to Meslin by his code-name of Morvain—" has given you some idea of our task. We have to try and crack this new Atlantic Wall." Someone, craning over the board, said " *Bien sûr patron*—and it's no easy one." And

Girard countered quickly, " It isn't impossible. Nothing is."
He looked up at the ring of faces. " Now here is what I propose
to do."

Girard had overlooked very little. As with all the networks
Renault had founded, the new network was to be run on the
lines of a French military general staff, with a marked division
of responsibility. To begin with, there were to be three classes
of agents—P-o's, occasional agents, who would go about their
normal business, P-1's, agents devoting at least half their time
to Resistance work, and P-2's, full-time agents. (The " P "
denoted " person.") Of the latter class, Girard intended to
have as few as possible. At their headquarters, as yet unchosen,
each aspect of the work would be sub-divided into dossiers:
casemates, anti-aircraft batteries, communications, beach-
obstacles.

Girard put Duchez, the painter, who had a wide circle of
friends, in charge of the P-1's. As a man noted for convivial
meetings in the town's cafés, he was likely to attract little
attention.

" We must think of this operation," Girard stressed, " in
terms of detail. Nothing is too small. We must know the
texture of the sand along every inch of that shore. If there is
barbed wire, we must find out not only how high it is but what
strand it is. If we find that they are building block-houses
along the coast, then we must not only find out where they are
but the thickness of the concrete. And we must find out about
the doors."

" Doors? " That was Thomas, who always liked to have
everything precise.

Girard explained, " If this is to be a Wall, it will have
doors. They have to move troops up to the forward areas from
Caen and other towns, don't they? Even at its nearest point
the railway runs more than a mile from the actual beach. At
intervals there must be channels, camouflaged so that they're
not easily recognised, going miles deep into the fortifications. They could be used by friend or foe—if the foe knew
how."

Once or twice as other townsmen drifted in to use the bar

he broke off, and the talk switched quickly to good-natured ribbing. " There now, move there and you've got him." " It's a sadness that I cannot play one hand without the advice of half-wits." Then, quietly, someone raised a query about the freedom of passage, and Girard explained to Duchez that as the P-1's would have to work under fictitious identities as well as their own, the faking of identity papers and travel permits would be the department of the painter's wife, Odette, a pleasant sweet-faced woman from Evreux, not present at the meeting. " Tell her we don't want to use fake identity papers," Girard said, " if we can possibly help it. Somebody must have access to the real thing and our job is to find them."

Methodically Girard allotted other tasks. Recruiting agents whose business normally took them through the forbidden zone was divided between Meslin and a liaison agent not then present, a dark strikingly-handsome young advocate named Léonard Gille. Daily liaison between Meslin and the agents and the distribution of funds would be Pierre Harivel's job. A solidly-built man with a broad forehead and an aquiline nose, Harivel's work as an insurance inspector for the company, *La Preservatrice*, gave him a limited freedom of passage throughout part of the zone. Once again, Renault's old and sure methods would be used to good advantage.

There was more to the conversation than these reconstructed extracts, of course. Other meetings were held at other times and places, between Girard and Meslin, between Meslin and his liaison agents, as points were thrashed out and settled, but within these first days there was a perceptible sense of the network clicking into operational shape. " It won't be any picnic," Girard warned them frequently. " We can't afford time—we haven't got any. And it'll be a bloody job, because there will be losses. We have to face that. Some of us are going to get caught."

No one said anything then or moved a domino, because the thought of Gestapo Headquarters in a converted doctor's surgery at 25 rue des Jacobins was something that one tried to isolate far back in one's mind. The legal penalty for intelligence work against the Gestapo was beheading by the axe, with the head strapped to a board, face up, but the chief of the Caen Gestapo, an effeminate pervert named Helmut Bernard, prided himself that he could always first obtain a confession implicating others. Beginning with such blandishments as cigarettes and good meals he progressed unhurriedly to immersion in ice-filled baths and electric charges administered through the rectum. This man, Girard knew, could be the greatest obstacle in their struggle to penetrate the secrets of the Wall.

" This is a mosaic job," Girard always wound up soberly, " putting together a thousand separate pieces." Then he added wryly, " And the devil of it is we shall never know which piece it is that counts."

The meetings broke up undramatically then; a last round of drinks at the bar, and slowly, in ones and twos, they would drift from the café into the spring night. After the birth of such a desperate and adult enterprise, it seemed an odd anti-climax that the curfew sent them meekly home like children at 7.30 p.m.

This, then, was " Commandant Passy's " idea taking shape in a new setting—as it turned out, the most important sector of the long Atlantic Wall in which any network could operate. Even Dewavrin did not yet know that, though he was soon to have an inkling, but the men of the Caen cell knew it still less. Two years had hardened them in this battle, in which the first rule was not to look ahead; two years had already coloured their feelings for neighbours who did not resist, and had given their unity something of the flavour of a grim personal battle in which each day was an enemy to be outlived. Girard, Meslin, Gille, Duchez—all of them knew the pathetic beginnings of other groups which had foundered and fumbled. There was almost nothing they did not know about the smudged sheets rolled off by patriots on forbidden roneos and dignified by the name of " secret newspapers," about blurred photos of de Gaulle, sold furtively to raise funds, about bizarre ways of passing on the word to resist. Gille and Chateau had even belonged to a dancing class where the instructor, under the guise of teaching new steps, had preached anti-Vichy propaganda.

If Resistance was now a personal matter, it was also considered, mature. It meant more than schoolboy antics like ripping down official posters behind the sentry's back or creeping out after curfew to fox the transport columns by changing the finger-posts. It was more than a blazing hatred of hearing jackboots on cobbled streets, or of seeing the swastika bannering against a blue sky. It even meant something normally most alien and distasteful to the French, a willingness to be organised. It meant now, in 1942, that you had heard the stories going the rounds and were intensely aware of the worst the invader could do: the father thrown violently into a deportees' truck while waiting outside an infant school to collect his five-year-old daughter, the youngster who bolted from the obscenities of a Gestapo interrogation to slash his wrists and die, much too slowly, on the pavement of the rue des Jacobins. If you resisted, it meant that you had weighed these factors and decided that there were bigger problems than how to stay alive.

Meslin, for instance. His first problem was to choose the nerve-centre of their war against the Wall. He thought hard about it for some days, conscious that through him things were hanging fire, but the decision was a hard one. As a bachelor, Meslin lived with a housekeeper in an old house overlooking the river, a full twenty minutes' walk from the office. The office, where he worked a twelve-hour day, was the real centre of his life, but if the office became his centre of Resistance, too, it meant bringing his secretary, a lively little redhead of seventeen named Jeanne Verinaud, into the network.

Meslin knew the girl would not betray him; over twelve months they had shared jokes as well as work, the favourite being the handful of gravel which the early-rising Meslin tossed at her bedroom window by way of reveille as he passed along the street. But he was a good and conscientious man who treated her like a favourite daughter. (It was typical of him that his desk in the office caught most draughts from the constantly-opening door.) Could he, in fairness, ask her to risk her life?

But in the end it seemed that there was no other way. One morning early, before the first callers had arrived, when Jeanne, as usual, was at the open window, tempting the sparrows with crumbs from her breakfast table, Meslin explained what he wanted to do. He ended up: " It's a big risk for you, Jeanne—bigger than for my friends, because they will risk less by coming here than by coming to my house."

Jeanne Verinaud laughed. Then she unlocked the top right-hand drawer of her desk and, in silence, took something out. She handed it to Meslin. It was the photograph of de Gaulle that she had prized for two years, so now Meslin had his answer.

On one thing the network was determined from the start: to profit by the past mistakes of embryo organisations. This meant that Torres, the security chief, also had his problems. Mulling over the security risk in his long cool drawing-room, hung with sporting prints, that overlooked the canal, he did not know of the disastrous blow that the careless Subsol had dealt Renault's radio link, but there was no need: he had an example right on the spot. One newly-fledged network of which he had heard rumours, working in the dark without guidance from London, had been wiped out only last month because an agent had carried a list of addresses. Seventeen of its members were still held in the gaol at Caen, awaiting trial.

Torres brooded for some time and then went to Meslin with a system of mnemonics all his own. " You know the way it's always been before," he said. " A liaison agent doing a job like Gille or Harivel couldn't remember the names of everyone he had to meet up with in cafés so he wrote them down. But now all they'll need to do is to carry a pocket dictionary."

It was absurd to think how simple it was—and how effective. Instead of writing down "Duchez," a man put a cross in his dictionary by the word " duchesse." Instead of " Torres" he put a cross by " torse." The Gestapo could do spot-checks as often as they liked but they would find nothing but innocent men eager to increase their word-power.

Duchez, too, had problems, being very busy on his wife's behalf. But the painter was a firm believer in the axiom that once a man has dipped a toe in the water he can often be induced to plunge in up to his knees. One morning at about this time, he drove his battered camionet down to the *Mairie*, a weathered yellow-plastered building on the rue Pasteur and asked to see Henri Caillet, the assistant to the Secretary-General. Duchez knew that Caillet, who had served with him as a private in the 21st Transport Group at Tours, was a man of integrity, besides being responsible for the issuing of food and identity cards to 57,500 people.

Caillet, a nervous heavily-built man with a diffident manner, at first received him cautiously—with good reason, since there were Germans working only twelve feet away from his own desk. Apparently untroubled by this, Duchez said chattily that few men seemed better in with the Germans than Caillet. Lately he had seen him riding with them in their shiny khaki-coloured staff cars and exchanging jokes. Caillet cast an agonised glance across the room at the genial *Hauptmann* (Captain) Kramm of Civil Affairs, who was so open-handed with cigars, and muttered that it was not of his seeking. He was almost a one-man bureaucracy and the Germans could hardly get along without him.

Duchez nodded with seeming sympathy. " And that," he said rather loudly, " is your kind of war? "

Caillet was understandably nettled. He hissed that it was not his kind of war at all. " So," Duchez said, " then you *don't* want to be well in with them? " And was relieved when Caillet answered quietly, with oddly-moving sincerity, " Most of all I want to be able to live with myself."

That was much better. In that case, for the sake of a poor devil on the run from the Gestapo, Caillet could no doubt provide a blank identity card and food cards, without which the *malheureux* could not eat, let alone escape. Caillet, unaware that the poor devil existed only in the painter's fertile mind, said he would, and Duchez had forged the first link in the chain of men leading double lives. Every three days thereafter, though Caillet did not know it, he would be back to ask for more.

Back to the battered camionet. Duchez did not believe in wasting time. The next call was at Police Headquarters to tell the same heartrending story to his friend, Inspector Roger Leblond. A dark, lively, young policeman with a bubbling sense of humour, Leblond knew and liked Duchez, who had several times painted his office, thinking that the painter's deceptive air of good fellowship would have been useful in police work. " There was never anyone for playing on your emotions like Duchez," he recalled later. " First he bought me a drink, then he wrung my heart with this tale, and when I brought him the card the next day he looked at me with a glint in his eye and said he could use 1,000 a week! I was in his network right up to my neck."

Now Leblond too was initiated into the mysteries of the Café des Touristes, and the disreputable broken boiler which the Germans scorned to touch became a receptacle for bundles of stolen identity cards.

Roger Deschambres, the plumber, now remembered that some weeks previously, while fixing the central heating, he had met a hotelier named Pierre Mayoraz who had expressed sympathetic views. He told Duchez and the painter drove down to the Hotel de Rouen, a quiet clean one-night hotel standing on the station approach, and found that Mayoraz, an enormous Swiss with a varnished wisp of moustache and grey unwinking eyes, appealed to him on sight. If his pale-green monogrammed silk shirts suggested prosperity, Mayoraz himself, enveloping a chair in his dark front bar, his belt threatening to snap across his stomach, suggested a very tough customer indeed.

Duchez made no bones about what he wanted—first an extra letter-box, but above and beyond that a haven for visiting agents. At the moment, he said, the network was small, but already his chief was shuttling between Paris and other towns, extending its coverage. It was going to be something big, this network, Mayoraz would see. Soon regional inspectors would be passing through Caen almost weekly to Cherbourg and St. Lô to Honfleur and Le Havre, collecting data from their sources along the Wall, and carrying it back to Caen.

Would Mayoraz be willing to receive such men as his guests? " Just send them to me," Mayoraz said.

" Do you have ideas for a letter-box? " the painter asked, trying to plumb his mind.

Mayoraz said patiently: " Of course. Behind the bar. Normal, you see, like any *poste-restante* in peacetime. They get you, you know, once you stop behaving normally."

Then Duchez asked the testing question: " You realise this is going to be dangerous? " And Mayoraz answered, without any emotion at all, " Sometimes you've got to live dangerously, or life is dull."

" *C'est le sang-froid,*" said Duchez approvingly.

Maroraz called for a calvados each, and they drank to Girard's network.

Chapter Six

OPERATION WALL

MIDWAY THROUGH April the network was ready for action. A constant stream of callers now came and went to Meslin's office; half a dozen times a day little Jeanne Verinaud felt her heart skip a beat when the door opened without warning and Lieutenant Karl Hoëfa, the blond good-looking young liaison officer from *Kriegsmarine Wehr* (Naval Defence) walked in on a heated Resistance conference between Meslin and three or four others.

But Meslin knew what he was doing and he had insisted from the start that those who visited him openly should be able to plead legitimate business. Duchez came to nose out painting contracts, Girard to discuss cement supplies, and they had all become adept at translating Resistance talk into terms of lorry-loads and labour gangs with the first turn of the door-knob. Nothing if not thorough, Meslin even took out a life insurance policy with Harivel's company, the premiums supplying a valid excuse for the money that often changed hands over the desk. Harivel now had the handling of 50,000 francs, the agents' working expenses, a fourth part of the money Renault had made available to Colonel Touny.

These men had convincing reasons to use the front stairs with impunity, but Meslin made the others, like the volatile Léonard Gille, the advocate, who always swept in like an actor taking a curtain call, use the back stairs, which led to an exit through a builder's yard.

At least once a week came Girard, always in a hurry, always with a fresh batch of instructions, pounding the table and talking so fast that Jeanne Verinaud almost developed stenographer's cramp taking notes.

" Thank God you did join us," Meslin groaned piously, " I couldn't remember half of this if you weren't getting it down."

The line of communication planned was not foolproof, but it was the best available. From the lanes and fields that ringed the Wall, the information would travel a risky 600-mile route to London. An agent would see a new blockhouse under way, scribble down details on a scrap of paper headed with his cover-name and drop it in the boiler at the Café des Touristes or seal it in a plain envelope and leave it behind the bar at the Hotel de Rouen. But that was only the beginning. Once a week Duchez or Harivel, the " postmen," had to clear the letter-boxes and carry the grubby incriminating scraps, like the contents of some treacherous suggestion-box, to Meslin's office. Then Meslin would classify the information according to subject matter, welding it into a lengthy report for typing.

Most of the typing Jeanne Verinaud squeezed into office hours—the Gestapo were suspicious of lights burning late—putting aside her new Imperial in favour of an old four-bank Underwood that was kept locked in a filing cabinet in the washroom annexe. " Officially we've never reported the serial number of this machine," she told the approving Meslin. " If they ever captured one of our reports, they couldn't trace it back to here."

Once a fortnight the courier ran the reports to Paris, passing them to Girard or to Berthelot, the ex-diplomat, who appended information that had come in from Touny's O.C.M. agents all over northern France, before passing them to Renault. It would be up to Renault then, either by Lysander pick-up from " Guardian Angel " or by maritime rendezvous, somehow to pile up all this information, plus the gleanings of his fourteen other networks, on Dewavrin's desk in London.

Meslin had picked Maurice Himbert, a leathery anonymous-looking little man who ran a motor-cycle repair shop, as the Caen-Paris courier. Because he had to visit the capital once a fortnight to buy spares, Gille had suggested him as the ideal man to carry the network's reports.

When there were any. That, at first, was the problem. Once the first flush of enthusiasm had paled both Girard and

Meslin had to admit that the results were slender. Despite the fake identities, only a handful of people had valid reasons to penetrate the coastal zone.

On 17th April, 1942, came the biggest chance to date.

Sometime during that night a group of anonymous saboteurs derailed a German troop train near the station of Moult-Argences, on the Paris-Cherbourg line. More than a score died in the wreckage and the German reprisals were swift and bloody. Five hundred Communists, whose names were supplied by Vichy's political police, and five hundred Jews, identified by the yellow stars sewn on their clothes, were deported and were not seen again. Of the seventeen conspirators who had given Torres such food for thought, three were shot on 9th May, without trial, in the barrack-yard of the 43rd Artillery Company, and the remainder transported for life. Sportsgrounds, cinemas and many restaurants were closed indefinitely. A 7 p.m. to 6 a.m. curfew was clamped down on Caen.

ALL TRAINS, ran a red-and-black lettered notice, WILL FROM NOW ON CARRY A PERCENTAGE OF CIVILIAN HOSTAGES.

The Germans had to find their hostages, twenty per journey, as and where they could. Busy housewives, arriving at the Gare Centrale to visit relatives in Evreux or Lisieux, would find themselves herded, protesting, on to troop trains, forced to endure not only the three-hour journey to Cherbourg but to stay overnight (all expenses paid) at the commandeered Hotel de Cherbourg. Their only freedom was to choose the time of their return next day. Even staunch collaborators shied from this duty, but not a stocky ruddy-faced cement contractor named Gilbert Michel, one of the network's most enterprising agents. Each week, whenever he could spare time, the obliging Michel reported to the Bureau Civil at the Prefecture and volunteered for the journey as an example to the irresponsible traitors who were sabotaging peaceful co-existence. If this was pitching it rather high, the Germans raised no objections; they were glad enough to find volunteers. Most other people in Caen had decided abruptly that their journeys were not really necessary.

"But after all," Michel told Girard, "there are compensations. If you pay to travel anywhere in wartime, you're mostly paying to stand in a packed corridor and be almost stifled." Hostages, as he pointed out, rode free, in the first-class carriages next to the engine.

There were risks, of course, despite their presence. Most railway sabotage was then staged by Communists, whose ideologies came a long way ahead of their regard for their neighbours and Michel did admit later that when the train jolted badly there was one second of lurching horror: in another minute we shall all be dead. But at the end, if you could rise above it, there were more compensations. Once outside the station, Michel would turn right along the Quai Caligny and then left on to the Place Napoleon, overlooking the inner harbour, walking free as air, with a German pass in his pocket, to savour the salt breeze, at the same time noting the distances between all those heavily-sandbagged machine-gun nests along the quays and where the minefields on the beaches began and ended.

Girard and Meslin were delighted. The Wall was developing eyes.

One of the sharpest eyes along the Wall belonged to Fernand Arsène. The expression is tragically literal, for Arsène, the second plumber to join the network in as many weeks, had lost the sight of one eye in a central heating explosion back in the 'thirties. He was a lean weather-beaten man, with steel spectacles and lank black untameable hair, contentious and brave as a lion. Sometimes, disconcertingly, he would imitate any object that cropped up in his conversation, from an electric drill to a fire engine, not to win laughter but to clarify his meaning. All Arsène's feelings were intense: his deep sense of religion, which gave him strength, his dislike of alcohol, his sense of frustration which made his life a hell of dyspepsia and kept him from sleeping almost all the war, his hatred of the invader which kept him resisting almost twenty-four hours a day. Because business was slack he doubled up his job delivering coal to German barracks round Caen, and wherever he drove his eye missed nothing.

66

It was some time that spring that he received a call, late one afternoon, from a woman whose central heating had developed indigestion somewhere beyond the town of Evrecy. Arsène got out his old camionet and drove south on the second-class road, C8; twice he was stopped at check-points and it occurred to him that if the job was a long one, he would be forced to make a twelve-mile drive back in the dark. He was not primarily thinking of the network or the Atlantic Wall.

Just south of Evrecy, the second-class road ran level for some 900 yards with a new feature of the defences—the stretch of rich cow pasture that was now the temporary dispersal 'drome at Ainchamps. The screening was by no means perfect, thick barbed wire tangling a hawthorn hedge, but Arsène, driving at a level 20 m.p.h. with his eyes on the road ahead, at first gave only a casual glance across the dispersal. And then a curious thing struck him. At that hour, just after five-thirty in the afternoon, the sun was a disc of beaten copper sinking slowly on the rim of the western horizon. Beyond the hedge a gaggle of Ju. 87s crouched in readiness; he knew them at once from the torpedo-shaped nose and the squat ugly wings. On several nights, at the cost of much eye-strain, he had sat up late mastering the small purple aircraft recognition silhouettes that Meslin had doled out to each agent.

Arsène's mind registered the planes, for reference, but he was almost beyond the boundary of the field before the inner realisation hit him. The whole western end of the field had been washed in the gold of the setting sun, yet no answering gleam winked back from the aircraft's wings.

Wood, Arsène thought, with a small secret glow of pleasure. *Wooden aeroplanes, drawn up at a dispersal like sitting ducks, a perfect pitifully easy target to tempt the R.A.F. Then what of the real planes?*

That afternoon he played the oldest and shiniest trump card—the wrong tools for the job—in the plumber's deck, arguing as only he could argue until the woman, like most of his friends, gave him best and told him to return on the morrow. Next day, making allowances for the sun, Arsène returned at the same hour to check his impressions, twisting his van in and out of the dead-end lanes north of Evrecy until at last he had spotted the real thing, cleverly camouflaged in tiny hangars over a square mile of woodland. The network had the news dispatched to London the same night.

New agents were being recruited almost weekly. Many were to prove shining examples of the faith of which Dewavrin had spoken; knowing neither Girard nor Meslin nor of the complex chain that linked their efforts with London, they still worked patiently on under the guidance of Gille or Harivel or Duchez until the Wall had crumbled. Among these were René Vauclin, the tiler and his wife, Olgvie.

Both seemed curious types for secret agents. Vauclin was a jolly roly-poly man, like a favourite uncle, who seemed to bubble over with the sheer joy of living. Olgvie, his wife, was a French countrywoman to the core, outspoken but kindly, with steady grey eyes, a firm chin and the habit of prefacing her sentences, " I will tell you very frankly . . ." No. 32 rue St. Martin, their home, was a high cool old-fashioned house, its floors glowing with linseed polish, its shadowed rooms echoing to the measured tick of ormolu clocks, the tooled leather surface of the great oaken desk, where Vauclin received his orders, accurately reflecting its owner's status as a prosperous *bon bourgeois*. The Vauclins were prepared to risk all this, and their lives besides, to give a first impetus to Girard's network.

Their first chance came at about two o'clock one April afternoon, just after lunch. A German pioneer officer called at Vauclin's door and ordered him to come at once. Outside a black Citroën was waiting, and they drove in silence through lanes clouded white with hawthorn to the village of Bretteville L'Orgeuilleuse. Before the great battle the fine Gothic belfry and steeple of Saint-Germain, Bretteville, stood 160 clear feet above the apple orchards, and at the foot of the tower Vauclin found a Colonel of pioneers, an elderly man with a lined grey face, waiting for him.

The Colonel began by explaining that Vauclin would be required to do work on the tower. The tiler merely nodded, and he went on, " I shall provide you with labour, monsieur, and with red lamps. You will install one of these lamps at each of the four corners of the tower and wire them for electricity."

"A red lamp at each corner?" Vauclin was thinking hard.

"Exactly. Now, then, the steeple itself." Vauclin followed the Colonel's outstretched finger, and he could see the steeple, pointing like a stone finger at the blue sky, the sun glittering faintly on the gilded cockerel which spans the weathervane of all French churches. The Colonel was still talking: "You see the weathervane? Very well, then, at the extreme ends of that, two more red lamps."

The implications hit Vauclin at just about the same time that the Colonel began elaborating, and they were considerable.

Five miles to the east lay the bomber airfield of Carpiquet. Vauclin was in no position to know that the squadrons of Focke-Wulf fighter-bombers based there were in the vanguard of the inexcusable "Baedeker" raids on old and unprotected cities like Exeter and Bath. Nor did the Colonel tell him, but he did explain that the red lights on tower and weathervane were a fix for homing aircraft, to be shut off immediately the last plane returned.

He was more astonished than ever when the Colonel added, "At the same time we shall switch on our landing lights at St. Manvieu." Vauclin knew a little about St. Manvieu, three miles south-east; a careful farmer had lost many acres of good earth because the Todt Organisation had decided to build an airfield there. Suddenly the ruse was very plain. What the Luftwaffe chiefs anticipated was something that the R.A.F. was in no position to carry out before the December of that year: a fighter retaliation offensive launched at night. Only if they *did* come they would not find Carpiquet, snug in the darkness of the Normandy night, at all. They would find the lime-lit nakedness of the false drome at St. Manvieu and bomb that. (In 1942, before radio-navigational aid was available, little more than one raid in three was really effective, and when "dirty" dark nights obscured targets, bombing open fields with German complicity was by no means unheard of.)

Vauclin spent the rest of the afternoon, aided by local labour, fixing the wiring like a good collaborator, hauling the lamps up to the belfry by means of winches. Later the Germans were good enough to drive him home, and just before 5 p.m. he was knocking on the door of Duchez the painter's house. In due course, " St. Manvieu " joined " Ainchamps " on the imposing list of non-existent aerodromes that the Air Ministry was building up in London.

It was not always so easy. Vauclin had completed his job and no questions asked; the R.A.F. had not bombed Carpiquet, but neither had they risked men and machines bombing St. Manvieu. Instead it was the Germans who had wasted time and effort, building one more adjunct to the Wall that fooled nobody. The R.A.F. instead found it more profitable to drop baskets of pigeons, and it was one of these that once more involved the Vauclins in the war against the Wall.

Some workmen found the pigeon late one afternoon, in the marshes north of Bayeux, and an hour later two of them were knocking at the one back door in the town·which instinct told them was safe. The door was opened by a dark, volatile, young law student named Jeanne Escolan, whom the workmen trusted because her parents had that day been arrested on suspicion of espionage. The girl decided that to keep the pigeon in the house that night was too dangerous. Instead she lodged it with a grain merchant named Lefort and the next day, concealing it in a basket, she cycled from Bayeux to Caen and knocked at Vauclin's door.

" You must be mad to come here on a day like this," Olgvie Vauclin remembers saying when she opened the door. " Why aren't you in hiding? They'll get you too." But the girl only stood there, pale and tense, repeating, " Never mind all that. The pigeon must go."

In theory, the procedure regarding pigeons was well known. At this time, by arrangement with the R.A.F., Dewavrin was having pigeons scattered in strategic sectors of France, a tentative attempt to ease the vastly overloaded radio traffic. (The system was dropped when German counter-espionage opened their own pigeon school at St. Lô.) Girard had made it plain enough to the network what to do. If you had vital information regarding troop movements behind the Wall, you scribbled a note of it, slipped it into the racing band on the bird's leg and released it in the early morning. If you had no urgent report to make, you passed the bird until you found someone who had.

Madame Vauclin *had* urgent information. On one of her periodic cycle trips through the countryside in search of butter and eggs, she had seen that the Bois de la Londe, a wood inside the forbidden zone near Carpiquet airfield, was now thick with troops and tanks. They were echelons of 24th Panzer Division establishing defences west of the Caen-St. Nazaire line, though she did not know that.

The penalty for possession of a racing pigeon was death, and of this at least she was painfully aware.

The night on which the pigeon arrived was cool but the Vauclins slept uneasily. At 5 a.m. Vauclin crawled heavy-eyed from bed and went upstairs in his nightgown to secure the pigeon from the loft. When the message was securely fastened in the racing band he crept downstairs again and Olgvie, very wide awake, sat up in bed. There was no one in the house but themselves and a maid-of-all-work sympathetic to the cause, but unconsciously both spoke in whispers.

" Is it all right? "

" It seems to be. I'd better release it now. . . ."

" Wait." Madame Vauclin climbed out of bed, a purposeful clear-thinking woman. " First I will look in the street and see if the coast is clear." Curfew still had ninety minutes to run, even German reveille would not sound for another hour, but if an early picket was on the march . . . In the stillness the opening shutter seemed to squeal down the whole length of the street, but there were only the pavements glistening in the early light, and the mellow steep-pitched roofs of Caen.

" All right—*now*! "

Pigeons are temperamental in unfamiliar hands, and the bird must suddenly have become aware of the tension. Vauclin felt it flutter and stir beneath his hands. His wife was holding the window wider, saying, " Now, René—quickly! " and Vauclin, trying to soothe the pigeon, shifted his grip. As he approached the window he tried to launch it upwards, as he

71

had seen the back-garden fanciers do, years ago, and the wire on which the lace curtains were strung ruffled the slate-grey plumage. The bird gave a short croon of protest, beating from Vauclin's hands, and seemed to go downwards over the sill like a stone.

Neither Vauclin nor his wife said anything for a moment, then, forgetting caution, they tore aside the lace curtains, craning over the sill. But as far as they could see there were only the shutters of their neighbours, tight-closed, revealing nothing. There was no movement of wings in the street, nothing stirred.

Olgvie Vauclin's jaw set tight with determination. " René, we've got to find the bird. Think, if *they* find it . . ."

" But how? If I go into the street I shall be seen. . . ."

" Then try from the ground-floor windows. Or it may have gone round to the back of the house. . . ." Both of them standing in their night-clothes, barefoot on the polished oak, their whispers seeming to fill the house. Chilled and frightened, Vauclin went downstairs. He crept from window to window, parting the curtains and shutters, seeing nothing. In the back-yard the raw air made him shudder, but the pigeon was not there. He crept upstairs again to find his wife still glued to the shutter. " I'd better get dressed," he was saying hopelessly. " For all we know it may be roosting on some window-sill down the street," when Olgvie suddenly blurted out, in a voice cracked with emotion, " Look! "

Vauclin's scalp crawled at the tone of her voice, but he looked, and there was the pigeon, sitting quite smugly and comfortably on the roof of No. 25, the grocer's store. He gestured at the bird fiercely, beginning to hate it, but the pigeon did not stir.

He was standing in the window, saying, with an edge in his voice, " Of all the stupid birds I ever saw——" when his wife cut in, " Come back inside or they'll see you from No. 36." And at the memory of No. 36 he felt his stomach turn over. At No. 36, the Hotel Florida, two houses down on their own side of the street and exactly opposite where the pigeon was roosting, a score of infantrymen from the 716th Division were billeted. Their bedroom was on a level with the Vauclins', and soon they would be all too visible, skylarking boisterously about the room as they did their ablutions.

With a woman's devastating common sense, Olgvie Vauclin decided they had better eat, but such *petit déjeuner* as they took that day was taken standing, still near the open window, gazing with a kind of mesmerised dread at the pigeon, which appeared to be drifting off to sleep. It had now occurred to both of them, though they did not voice it, that the pigeon might decide to fly through the Germans' window. Unlike the more prudent French, the Germans kept their shutters wide open all night, defying the worst the weather could do.

Soon after that they heard a clock strike six, and Vauclin suddenly said, " Oh, God," and they stood there very still. Shutters were banging back along the street now, and he had begun to believe that no worse could come, when suddenly and cruelly the sun was steeping the roof-tops, and its light was trapped, winking and sparkling, in the bird's pink polished claws. Six-twenty. Someone would see that tell-tale light, Vauclin thought trembling, would see it and report it. They were not all Resistants in that street.

Six-thirty. At the Hotel Florida the Germans would have finished dressing. Soon they would be ready to leave for breakfast. They would come piling into the street as they always did, their nailed boots ringing on the stone. They would turn right, past the Vauclins' house and they could not fail to see the bird. One good rifle shot would bring it down like a stone, and it would not take them long to check the handwriting. Dry-mouthed and sweating, Vauclin closed his eyes in prayer.

The pigeon seemed to come to a decision. The wings spread suddenly and wonderfully like a soft grey fan; it stirred and became briefly airborne. For one agonising second it hovered above the grocer's chimney tops. Then, with a long soaring ripple of flight, it rose eastwards and out of sight, climbing towards the sun.

At nine-thirty on the Saturday night, crouched in their coal cellar by a forbidden receiver, they heard the measured dispassionate tones of the B.B.C. announcer telling " Madame

Marthe," as the Underground knew Olgvie Vauclin, that her message had been received. Another small link in the Wall's defences had been faithfully charted. Vauclin looked across at his wife, but for a while he could say nothing, nothing at all.

Gille, meantime, had had a somewhat off-beat interview in a cluttered studio off the rue Geôle. He had gone there to make a new recruit, a man named Robert Douin, and it struck him in retrospect that, aside from Duchez, Douin would probably figure as the network's most picturesque agent. But where Duchez was gay and insouciant, Douin was a man afire, who made small attempt to conceal his emotions. Bearded, his hair poking in wild spikes from beneath his beret, he started by asking the advocate in quivering fury: " Are you asking me to work for the English, m'sieu? "

Gille said diplomatically that he was asking Douin to work for France and for humanity, but the peppery little sculptor was only partially mollified. " I must make this very plain to you, monsieur. *I* am a Royalist. You may work for whom you please, but I shall be working for the King of France. I do not recognise the Republic of France, any more than I recognise the English."

Gille was so taken aback that he lost track of the complex historical reasoning whereby Douin held the English directly responsible for the French Revolution, but he left in no doubt that the sculptor found his bread and butter work extremely distasteful. Most of his commissions were to sculpt the head of the legendary woman called Marianne, the accepted symbol of the Republic, which appears over every public building.

A former Professor at the École des Beaux Arts, and the last of a long line of sculptors, Douin was a perfect addition to the Caen cell. In the most sanctified way imaginable, he had endless opportunities to penetrate the zone. He was a restorer of church statues.

In the first week of May, Douin was scheduled to carry out repairs to the statues and carvings in the belfry of Notre Dame de Ranville. The weather was clear, without hint of haze, and Douin, who bicycled to and from his sites, worked undisturbed for several days, seeing few people apart from the Abbé Georges Duhamel, the *curé*.

North of Caen the land is flat and lonely and the only vantage points are the high belfries of the village churches. From the belfry of Notre Dame in the village of Ranville, 75 feet high, Douin could see all the land lying between Caen and the sea with vivid clarity. It was as if a photograph had taken on a third dimension: the green candelabra of branches, the toy roofs of barns, the Orne, twisting like a silver filament between gentle river meadows. At the most he reckoned he could see three miles in any direction, for the land was as level as a table, and in this small section of the Wall he could see a number of things that interested him.

Due north, two miles away on the secondary road running from St. Aubin d'Arquenay to Ouistreham, was the water-works. Douin was glad he knew the landmark, for it helped him to define precisely that only a hundred yards or so due north of that was a battery of short-range 155s. He could determine the range through his experience in an artillery regiment, and there was one large piece of artillery—impossible at this distance to tell what. There were barracks, too, in Douin's bird's eye view; he spread a scrap of paper on the worn grey stone, sketching intently as his eyes strove to compass the distance. That was an observatory, a little west of the barracks, on the Colleville-sur-Orne road, and farther on, at Colleville itself, loomed the outline of the Charot factory; Douin had no idea what they manufactured and an early instance of teamwork came later in a bulletin from one of Duchez's scouts: industrial alcohol for the Germans.

Douin worked and chipped with mallet and chisel, pausing now and then to let his eyes roam the countryside. Now he was looking south of Colleville, toward Benville, on the road back to Caen. Concrete works were going up there, the dark ant-figures of labourers teeming like an upturned nest, and for artillery by the look of it. That was the first step, noted down, and it would be up to Duchez to find a means for one of the part-timers to penetrate that road and spy out further details. To his right, among the golden kingcups of the river meadows, was another battery of 155s—long range, this time. That was almost all, apart from the pom-pom guns for anti-aircraft, very close to the Ranville bridge, only a mile away from where he crouched in his eyrie.

Douin took his findings back to his studio and worked them all into a map, using an accepted military scale of one-in-fifty-thousand, or just over one inch to the mile. Other information had dribbled in from Chateau and Deschambres by the time it was ready to deliver to Gille, so Douin also incorporated that. It made an encouraging start, too: a munitions dump on the left-hand side of the road running from Riva-Bella to the sea, and two more batteries of 155s, with an anti-tank cannon, both going under concrete, eastwards along the coast from Riva-Bella. The Wall seemed more guns than concrete in this stereoscopic view, and that, although they didn't know it, was then the pattern along its whole 2,000 miles' length.

" Good work," Gille told Douin. " If you ever get an opportunity like that again, seize it." He was leaving the studio when Douin said: " One moment, m'sieu—there is one thing I wish to emphasise."

" I am listening."

" You must please make clear my motives to your chief. What I have done is firstly for the King of France—that must be understood. Secondly, for my country, even though she is now a Republic. There must be no misconception."

Gille said gravely that there wouldn't be. And there never was.

Over some of these ingenious methods Girard chuckled dryly, but by the end of April it seemed to him that progress was slow, and he said as much to Meslin. The Caen cell had been only able to cover five per cent of the territory available, and much of this information concerned secondary defensive positions rather than those guarding the beachhead.

" Even if we do solve the problem of getting people into the zone in quantity," Girard added, " I can think of another. A man takes perhaps a week to report on a few hundred yards of coast, if he's lucky enough to get close, and his chance may never come again. Supposing, after that, the Germans start making changes? We shall never catch up with them."

" Surely aerial reconnaissance would take care of that? "

Girard said gloomily that Meslin was probably right. In any case, he thought that it was not worth losing sleep over, because London probably had all those details anyway.

Chapter Seven

THE MAP AND THE MIRROR

EARLY IN May a black-lettered notice printed on coarse buff paper was pinned to the official announcements board outside the *Mairie* in Caen. The date on which it first appeared is uncertain, but it was about mid-morning on 7th May, a Thursday, that Duchez drew his battered grey camionet to a halt beside the board and read it.

The text of the notice, which was in French, asked for decorators to submit estimates to the *Mairie* in connection with minor repairs to be carried out at the headquarters of the Todt Organisation. The final date for submissions had been at 5 p.m. the previous day.

Duchez sat and thought about it. The deadline suggested that he had missed his chance, but Duchez was never a man to underestimate the value of *monnaie de singe*—an extremely French phrase, roughly translatable as blarney. Beneath his bland spoofing exterior was a clever cold brain, which told him he could be of more value to the network inside the Todt Organisation than any of his colleagues. The painter could recall vividly the long hot summers of his childhood in occupied Lorraine, playing on the stoop of his father, the architect's, house in Nancy. The tall blond German soldiers would stop to banter with the boy, and his brain had retained much of the patois. The Todt Organisation were building the Wall, and if they were to let drop any crumb of information on that score, Duchez stood more chance than most of understanding and retaining it.

And then, was he not Duchez? Later Arsène said this of him: " His greatest pride was that he could make fun of the

Germans without their knowing it," and it is likely that this motive influenced him as much as any. To beard the Germans in their own territory could, with luck, emerge as a really gorgeous hoax, a good tale to tell over a calvados—and, at any rate, it could do no harm to try.

In the gloomy tiled lobby of the *Mairie* he made inquiries and was finally directed to the Bureau Civil, run by a man named Postel. Postel, however, pursed his lips dubiously. " I think you're too late," he said. " All the estimates were in twenty-four hours ago." Then, since he liked Duchez, he added: " On the other hand, they haven't told us yet that they've accepted any tenders. You could always try direct."

This was Duchez's version of what happened after that.

No one seemed too certain whom to approach, so the painter went back to his camionet and turned left across the first intersection into the Avenue Bagatelle. The Todt Organisation in Caen was not of first importance, being what the Germans called a *Bauleitung* (Works sub-sector) of the main headquarters at St. Malo, but they had taken over three buildings in the city: one for camouflage, one for administering forward area personnel, and a third for the *Abteilung Technik*, which dealt with mapping and works contracts. Duchez had no clue that he was driving towards the most important of the three buildings at that moment, a four-storey stone mansion faced in brick with stone-sashed windows, fronting directly on the street.

Fifty yards from the main entrance this street was blocked by a picket fence barrier wound with a cat's cradle of barbed-wire. Duchez brought the camionet to a shuddering halt within a few feet of it, then dismounted, grinning amiably. A sentry came out of the black-and-white striped control box on the left and brought his rifle to the ready: " *Halten!* "

Duchez beamed at him in a fuddled way and kept going. The rifle-barrel came hard against his ribs. " *Halten!* Your *ausweis.*"

Duchez explained that he had come to apply for the painting estimate, but the sentry did not follow his schoolboy German and was all the time motioning him backwards. Mystified by the rumpus, another sentry, guarding the main

entrance, came forward to investigate. Then, so they say, there
followed several indescribable moments of pure low comedy,
as Duchez tried in desperation to bridge the language barrier
by mimicking the actions of a man painting the side of a house,
using the side of the sentry-box by way of demonstration. The
reaction was brisker than he had anticipated. A savage blow
with the flat of the hand almost knocked him senseless, and to
a running accompaniment of cuffs and kicks he was hustled
along the street through a moulded stone doorway and into a
ground-floor office.

A torrent of German followed, too fast for him to understand, and at last a monocled *Hauptbauführer* (Todt Captain)
with some knowledge of French asked icily whether he was
aware of the penalties meted out to wretched Frenchmen who
dared to poke fun at the Fuehrer. Duchez stared at him for a
moment before the full savour of the jest hit him, then, controlling himself with difficulty, explained that he had cast no
aspersions on the Fuehrer, nor indeed on house-painters in
general; he himself was a house-painter in search of work.
The man began to chuckle dryly, dismissed the sentries and
sent an orderly for a junior officer in charge of the painting
estimates.

A young officer led him up two flights of uncarpeted stairs;
in peacetime these had been solid merchants' houses, and the
steel filing cabinets, the jackboots, the whiplash precision of the
" *Heil Hitlers* " seemed in bleak contrast to the moulded pillars
and the ornate plaster friezes. The *Oberbauführer* (Todt
lieutenant) was explaining that it was merely a simple papering
job, involving two offices on the second floor. Would Duchez
submit an estimate?

The painter thought fast. He could gauge pretty accurately
what his competitors would be charging. They would take
only a small margin of profit, because work was scarce and
anyone who did a good job for the Todt Organisation might
expect to be called on again. But a margin, just the same.

Duchez breathed a silent apology to his competitors and
decided that for the sake of the network this was one job that
would have to be done at a loss. " Twelve thousand francs,"

he said, conscious that this was at least one-third below anyone else's estimate, and before the officer even opened his mouth to speak he knew that the job was his.

" You will report in person," the *Oberbauführer* told him, " to *Bauleiter* (Todt Major) Schnedderer."

Duchez could never understand, even afterwards, why Schnedderer, whose office was not involved, should take a personal interest in the decoration of other offices. Possibly as *Gebitsingenieur* (Army liaison officer) he had a personal interest in the costing but from subsequent events Duchez thought it likely that the *Bauleiter* had a streak of frustrated interior decorator in his make-up. A bald, powerfully-built man with a thick crease of duelling scar on his right cheek, wearing the silver-lined Todt uniform collar and swastika brassard, Schnedderer received the painter jovially in his second-floor office. Then he began to expound at length on the patterns he had envisaged. Blue horsemen carrying flags on a light-yellow background might look good. Or silver cannons against a background of navy blue.

Wallpaper, like most other items, was in short supply, but Duchez promised to return next day with some likely samples. He spent the rest of the day in his *atelier* near the rue Grusse, hunting through pattern books, and that evening, at the Café des Touristes, he did not hesitate to tell little Dumis, the courteous ex-garage proprietor, and Deschambres, the red-haired plumber, that he had got a job with the Todt Organisation and that much might come of it.

Dumis, who worshipped this reckless swashbuckler, remembers that he begged him to be careful, but Duchez, his eyes gleaming with mischief, replied, " Now, look, *mon ami*, *I* am Duchez. I can do things with the Germans that others cannot do. Why? Simply because they think I am all sorts of a cretin, and they don't care what they say in front of me. *C'est le sang-froid*, my friend—*c'est toujours le sang-froid*."

Then, seeing " Albert " sitting in one corner, lost in thought over a cognac, he did not neglect to nod to him politely. " Albert " was an elderly German *Hauptmann*, whose real name they never knew; the only German who ever used the Café

81

des Touristes, he had frequented it long before the network was formed. At first the agents had mistrusted him profoundly, giving the café a wide berth, but carefully-laid traps had revealed that the man neither spoke nor understood a word of French.

And in a strange, irrational way Duchez and the rest now welcomed " Albert's " visits; his presence was soothing rather than otherwise and he was such a good front that the network's business could be discussed freely before him. In turn, the shy elderly man seemed to derive comfort from watching what he evidently believed were the little traders of a French town, gossiping about life over a glass of *ordinaire*.

It was on Friday, 8th May, that things started to happen.

Soon after ten o'clock Duchez presented himself at the Todt building. This time he had no trouble in gaining access to Schnedderer, and the liaison officer began to pore over the pattern books, sometimes grunting as one caught his fancy. Duchez was standing facing him, on the other side of his wide paper-littered desk. Schnedderer was debating between two particular patterns, when a knock sounded at the door. Still turning the pages, he called, " Come in."

A junior officer whom the painter had not seen before entered carrying a thick pile of what looked like papers. A " *Heil Hitler* " and a click of heels. Still browsing, Schnedderer said absently, " Put them down there," and then, a minute later, " *Danke schön, Oberbauführer.* I was waiting for these." As he put the pattern book aside and began to unfold the pile of papers lengthwise, Duchez saw from the corner of his eye that they were not papers but maps.

Duchez stood quite still, watching, but after a moment it was obvious that Schnedderer, studying the maps intently, had temporarily forgotten his existence. Ostensibly the painter went on staring at the cypress trees outside the window, with the expression of amiable idiocy that he always wore when dealing with the Germans, but all the time his heart was going hard. The liaison officer had now thrown back his bald bullet-head to study a section of the map (it was too long to unfold in its entirety) at arm's length, and Duchez could see some of the details outlined plainly in reverse through the back. That was the narrow bottle-neck mouth of the Seine at Quillebeuf in the far corner and, beyond it, the Risle, winding down to Pont-Audemer; the coastline, smooth and rounded as far as Honfleur, then plunging abruptly downwards to the smart watering places, Trouville and Deauville, and the cliffs north of Houlgate and Cabourg.

With an odd sense of hysteria, Duchez realised he was looking at a Todt Organisation map of the coastline of Normandy.

From that moment he always had the confused impression that everything happened at once. Still dazed with the possible implications, he saw Schnedderer replace the top map from the pile, push the maps to the left-hand corner of his desk nearest Duchez, and return to the pattern-book. But it seemed to be a busy morning on the Avenue Bagatelle. Another knock sounded, and this time it was a *Truppführer* (Todt Sergeant) who entered, repeating something that sounded like a message, which Duchez could not catch. Whatever it was it made Schnedderer get up, turn his back on the painter and open the door leading to an inner office immediately behind his desk. The *Truppführer* withdrew, and Schnedderer, looming in the doorway with his back to the room, one hand propped on the jamb, seemed to be dictating to a clerk.

Duchez was left alone with the maps.

They were still lying on the table where the Germans had left them. Cautiously, as if it had been a red-hot stove-lid, Duchez lifted the top one. It was printed, by the ozalide system of mimeograph, on deep blue cartographic paper, the great red letters, SONDERZEICHUNGEN—STRENG GEHEIM—meaning " Special Blueprint—Top Secret "—prominent in one corner. Duchez thought for a moment that he was going to be ill; although the map was too bulky to risk opening out in full, it seemed to be a blueprint for defence, right enough, though of what order he had no time to find out. Chance phrases like " Blockhauss " caught his eye and " Sofort-program " (highest priority construction).

He cast a scared glance towards the door, but Schnedderer

was still dictating. All the time a nagging irresistible voice inside his brain was saying, Take it, you fool, take it. There may never be a chance like this, *now*, while he's not looking. . . .

He took three steps backwards across the room, still holding the map, and there was the fireplace ; that was no good, but above it was a heavy mirror, perhaps two feet square, with a chased gilt frame, like an oil painting. With his right hand Duchez slid the map behind the mirror lengthways, so that the inward cant of the frame prevented it from falling. Then, treading lightly, he went back and took up his old innocent stand by the desk. Afterwards he said that he was wet through with sweat and that there was a sick dead feeling in his throat and down to his stomach, because if Schnedderer found out what he had done, whether the map was important or not, it would be the last foolish and gallant *beau geste* that he would ever make.

Then he just waited for Schnedderer to stop dictating, which was the worst time of all, because he could not, in the few brief minutes remaining, collect his thoughts sufficiently to go over what he had done, looking for loopholes. It had not even occurred to him to check whether the maps differed; if they did then the loss might be discovered before he was even out of the building. In the back of his mind was the idea that somehow, at some future date, he could abstract the map without anyone knowing, but beyond a fervent prayer that he might leave the building alive he had no other plans.

Almost before he realised it, Schnedderer had closed the inner door and was back at the desk again, selecting two patterns and making it plain that the interview was over. " Monday then," said the *Bauleiter*, and Duchez thought guiltily that Schnedderer gave him a suspicious glance, but later he told himself it was only imagination, for the officer returned to his papers without even glancing at the maps again, apparently suspecting nothing.

Duchez walked two flights of stairs to street level, quivering and rigid with fear, waiting for something to hit him. Nothing did. Then feeling a lot older than his forty years, he went to the Café des Touristes and had a drink. He felt he had earned it.

By afternoon the paralysing sense of dread had worn off, and he was almost his old self again. Before he went back to the café that evening, when his children Jacques, aged eleven, and Monique, aged three, were safely tucked up in bed, he told Odette what he had done, and the good placid woman, who had come to accept her husband's pranks the way a mother indulges a mischievous youngster, said, " That's very good," and meant it. Thinking about it afterwards she had to confess that the news didn't surprise her. In her own words, " He was always doing funny things like that."

At the time she was more concerned with persuading René to eat regular meals; the war was taking more toll of him than people realised, and unless she offered him cold chicken for almost every meal, the chances were he would push his plate away after a few mouthfuls. " Sorry, *chérie* . . . just not hungry." From the windows of their old-fashioned house she watched him slope off across the courtyard towards the café, with his peculiar shambling gait, and thought, with the blessed treason of her sex, He's never really grown up at all.

And she was not far wrong. At the café that evening Duchez was in great form, treating everyone. " No, no, *mon ami*, this is with me. . . . Do you know, a most extraordinary thing happened to me to-day? Yes, this very morning, while I was with an officer at the Todt Organisation . . ."

Duchez was lucky in his loyalties. No one talked. Yet, by curfew-time that night half a dozen of the network had heard his story and perhaps it was lucky too, that not everyone believed him; Duchez was a famous man for crying " Wolf." Arsène, the argumentative one-eyed plumber, did not believe it for one, and never did, and another disbeliever was the shy fair-haired young Robert Thomas. " He's full of such stupidities," Thomas grumbled when he heard the story. There was no denying the truth of that. Without such indiscretions, Dewavrin himself once said, his networks would have functioned more smoothly, admitting the wry paradox that without such bravery they would not have functioned at all.

Duchez, of course, slept soundly that night. He had already decided that on the Monday, when he started work, he could

85

make an excuse to see Schnedderer and a way would present itself for him to remove the map. It had to, for he was Duchez. Only Odette lay still and awake, remembering the Gestapo officers billeted only two doors up the street, wondering each time a car's headlamps swept a white windmill of light across the bedroom: Is it for us? Or the wheels of a car, cornering with a faint thin scream on the wet tarmac: Is it for us? Then the engine cutting out, a door slamming, feet scrunching on wet gravel, a second of eternity, of whispering a prayer, please, God, dear God, not for us, not for our children. Then the feet dying away, the thick silence like a curtain, and the numb sick feeling of having lived all the fears and anguish of your life in the space of this minute.

Sleepless by her husband's side, Odette fought her war.

On the Monday, Duchez reported at the Todt Organisation at half-past eight, armed with buckets, cans of size and rolls of wallpaper; it was his habit to start work early in order to knock off at four, leaving good time for meetings at the Touristes. At that hour the building was cold and silent, only the clerks and orderlies had arrived, and for about two hours he worked, washing the walls down to the plaster and sizing them, singing abominably through his nose, until an outraged orderly came and told him to cease.

The painter apologised profusely, saying, " When it is convenient, please, I would like to see *Bauleiter* Schnedderer."

The orderly said unsympathetically, " Well, you'd better take the train to St. Malo then, if you do."

Duchez saw the green light. If Schnedderer's office was unoccupied . . . " Any time will do," he said pacifically. " When will he be back? "

" Back? " The orderly stared. " Never here. He's been transferred to another unit. *Bauleiter* Keller is the new liaison officer.

Duchez was electrified.

The orderly stared at him curiously for a moment, then walked away. The painter spent the rest of the day in silence and misery, too depressed even to sing, and he said later that for a moment the idea crossed his mind that Schnedderer's abrupt departure had something to do with the missing map. Yet if it had he would surely have been rounded up for questioning. He could make nothing of it. Hadn't they even missed the map? And if they hadn't how could he get it out of the building before they did?

Some time during the next twenty-four hours he did a lot of thinking, though as was usual when he really had a plan brewing he said nothing, not even to Odette. He began his campaign about ten on the Tuesday morning by asking to see the young *Oberbauführer* in charge of the painting. When the officer appeared, Duchez asked, with great deference, when *Bauleiter* Keller would be ready for him to begin. Begin what? the young man wanted to know. Why, the papering, of course, said Duchez innocently. The arrangement had been that some time on the Tuesday he would also paper Schnedderer's room. *Bauleiter* Keller would know all about it.

He waited almost half an hour while the young officer made inquiries, before the man came back and said curtly that Duchez was mistaken: the requisition showed nothing but the papering of two offices on the second floor. " It wouldn't be on the requisition," Duchez pointed out. " It was a last-minute decision of *Bauleiter* Schnedderer's but he certainly wrote down some details on a scrap pad."

Anxious to settle it one way or the other, the *Oberbauführer* beckoned Duchez upstairs, and within a few minutes, his heart pounding beneath his ribs, the painter was ushered back into the office where it had all started. Everything looked much the same. . . . An uncomprehending N.C.O., apparently Schnedderer's chief clerk, was brought into the argument. Soon he heard a voice asking irritably, " What is all this nonsense about wallpaper? " And *Bauleiter* Adalbert Keller came out of the inner office to investigate the fuss.

More explanations. More mutual incomprehension. Keller said tersely—perhaps, Duchez wondered, rather wistfully— that the budget did not permit this extra expense at the present time. But surely, Duchez said, there had been some misapprehension. He had offered to paper the room free, as a gesture of good-will. *Bauleiter* Schnedderer had done him the honour of accepting. If his successor would be similarly gracious. . . . Both the *Oberbauführer* and *Truppführer* now looked a little put out, in the manner of men who had too hastily misjudged another's motives.

Bauleiter Keller, his face wreathed in smiles, slapped the painter on the back and said in measured but execrable French, " *Vous êtes un bon français.*"

Unfortunately, Keller said, the papering could not begin that day. He also asked how long the job would be likely to take, and Duchez, reckoning quickly, said two days. Arrangements were made for the room to be cleared of furniture when work was finished for the day, but Duchez said hastily that there was no need for that. If the furniture was just moved to the centre of the room, he could cover it with his own dustsheets and work perfectly well.

At 8 a.m. on the morning of Wednesday, 13th May, Duchez moved in and started work.

Chapter Eight
A PLAN IN JEOPARDY

In Paris, at approximately the same time, Renault had other things than Girard's network on his mind. For the first time since the networks began, he felt trapped. It was the feeling a man has in a nightmare, when appalling things begin to happen and his subconscious maliciously robs him of the power to defend himself or hide.

Subsol, the radio operator, had talked. Not under torture, which would have demanded compassion, but quietly and exhaustively, as part of a bargain with the Gestapo, and the waking nightmare had begun: one by one the contacts were being rounded up, everyone whom Subsol had known even vaguely. Jean Pelletier, who did the Confrérie's micro-films, copying every document that went to London, had been dragged fighting from his studio in Asnières; Dumont, the ex-fighter pilot, who had supplied details for the British raid on Bruneval; other contact men, known only to Renault's lieutenants. The one consolation was that Subsol had never met Renault. He had been appointed by Guy Julitte, the technician, who was safely back in England with Dewavrin.

But the others knew Renault, and one of them, by the cruel law that governs such averages, would crack under torture. Renault kept Edith and the children, still in Brittany with Madame Le Crom-Hubert, a trusted family friend, ignorant of the danger. With cold clear fatalism he gave himself a fortnight at the most.

His radio link with London was as tenuous as it had ever been. Papa Fleuret, the pilot of the port, had sent a transmitter from Bordeaux, and it was set up in an office near the Porte

St. Martin, but within twenty-four hours a detector van was prowling round the square, and since then the transmitter had stayed there, useless and silent. Even the reserve equipment depots that Julitte had organised couldn't be touched, because Subsol had known the addresses and they would now be watched.

Only one radio remained intact, at the house of an agent named Jean Tillier in the Avenue Mozart, and with this transmitter Renault signalled Dewavrin to send replacements as priority. But even this plan misfired. A plane took off two days later and reported its containers jettisoned, but the radios never reached the dropping-ground in the Aisne country that Renault's scouts had indicated. They thought that the pilot must have mistaken other lights for the reception committee and dropped the radios off target. With only one radio, aerial pick-ups were almost at a standstill and meantime dispatches were piling up.

News came from his scout in Lorient during the first week of May that a fishing vessel had been bought for a first attempt at sea liaison. To give Renault another method of sending his dispatches Dewavrin had worked out a sea-route from the great fishing bank that stretches out opposite the Ile des Glenans, between Lorient and Concarneau, to Tresco in the Scilly Isles. Dispatches would now be picked up by Lysander from " Guardian Angel " near Rouen only during the moon phase. In pre-moon periods the N51, a British trawler manned by a crew of ten, disguised as a Camaret fishing vessel, would pick them up at a rendezvous with Renault's craft.

Renault travelled down to Lorient to find Alex Tanguy, his local scout, waiting for him on the platform, shrouded as usual in an old and filthy trench coat. He was a fair bullet-headed ex-naval officer who spoke in short clipped sentences like a German. Renault had at first been put off by his brusque grumbling manner, but Alex was now one of his most trusted agents.

Alex said, " Well, I've done what you wanted, I've got the boat, but it wasn't easy, don't think it," spitting the words out as if he positively disliked them. They walked down to the harbour and along the quay, until finally the agent said gruffly, " Well—that's her," and Renault felt his heart sink.

Never in his most pessimistic moments had he pictured a boat as totally unsuitable as this. In length she was about thirty-five feet, with a foredeck, the paint long since chipped from her sides and the white stains of salt crusted on her hatches and lockers. She looked as if one lively spring squall would put paid to her for good. At her masthead the Tricolour fluttered wanly above the furled rust-coloured sail. Worn lettering on her port bow identified her as CC.2900 the *Deux Anges* (Two Angels) out of Concarneau.

They went aboard, the little man's nose bridling at the odour. " What," he said finally, " did they use her for? "

Alex grumbled into his coat collar: " I don't know. Lobster, I think—or conger-eel fishing. Something like that."

Renault looked her over hopelessly, the dead feeling of despair like a weight in his chest. With a 20-h.p. Beaudouin engine to help out, Alex was explaining, she could make thirteen knots, but Renault, rummaging vainly for a hiding place suitable for documents or agents, scarcely heard him. Apart from the lockers, about six feet by three and a half by two, there was scarcely room for a ship's cat to hide, even supposing a cat had condescended to patronise her. Restraining himself with difficulty, he said: " Alex, I know it can't have been easy, but don't you think—I mean—surely there was *some* other boat? . . ."

But Alex said obstinately that there hadn't been. She was seaworthy, he had paid 75,000 francs for her, and he now proposed rounding up a crew in the nearby fishing village of Pont-Aven. " Let's hope they're at least as seaworthy," said Renault acidly. " When can I arrange a rendezvous with London? "

" About 20th May, I should think. I want to overhaul the engine first."

Renault went back to Paris by train. A maritime liaison was not much, but at least he could send a detailed report of his plight to Dewavrin, which was not possible by radio, and all the dispatches that had been piling up in Paris since the beginning of April could go too. On the 15th, if he was still alive, he would travel back to Lorient and supervise the rendezvous.

At 5.30 p.m. on 13th May, Girard arrived in Caen from Le Mans. On this day, by previous arrangement, he was to contact Duchez on his way through, but on the train journey that afternoon he had no knowledge of Duchez's map or that the painter had secured a temporary job with the Todt Organisation. Nor was he aware of the complications that had arisen at the Café des Touristes in the hour before his arrival.

One or two others had drifted in that afternoon to take a hand at dominoes: Deschambres, the ginger-haired plumber, little Léon Dumis, the ex-garage proprietor, and the insurance agent, Harivel. There was no sign of Duchez. The main subject under discussion was the map that Duchez claimed to have secreted somewhere inside the building on the Avenue Bagatelle, and how to retrieve it—if it existed. In view of Duchez's talent for tall stories, the melancholy Deschambres was inclined to doubt the whole yarn. Only Léon Dumis, staunchly loyal to his friend, had implicit faith.

The quiet authoritative Harivel drummed his fingers on the table-top as various suggestions were talked over; none of them, it seemed to him, stood much chance of working. One idea, an agent dressed as a German officer walking in to retrieve the map, seemed feasible, but only just. A shadow fell across their table and instinctively they froze, lowering their voices, but it was only " Albert," the elderly German captain. Stripping off his heavy greatcoat, the German hung it on a coat-stand, ordered a cognac and sat down a few tables away.

These three were not anticipating Girard, and towards five they were on the point of adjourning the meeting when Duchez ambled in.

Harivel was intrigued by the persistent buzz of rumours about Duchez's map, but he had heard the painter's gay fabrications before. He thought that they had better hear what Duchez had to say, and sat down again. " We might as well play another hand," he said. " Deschambres, I'll take you on." They nodded amiably to the painter, but, perhaps because of " Albert's " presence, Duchez seemed in no hurry to join them. He ordered a calvados from Paul's wife behind the *zinc*, hung his heavy paint-streaked topcoat on the coat-stand then came over to join them.

" Double-six," Deschambres said. " How is it, René, *mon ami? Ça va?* "

Duchez nodded amiably, said, " *Ça va bien*," and then, almost at once, got up again and wandered to the door. Silently the three others exchanged glances. They could not see what the painter was doing, but each man, without knowing why, could feel the tension mounting.

In the doorway Duchez was watching the Boulevard des Alliés. Across the roughly-paved street, beneath the Église St. Pierre, the flower market spread its multi-coloured profusion: old peasant women, as brown as berries, were hawking wicker baskets of Easter anemones, crimson, purple and white. Duchez stayed in the doorway, like a man savouring the afternoon sun, long enough to see the black Citroën with police markings nose its way into the square, two men in raincoats and grey felt hats sitting silently in the back.

He came back into the café, humming, as he often did, loudly and discordantly. " With you in a moment, my friends," he said. " I need my cigarettes." And for a moment that awful discordant hum droned on before he joined them with a crumpled blue packet of Gauloises.

" You appear to have done a good job," Harivel said in low, conversational tones. " We have been an hour discussing how to get this German map out of that hornet's nest. Always supposing, of course, that there is a map. Your move, Deschambres."

" Pass," said Deschambres.

Duchez said, almost mildly, " I have the map."

No one spoke. Deschambres's fingers remained glued to the domino board. Almost instinctively they glanced quickly at " Albert," but the *Hauptmann* had not moved. Then Harivel said in a cracked voice, " Not *here*, for heaven's sake? But you must get outside. . . ."

93

" No time," said Duchez evenly. " The Gestapo are out-side. There's no time to do anything now but sit tight. And play dominoes."

Harivel said carefully, " Why are *they* outside? Do they suspect you? "

" I don't think so. They may have followed me in a routine way, but no one seems to have missed the map yet. That's what seems so queer. *Prenez garde, mes amis*—here they come."

They bent diligently to their dominoes. No one could summon the courage to look up, yet Dumis swore later that he almost *felt* the physical presence of the car pass the door, and could distinguish the faint hiss of the tyres on the paving from all the other street sounds filtering in. A voice in everyone's head was saying: They're coming, they're coming, now, now, *now*. . . .

The minutes crawled. It was Duchez who got up finally. He walked to the *zinc*, ordering another calvados. He leant at such an angle against the bar that he could survey the whole street. At last an imperceptible nod of his head told them the Gestapo car had gone. And they relaxed, drawing a deep breath.

" Now then," Harivel said, when the painter had returned to the table, " be good enough to tell us . . ."

But this seemed to be one of Duchez's restless days. " Albert," the *Hauptmann*, having finished his drink, had risen to go. Duchez also got up, and the two men almost collided by the coat-stand. Bewildered, the others saw Duchez stiffly beg " Albert's " pardon, relieve him of the Army greatcoat, which the German had lifted from the coat-stand, and help him into it. Gratified, " Albert " inclined slightly from the waist, wished Paul's wife good afternoon and left the café.

Almost at once more Germans marched stolidly in to form a thick phalanx of field-grey at the bar, and about five minutes later came the chunky figure of Girard, weaving among the tables. Duchez hailed him noisily: " *Ça va, vieux? Que prenez-vous?* " Girard accepted a cognac, sitting well forward on his chair, anxious to be gone. Only one more train was due to leave for Paris that day. He asked Duchez, " What have you got for me? "

Duchez beamed, enjoying the suspense. " A nice pile of dispatches from the P-1's. Things are not coming along too badly there. . . ."

Girard nodded imperturbably. These he had contracted to collect, since Himbert, the courier, was not due to visit Paris for another ten days, and Meslin had reported a back-log of dispatches.

" And," Duchez recounted smugly, " a map of what I think are German defences that 1 took from the Todt Organisation."

Girard was aghast. " In the name of God, how did you get that? Break into the place? "

Grinning, Duchez recounted the story of his coup, explaining that once *Bauleiter* Keller had accepted his story on the second visit, the rest had been eays. The mirror had not been moved, and the map was still in the same position as he had put it. He had worked in Keller's office all that day, and until finishing work he had not even touched the map. He concluded innocently, " Then I just put it in the cylinder that holds my paint brushes and walked out."

There was a shocked silence. Then Girard said harshly, " And you brought it *here*, instead of putting it in the boiler? You must be mad, raving mad. For God's sake give it to me quickly with the other reports while there's still time."

The others had a fleeting glimpse of the thick envelope that Duchez, ignoring the Germans at the bar, passed over before Girard, not without difficulty, stuffed its bulk into his breast pocket. " The sooner I get this to Paris," he said, " the better I shall like it. And next time, for God's sake, use your head a little. If the Gestapo had come into the café and found that on you, we should have been finished."

Duchez was bland. " The Gestapo would have searched in vain, *mon vieux*."

" But how——? "

" The Gestapo were around a while back, so when I went to get my cigarettes, I put it in " Albert's " pocket. I thought it would be safer in case they came in. Then, when he rose to go, I played the gentleman, helped him on with his coat, and removed it again. After all, we do not want " Albert " to get the firing squad."

He beamed at all of them with cheerful rascality. " *C'est le sang-froid*, my friends—*c'est toujours le sang-froid*."

" Your insanity is unquestionable," said Girard with a flash of anger, then grinned broadly and added: " But so also is your courage."

In wartime the Paris express departed from Platform 2 of the Gare Centrale at Caen punctually at six. On that same night, 13th May, the map began its fantastic journey, when with ten minutes to spare Girard boarded the train. People, too many people, dislodged by the shifts and shortages of war, jammed its corridors; sallow lads in threadbare jackets with pinched hungry faces, old peasant women in rusty black, beards, bonnets, babies gurgling in shawls, haversacks and brown-paper parcels. Sweating straining humanity. German railway police in their black uniforms with silver piping fought through the crush, checking tickets. At every stop the luggage from the corridors had to be manhandled through the compartment windows.

Girard, travelling second, was conscious of a quiet satisfaction, feeling the solid reality of the envelope wadded in his breast pocket. The hiding-place was another of Girard's " normal " precautions, based on acute observation. On the train the Gestapo or railway police might demand papers or search your luggage as a matter of routine. But they had to be deeply suspicious before they asked you to turn out your pockets.

About the significance of the map itself he thought hardly at all. (" My God," he said later, feelingly, " if I'd known what dynamite I had in my breast pocket . . ." Then paused, overcome by the sheer horror of the thought.) But as yet he had had no opportunity to glance at the plan, and, being Girard, never permitted himself to so much as speculate on any subject he had not fully explored. Duchez, he contented himself with

*André Dewavrin
('Colonel Passy')*

Fernand Arsène

False identity card of René ('Third Fool') Duchez

thinking, had done a good job. That was the first stage. Now it was up to him, Girard, to get all this stuff past the check-points at the Gare St. Lazare. That was the second.

The chances of being stopped were perhaps a hundred to one against. And after that? Stage Three, the map must be copied and passed to Renault. Beyond that, on this particular journey, Girard did not allow himself to think.

Much later the legend was to arise that Duchez's approach to the Todt Organisation was a carefully-planned coup, thought up by Girard, to steal the map from under the noses of the Germans. Nothing could have been further from the truth. As much as any of his subordinates, Girard was working in the dark, as Dewavrin had prophesied, a man sustained by faith. His target was the Normandy sector of the Atlantic Wall, and his network would not give up until they had ferreted out every detail they could, but for the rest . . . Who knew whether the Allies would ever land, and if so where? And wasn't it likely that they knew most of the important details on the coastal defences from other sources? One could do only one's best, day by day, thinking of it clinically, as a job to be done, pressing back the terror and the sense of loneliness and the knowledge that a man could manufacture his own defeat in the recesses of his heart, because he was sick of lying and hiding and fearing and came to believe that death was the better bargain.

The train pulled into the Gare St. Lazare just before ten. Girard walked briskly among the hurrying crowds and the bellying steam, clutching his overnight bag, keeping well in the centre of the throng as he passed the barrier. Once past the barrier, it was harder to appear one of a crowd. The Metro ceased running at nine and the concourse was almost empty. Small knots of people scurried in the gloom anxious to beat the ten o'clock curfew, their footsteps echoing hollow beneath the great glass-roofed vault. Armed soldiers of the *Feldengendarmerie* paused watchfully in the shadows. With perhaps as much reason to hurry as any man on the streets of Paris that night, Girard forced himself to walk at an even pace. He passed a group of soldiers, and for a moment one of them seemed to hesitate; he felt his heart pounding, and then he was out in the cool night air, unchallenged, with a million stars glowing gently over the white cupola of Sacré-Coeur.

It would have been too late to consult Berthelot or Colonel Touny about the plan that night, even if it had seemed that important. Following normal procedure he would take it, with all the dispatches, to Berthelot's flat on the Boulevard Flandrin first thing next morning. Meantime the curfew was due any second. Outside the Printemps department store he hailed a velo-taxi and grunted his address, easing his bulk gingerly into the two-seater wooden trailer which fitted behind the cycle on which the driver pedalled.

His apartment—or apartments—were in the rue Cardinal Lemoine, high on the Left Bank. Once the velo had laboured painfully up the cobbled incline from the river, and the high stone archway of No. 71 came in sight, he felt better. The best security device he had was here, better than any fictitious job, better than any cover-names. At the entrance gateway he paid off the driver, walking briskly up an alleyway running between high moss-covered walls into an old-world courtyard cloistered by trees. It was peaceful here. A fountain rippled softly under the stars, and with the morning sun, he knew, would come flocks of pigeons, grey and murmurous. Surrounding the court-yard were buildings made up of all types of dwellings, including the modern apartment block that Girard entered. In wartime the lift was not running, but despite the pull on his injured knee, he felt better with each flight of pitch-black stairs.

He reached the sixth floor and turned left. Now, from the wide window of the hallway he could see all Paris: the sleeping river, the sombre bulk of Notre-Dame, the old houses massed steeply on the Montmartre slope. In this hallway the doors of three apartments faced, two at right angles to the third, but curiously Girard did not pause by the door of the first apart-ment, nearest the lift, which he officially rented. Briefly he glanced upwards at the opaque blur of glass above his head, which was the skylight offering an escape route to the roof—the first part of his security device. Then, selecting a key from his pocket, he unlocked the door of the next apartment, locking it carefully behind him. The room smelt unlived in, the dry resinous smell of old wood and central heating. This was his second token of security. He switched on a shaded desk-lamp and sat down to take his first hasty glimpse of Duchez's map.

The first thing that hit him was the size of it; he was too nervous, in too much of a hurry, to measure it, but it seemed an age before he had unfolded the pleats and got it in perspective. His second sensation was disappointment, spreading quietly like a chill through his stocky frame. If he had thought about it, he might have guessed it would be in German!

It was a map of the coastline, all right, from the mouth of the Seine to just below Cherbourg, but Girard knew not one word of German. It might, for all he knew, be a map of military telephone installations. Little black roundels and hatchings were dotted across the deep blue expanse, all crowded together with terms like " Flammenwerfer " and " Gross-program," but Girard had no way of penetrating their real significance—" Flame-thrower " and " Large-scale construction, fortifications, underground tunnels."

He studied it with scowling incomprehension for a few minutes before hastily folding it again and stuffing it, together with the other papers, down the side of the *banquette*, the padded window-seat on the far side of the room. Studying papers, even in solitude, was a dangerous luxury when the Gestapo possessed skeleton keys capable of opening any door in Paris.

He left the second apartment, again locking the door behind him, crossed the landing and unlocked the third. This was his final guarantee of security. Only a handful of people knew that he slept alternately in the second and third apartments, which were connected by an inner door, never the first. As he climbed into bed and put out the light, he thought that the third was his favourite. From the keyhole a man had a useful view of the entire hallway, as well as the head of the stairs. A Resistant stayed alive longer through knowing things like that.

Next morning, the 14th, Girard was early at Berthelot's flat on the Boulevard Flandrin, but here again he drew a blank.

Berthelot peered at the map for some time through his gold-rimmed glasses, but despite his diplomatic past his German was not much stronger than Girard's. In his prim unhurried way he refolded it, together with the other dispatches, and took it to Colonel Touny's small office, camouflaged as a Red Cross branch office, opposite the Pompe Metro station.

For a time the Colonel studied the map in silence, absorbed. Then his strongly-marked eyebrows went up. " Here," he said, " I really think we have something."

Touny's working knowledge of German was good. Good enough to know, incredibly but indisputably, that stretched between his white well-manicured hands was a top-secret blueprint of the Atlantic Wall in Normandy, apparently the minutest details of every coastal defence in the hundred miles between Quillebeuf and Cherbourg, together with troop dispositions on a scale of one-in-fifty-thousand—just over an inch to the mile. The one thing that both dismayed and elated him was that the construction of the Atlantic Wall had progressed much farther than anyone could have dreamed. True, there were sizeable gaps—but, on the debit side, a truly mighty concentration of *Stuetzpunkt* (strong points) on the coast above Grandcamp-les-Bains, machine-gun nests along the cliffs above all the seaside resorts north of Caen, even a heavy strong-point in the village of Langrune, where Duclos and Beresnikoff had watched the preparations mounting for " Operation Sea-Lion." Of course Girard had lacked agents right on the coast to report this progress, but just the same . . .

Touny came to a decision. " I think this may be the most important thing we have ever got hold of," he said levelly. " We must have it copied and passed to the Confrérie Notre-Dame before the day is out."

But to copy the map quickly presented a fresh problem. Until the arrest of Jean Pelletier, Renault's expert, the system had been simple: plans and dispatches had been micro-filmed in his studio at Asnières, the copy retained until the original reached London and then destroyed. Now anything in the nature of a map would have to be copied by a trained cartographer and it was a stroke of the purest luck that Renault had put Berthelot in touch with a two-man team only a few weeks previously: an architect named René Bourdon and Paul Mollet, an industrial draughtsman. Berthelot took the plan along to them before the morning was out and pressed them to make a rough reduced-scale drawing within the next few hours.

He treated it as a matter of routine urgency, not, in fact, realising how desperately urgent it was. Renault was leaving for Brittany and the sea liaison the next night.

At four that afternoon, with the enemy all around him, Renault was drinking coffee on the terrace of a café in the Avenue Carnot. Across the street German soldiers on leave were clustered round a revolving rack, admiring coloured post-cards of the Champs-Elysées; a few hundred yards away the red and black of the Swastika snap-snapped in a faint breeze atop the Arc de Triomphe. Presently Berthelot dropped into a seat beside him, and Renault, looking at him, remembered afterwards that he was " quite excited about something."

Berthelot passed across a thick buff envelope and said, " There is something that I think London may be very pleased to see." And then, lowering his voice almost to a murmur, " A map from our friend Malherbe. He got it through the help of the government engineer in Caen." Afterwards Renault had time to realise how strangely this whole day lacked drama; that same morning he had run into Girard, who told him, " I have something very important for you—a map of all the defences along the coast." Berthelot waited expectantly for some show of enthusiasm, but Renault only said abruptly: " All this should be very good. I will have a look at it some-time. . . ." All the time his mind was moving ahead, checking rendezvous, memorising train times. Was there anything he had overlooked?

The rendezvous of the *Deux Anges* with the English trawler was timed for the following Wednesday, 20th May. Alex had hired a crew of three without trouble, and now it only remained to confirm the rendezvous with Dewavrin at the week-end. But Renault was haunted by fears and doubts that he could not dispel: the sense that the *Abwehr* were closing in, the memories of Pelletier and Dumont and now François Faure, his No. 2, only recently returned from London but pounced on by the Gestapo in the Boulevard Montparnasse that same morning. God alone knew what tortures the Germans had devised to break them down. Under the circumstances Renault can be excused for paying little attention to what Berthelot was telling him.

But at least, he thought, there would be no difficulty in getting the map to England. That aspect of the operation was already settled: the map would go, along with all the other dispatches that had been piling up, in the custody of young Paul Mauger. Until now Mauger, the youngest of all his recruits, had been a humble liaison agent, but this seemed the best chance of fulfilling his heart's desire, which was to join the Free French Air Force. The knowledge that he was going on a secret mission to the famous " Commandant Passy " had sent the boy wild with excitement. He was slender and small-boned, with the sensitive face of a young gazelle, and blushed every time you spoke to him. He had just turned eighteen.

On Friday, 15th May, Renault left for Lorient on the nine twenty-five from the Gare Montparnasse, in company with the hatchet-faced Robert Delattre, his personal radio officer, and their last remaining transmitter, wrapped up in newspaper. The map of the Atlantic Wall was packed with other dispatches in a brief-case on his knees. (It had spent the night at Renault's Champs-Elysées headquarters only four blocks away from the H.Q. of the Todt Organisation in France.) In the crisp dawn of the Saturday morning, they arrived at Lorient, and Alex Tanguy, as brusque and forbidding as ever, met them at the station with Paul Mauger. They drove in his battered old car to an apartment on the Cours de la Bove, where Delattre and the transmitter could function in peace.

All morning the thought nagged Renault: Could they get through to London? In despair, he confided his fears to Alex, but the sailor only said bluntly: " Well, if you can't the operation's off then, isn't it? " Which was small consolation. In the afternoon he drove off to buy the petrol for the trip through one of three intermediaries who bought it for him from the German naval base, and Renault and young Paul Mauger were left gnawing their nails in the front room of the apartment. Upstairs, in a small attic bedroom overlooking the port, Delattre was trying to raise London and confirm the rendezvous.

He had been trying for only ten minutes when Renault, through the bay-window of the dining-room, saw the cream-coloured ambulance swing into the street. Sheer animal instinct told him that it was moving too slowly for any errand of mercy, and he took the stairs two at a time to find Delattre just disconnecting his earphones. The technician said, " Well, I got through all right—we'll probably get an answer some time to-morrow." And Renault answered tersely: " If we're all still here. There's a radio detector van outside! Let's go."

Hastily they swaddled the transmitter in newspaper again and clattered down the stairs. All three of them came out of the front door, moving in a tight body, into the windy street, and there were ten nerve-stretching seconds as they met the " ambulance," still crawling tortoise-like, face to face. But nothing happened, and they set off, walking briskly through the streets, to shake off possible pursuers.

At one shop, a small grocer's, Renault stopped and bought a box of biscuits, a Breton delicacy called Crêpes Dentelles; the others glanced at him curiously, but he offered no explanation, and it was only when they came to the small villa in the suburbs where Alex's sister lived that they understood. While the quiet placid woman brewed them coffee, Renault got busy discharging the contents of the tin and packing in the envelope that Berthelot had given him. He was taking no chances with Girard's map. The box was about twelve inches square, and it fitted nicely, and Renault sealed it with adhesive tape to prevent moisture leaking in.

" You may be in for a damp trip," he told Paul. " This plan is important and you must take great care of it."

The youngster nodded eagerly, unable to say anything adequate. The excitement and importance of his mission were still too much for him.

It was almost too much for Renault. Up to that time he had not even broken the seal of the envelope to examine the map. In his dispatch case there were piles of closely-written reports from other agents, which had arrived in Paris too late for typing, and Renault, always methodical, wanted to sift through them and classify them. Curiosity about Girard's map had to take second place to necessity. On the Sunday morning Alex drove the three of them to Madame Le Crom-Hubert's house, eleven miles away at Baud, and Renault enjoyed another of those bitter-sweet reunions with Edith and the children. No answer came from London and for the next thirty-six hours he worked at the dispatches. It was like the old days at Perpignan, he thought whimsically, when he had been travelling weekly to Bordeaux and Lorient to found the first networks: himself working upstairs, encoding vital information, while downstairs Edith was feeding the baby. Often, when he needed heat to bring up the secret ink on a wrapping paper, Edith had to put aside the children's laundry to lend him the iron.

At lunch-time on the Monday, Delattre, who had set up his transmitter in an upper room of the villa, was jubilant. " It's on, chief—it's really on! Rendezvous on Wednesday, 4 p.m., Greenwich mean time."

In setting up the operation, Dewavrin had not taken any chances. If the first rendezvous failed, there was to be a second, on Thursday, 21st May, at 10 a.m. G.M.T. If that again failed, there would be one final try, at 4 p.m. the same day. The captain of the N51, Renault knew, was the finest choice for the job. He was a young curly-haired Breton, named Daniel Lomenech, and de Gaulle had loaned him to the Royal Navy for special operations because he knew the coast of Brittany so well.

For Renault the Monday passed all too quickly: there were still many dispatches to be coded before young Paul left on the afternoon bus to Lorient. Paul was to stay that night with Alex's sister, and on the Tuesday he and the bullet-headed Alex were to take the boat to Pont Aven, twelve miles awya, to pick up the crew. Paul shook hands solemnly with all of them before leaving, and Renault thought that he looked absurdly young and defenceless as he stood there in his fisherman's jersey, clutching the biscuit box and the brief-case. Edith and Cécile were crying quietly. " I almost feel as if my own son was going away from me," Edith said.

To comfort her Renault promised that he would stay on in Baud until the operation had been completed successfully. But now that Girard's map was on its way to England, he felt a strange lightness of spirit. A German plan of coastal defences was an uneasy item among one's personal baggage.

He spent the morning of the 20th away from the house watching Michel, the youngest, take his first toddling inadequate steps. Among the green fields, with the soft silken rustle of the sea, and the baby's small grunts of concentration as he tumbled and tried again, the momentary peace was like an opiate, dulling the pain he felt for Faure and Dumont and Pelletier and all the others who would endure indescribable agonies but would not talk. Back at the house, after lunch, he rested, talking to the children, trying to plumb what had passed through their minds all the time he had been away: Jean-Claude, painfully earnest with his fair curly hair and steady blue eyes, Catherine, with all the poise and self-assurance of eleven, brown-eyed Cécile, lively and irrepressible. It struck him that in view of the dangerous mission which was now, he thought, completed, it would be safer for them to change their names once more. At an age when make-believe comes easily, it was simpler for them than for Edith to keep pace with their father's swift changes of identity.

" One thing, children," Renault told them. " From to-day our name is no longer Renault. It is Recordier." He never knew why he had picked on the name.

" Recordier," they all repeated solemnly, as if they were learning a lesson, and five minutes later, when they left the room, he knew that the lesson was absorbed. The decent Renault was left there hating himself, thinking: What kind of a life of deceit am I training them for, they've got to get away from all this, with a chance to live like free people, and then suddenly he felt his stomach knot up because outside Edith and Madame Le Crom-Hubert were greeting someone he knew, and in a moment Paul walked in, pale and frightened, still carrying the dispatch case and the biscuit box.

The map had come back.

And suddenly Renault's control went altogether; he jumped up, shouting violently " In God's name why are *you* here? " And for a few moments there was an ugly scene, as Edith tried to calm him, and Paul stood there, almost blubbering, too upset to speak, but finally in fits and starts, the story came out, as bad as it could be: at the last moment, as they were leaving Lorient the day before, the engine of the *Deux Anges* had broken down. (It turned out later to be a faulty spark-plug.) Alex had repaired it too late to keep the Wednesday appointment, but consoled himself there was still a chance of keeping one of those scheduled for Thursday. Then, during the night, had come the worst and most fantastic luck of all. British bombers, passing south over Lorient, had dropped mines at the port entrance. The *Kriegsmarine* had forbidden all shipping to leave port until the channel had been swept.

After five days of tension, the map rarely absent from his mind, Renault was too strung up to bear it; he had told Alex the boat was useless and now this damned map of Girard's seemed to have laid a jinx on everything. " You young fool," he shouted. " Why didn't you warn me yesterday? We could have warned London, couldn't we, and transferred the appointment? You're not fit to be sent on a mission to General de Gaulle, you . . ." Then he cut short the tirade for which he has never since forgiven himself, because Paul, his eyes filling with tears, had blundered from the room.

Now there was nothing to do but compose a message for Delattre to transmit, explaining the failure of the operation. Sick at heart, the little man apologised to Mauger, realising, too late, that as Madame Le Crom-Hubert had no telephone there would have been no way for the youngster to get in touch —and made preparations to return to Paris. This time Edith went with him, and the children were left with Madame Le Crom-Hubert, but after five days Renault sent her back to them at Baud, staying on alone at the apartment in the Square Henri-Paté.

I have this in my notes from Renault: " Up to now I had not examined this map of Girard's. It remained in the biscuit box in a cabin-trunk in the basement of my apartment block. But obviously the possession of it was dangerous, and it was unthinkable to leave it in a small country house where my wife and children were hidden or even to have my wife with me any longer. I had to stay in Paris with the map and transfer the danger to myself."

That was 29th May—three weeks to the day since Duchez had concealed the map behind the mirror.

Chapter Nine

OPERATION MARIE-LOUISE

GIRARD, in the meantime, had been extending his coverage along the Wall. If Renault had vindicated Dewavrin's theories for the southern Atlantic coast, he would do the same in the north-west. His life became a kaleidoscope of pounding train wheels, the blare and chaos of big junctions, subsisting on ham rolls and sour red wine at railway buffets, feigning nonchalance under the hard electric stares of the *Sicherheitsdienst* when it came to pass-checks at the barriers. With identity papers abstracted by Caillet from the *Mairie* at Caen, forged for him in Odette Duchez's dining-room, he was extending his identities too. In Paris, Malherbe, in Caen, Moreau, but in Argentan and Le Mans and Rouen, Rivière, Mallet, Lebret, Garnier—he no longer remembers which cover-names he used in which towns.

As he appointed local agency heads, they, in turn recruited agents, and new cells were set up. For the most part their membership was drawn from the anonymous working-class of Dewavrin's dreams, intelligence agents with work-calloused fingers who wore shopkeepers' aprons or labourers' denims. In Rouen it was an Alsatian coal merchant with a taste for drama calling himself " The Fox "; in Argentan a cheerful squarely-built electricity board inspector named Robert Aubin, who used the cover-name " Jonquet." By late May Girard had already appointed three departmental chiefs for the districts girdling the Wall inland, the Orne, round Argentan, the Sarthe, which was the region of Le Mans, and the Eure, the farming region of Evreux.

With the network only five weeks old, the results had been

staggering, and it would be pleasant to record that Girard felt a genuine glow of satisfaction. Pleasant, but untrue. Now that Touny had pronounced judgment, he admitted freely that Duchez had done a good job—but where did the Caen cell go from here? There were no signs that the Todt Organisation had missed the map—and that was puzzling—but Duchez was the obvious suspect when the search started. If he or his wife should crack under torture, almost every member of the network would come under the axe. A bitter price to pay for one success.

And could you call it a success? Wasn't it likely that London would see the map as just so much confirmation of what they knew from aerial reconnaissance? Lacking agents in the immediate coastal zone, neither Girard nor Touny nor any member of the network realised that even unlimited aerial reconnaissance (which the Allies then lacked in any case) could not have picked out the strongpoints on Duchez's plan.

The Allies knew a little about the Normandy coast at that time. They knew, for instance, about five medium and heavy batteries sited between the north-eastern tip of the Cherbourg peninsula and Port-en-Bessein. But no aerial photography had spotlit Duchez's defences, and for one simple reason: *they had not been built.* Duchez had stolen a mighty march on Hitler's Atlantic Wall, and it is an ironic paradox of the Intelligence game that no one realised it less than the painter or his chiefs.

In the meantime Girard had another pressing problem. Once or twice recently, a casual glance along a crowded street had given him the uneasy feeling that the Gestapo were taking an interest in him. On Berthelot's advice, he appointed a woman as his secretary-cum-shadow.

Denise Fernande Geninatti Banck—known to the Resistance as " Dany "—was tall and as slim as a wand, with a delicately modelled face and a restful air of sympathetic understanding. An early member of Touny's O.C.M. she had used her job as a secretary with S.V.P.—a Parisian agency furnishing everything from a client's family tree to a fourth at bridge—to receive and pass on information. Girard admired her from the first. He liked her sense of humour, her air of cool competence, the quickness of her wit and, above all, of her reflexes. To signal messages she would change the click of her heels on the pavement, stop suddenly to adjust her make-up, shift her hand-bag from right to left or touch a button. Once, leaving an office that Berthelot used on the Place Madeleine, Girard glanced across the street, and, in the shadow of the great white temple, saw Dany drop a glove. At once he had bundled into a velo-taxi and was off too quickly for the lounger on the corner to hail another and give chase.

Girard liked to play down such heart-stopping dilemmas which made up an agent's life (" just a little anecdote, that's all, nothing extraordinary about it "), but it was noticeable that he never tired of telling how Dany, disguised as an old woman, once shared her lunch-basket on a train journey with three members of the *Wehrmacht*, who never guessed that the " old lady's " box of good cream cheese concealed some important documents.

Dany's first judgment of her boss carried more reservations, being expressed by a significant shrug of the shoulders: " If only he listened to what people said or let anyone get a word in edgeways. . . ." But time was to bring many changes.

As to the whereabouts of Duchez's map, Girard saw that as the least of his worries. In theory, with no search forth-coming, the network had gained valuable time, and he assumed that it was by now in London where those responsible would make what use of it they saw fit.

In practice, the network had gained no time at all. The map was still lying in the trunk in the basement of Renault's apartment a few miles from Girard's own flat, and 32,000 Gestapo agents in Paris now had Renault's description.

Renault was made aware of this on the Pont Mirabeau, which spans the Seine below the Eiffel Tower, at approximately 2.30 p.m. on Saturday, 30th May. The news came from one of his agents, Maurice Rossi, a small smiling dumpling of a man who to the world was the polished and patient *maître d'hotel* of the Restaurant Traktir on the Avenue Victor Hugo.

On Renault's behalf Rossi had organised a network of all

the head waiters in the capital, to report the lunch-time indiscretions of such guests as General von Stulpenagel, the military governor, and he had rushed from duty in a great hurry to report some advice given to him that day by a friendly client in the lower echelons of the Gestapo.

"This man actually warned me," Maurice was telling Renault. "My name is on the Gestapo's suspected list. It was in François Faure's notebook when they arrested him and yours too. To-day they were at the restaurant asking about you."

Renault considered. "What do they know?"

Enough, Maurice told him, to know that they were looking for a bald not very tall man who called himself Morin or Jean-Luc, who posed as an insurance inspector for the Eagle Star and who always wore a silk handkerchief the same colour as his tie in his breast pocket. Maurice urged, "You've got to get away, monsieur. They are getting very close to you."

But Renault, hastily tucking a green silk handkerchief out of sight, did not think he could go. In London, Dewavrin had lost no time, and during the abortive trip to Lorient, six more transmitters and two operators had landed successfully on the dropping-ground at Aisne. One of them, Olivier Courtaud, a calm solid man in his forties, had already arrived in Paris with a transmitter. Four other sets had been buried close to the ground for future emergencies, and Delattre, Renault's personal radio officer, and the other operator were bringing another back to Paris. Alex was standing by for another attempt at a maritime rendezvous on June 17.

And there were three trump cards that he still held. The Gestapo did not know about his other aliases. They did not know about his family. They could not connect him with Girard's map, which had apparently not been missed.

He came to a decision. "I can't go yet," he told Maurice. "Instead, *mon ami*, you must go, because *you* can compromise me. Take your friend's advice—get through to the Unoccupied Zone and forget you ever heard of a Paris network." Then he left Maurice staring gloomily at the sunlight on the Seine.

The news that came next day left him shaken and sick and

wondering, for the first time, whether Maurice had not been right. On their way back from the dropping-ground Delattre and the second operator, a man named René-Georges Weil, had been stopped by black-market inspectors, suspicious of the suit-cases they carried, at the Gare du Nord. Delattre and Weil took advantage of the official's consternation at un-earthing a transmitter to make a bolt for it. They enjoyed seven hours of liberty before the Gestapo, now furnished with their descriptions, had arrested them on the Boulevard Hauss-mann. Delattre, again trying to escape, had been shot in the arm and dragged away. Weil was already dead, doubled up on the pavement in the agonies of a cyanide pill.

Young Paul Mauger, who had gone to meet them at the Gare du Nord, knew that Delattre had deposited a second trans-mitter with the left-luggage office; as a precaution Delattre had handed him the ticket just before the black-market officials stopped him. Rashly, Paul had gone back, a few hours later, to claim the suit-case and the Gestapo had been waiting. He, too, had been arrested.

Renault heard the news and could not speak. Little Paul. He had been so eager to take Girard's map to England, so bitterly hurt by Renault's injustice over the boat. It was safe to say he would never see England now. He would rot in the stinking twilight of a concentration camp, if the Gestapo did not tear him apart in an effort to find out what he knew. Renault felt himself shaking all over, he wanted to howl like an animal in his grief and shame, and the agent who had broken the news went quietly away.

On 10th June Pierre Brossolette, the dark dynamic journalist, returned from London. His burning sincerity had so impressed de Gaulle and Dewavrin that they had entrusted him with a political mission. He brought Renault a letter from Dewavrin, and watched the little man's lips set in a tight line as he opened and read it. The contents admitted no compromise. " You will return to England as soon as possible and bring your family. The remains of your network must be entrusted to other hands."

" You know what's in it? " Renault asked, and the

journalist nodded, embarrassed. It was Renault, after all, who had arranged his Lysander pick-up to London, shortly after their second meeting. Renault said, " Well, I'm not going and that's final. Dewavrin doesn't know what's going on here, he probably thinks that every network is under the axe. . . ."

After all, what had been destroyed to date? He had had to close the headquarters at 72 Champs Elysées for safety, but what of it? Was everything to be disbanded overnight because the central transmission agency was hard hit? Networks like Girard's were unaffected, and were still sending in dispatches weekly. He had the promise of a new headquarters above a warehouse in the Boulevard de la Chapelle. He must carry on.

The way Renault felt, if unrealistic, was human enough. It was he who had founded the provincial networks, it was he whom they knew and trusted, and it is hard for any man to believe that things can run as smoothly without him. Only if he believed he was a danger to his friends would he go.

It was not until Friday, 12th June—five weeks since Duchez had hidden the plan—that he saw the red light.

At six o'clock that morning he had sent Courtaud to the one safe transmission post, the house of a Madame Chedeville at Pont-Audemer, sixty miles from Paris, to get in touch with London about the sea rendezvous. Now at nine o'clock he was sitting on the bench in the Muette Metro station, talking to Georgina Dufour, the chic middle-aged Parisienne who acted as a combined *femme-de-chambre* for himself at Auteuil and for his sisters at his former apartment in the Avenue de la Motte-Picquet. For five nights he had stayed in hotels, not daring to use his own flat, and he was anxious for a bulletin. He remembers that Georgina began conversationally, " Your sisters were arrested by the Gestapo yesterday . . ." and he felt his stomach turn over, but for a moment the rest of it was drowned by the rumbling of a new train, the slam of doors as workers hurried aboard.

Georgina was still talking. " But it was all right, monsieur, you understand—only routine, because it had once been your apartment before you gave it over to them. They took Mademoiselle Maisie and Mademoiselle Isabelle to the rue des Saussaies and questioned them, but they had to release them, monsieur. It is not they who are in danger, it is you."

Renault was tense. " Why me? "

" They know all about you, monsieur—everything." But that one Renault tried to laugh off. " They always pretend that, Georgina. It's an old trick to pump more out of you."

Georgina's handsome face was lined with anxiety. " But, no, monsieur—believe me. To put them off the scent Mademoiselle Maisie, said—forgive me, monsieur—that you could not be a spy as they suggested, you were a good-for-nothing idler. The Gestapo man was very angry and to convince her he gave a list of your cover-names. Morin, Watteau, Renault, Rémy, Raymond—he knew them all."

Who had talked? Bob Delattre? Faure? Little Paul? Whoever it was Renault could feel no bitterness, only an appalling despair which to any Catholic as devout as himself was the truly unforgivable sin. He could not blame the others, and it was characteristic of the man that he never, at any time, tried to discover the source of the leak. No one could predict what would happen to a man's mind when Himmler's specialists got to work on it. Georgina was still talking.

" And then, monsieur, they asked your sisters for a photograph of your family. Mademoiselle Isabelle pretended that they would disdain to keep such a memento because they had quarrelled with you, but the Gestapo man said it didn't matter. He said, We know he has a wife and four children and that they are hiding somewhere in Brittany, near the coast.

So that was it, and they knew, and there was no way round this one. He was finished. A Frenchman—and therefore an individualist—to the last, Renault would have defied his chief and risked the agonies of the damned to stay in France with his men, but the sacred unit, his family, must not be involved. He must obey Dewavrin's orders, remove his hostages from the grasp of fortune, and then return.

" Oh, Monsieur Gilbert," Georgina said hopelessly. " What are you going to do? " And her employer, rising to vanish among the crowds, patted her shoulder reassuringly.

" I am taking them all to a place of safety," Renault said.

Renault worked fast after that. There was so little time. He had a brief meeting with his deputy, a quiet patient man named Max Petit, entrusting the care of the networks to him until he returned. Then he sent a message to Alex, asking him to meet the night train from Paris at Hennebont Station next morning. (Hennebont was six miles from Lorient and seemed a quiet place for a rendezvous.) Then, back in the basement of his apartment block, he worked for some time, transferring the biscuit box with Duchez's map of the Wall, together with many dispatches, into a suit-case. A second suit-case he packed with clothes taken from the trunk. Then he rang one of his agents, Renaud de Saint-Georges, who kept a garage, and asked him to send a van. The trunk, which was harmless, he moved to a friend's apartment (thinking dryly that when a man is hunted he has no option but to travel light). The suit-case with the dispatches he took to the Gare Montparnasse and registered for Hennebont.

He was still lugging the suit-case full of clothes at six that evening when he climbed the steep stairs to Courtaud's room at the Hotel de Royan, by the Gare Montparnasse, and one look at the operator's face told him the news. Short-wave transmission is a complex process, and over the 500-mile distance the ionosphere often caused the waves to bounce back before they reached the receiving area. Courtaud had been unable to get in touch with London.

Renault calculated hard. Four days. To be at the rendezvous the following Wednesday the trawler N51 would have to leave the Scilly Isles on the Tuesday evening, but to lay on the operation London would still need twenty-four hours' notice. Dewavrin would have to state his requirements by Monday morning. That meant raising London by to-morrow, Saturday, at the latest, in case a full staff was not on duty Sunday.

Renault sat down on the operator's bed. He said, " Now, listen, Courtaud. This is what we do. To-night we travel separately to Hennebont. Your transmitter can go in my suit-case. We'll register it and you'll keep the ticket. And you'll keep this ticket too—that's for a suit-case containing dispatches, that I've already registered." He looked at Courtaud squarely, thinking, I wonder how this seems to him. Only two weeks here and he's plunged into a nightmare. " One more thing— if I'm arrested on the journey before joining the train you won't see me at Hennebont. That is obvious. So what you do then is check out the suit-cases, join up with Alex and somehow see that those dispatches *and* my wife and children get to England. Only you won't tell my wife I've been arrested. If necessary you will lie unashamedly, but you will somehow convince them that I am to join the boat a few minutes before sailing."

The radio operator seemed pale but composed. " I understand," he said.

Renault had a last dinner at Schubert's with friends, listening to Spanish music and trying to get drunk, but no matter how much wine he put away it could not cushion his feelings against the agonising reality of the danger. He caught the nine twenty-five from the Gare Montparnasse; rain sifted like a curtain over the boulevards as he reached the station and the street lights wavered moltenly, but he boarded the train without trouble and went straight to the two-berth sleeper he had reserved with Cooks'. In the lower bunk a German officer, preparing for bed, wished him a quiet *Guten abend.*

The sleeping-car attendant came to check the reservation card with his identity papers, and there was an agonising moment when he said:

" You are Monsieur Morin? "

(Morin! He'd forgotten and reserved as Morin! And the Gestapo had known the cover-name for a fortnight!)

There was no way to rectify the mistake. " I'm Morin," he said quietly. He undressed and got into the upper bunk, trying to control his trembling, but the German, putting on his bedroom slippers, hadn't even looked up.

The train drew in to Hennebont the next morning just after seven. Courtaud had already descended to the platform. Across the tracks Renault could see Alex, dour and imperturbable, his assistant, Alain de Beaufort, a slight crew-cropped lad with a

116

hint of moustache waiting beside him, and a faint hope stirred in him at the sight of friends. Perhaps even now there was a chance. . . . While these two waited in Alex's battered old Peugeot, Renault and Courtaud went to the luggage office to claim the two registered suit-cases. The baggage clerk, a thin restless man, his face pinched tight with hunger, handed up the brown case containing the dispatches.

So far so good. The map was safe.

Renault said, " *Un moment, Monsieur*; there are two."

The clerk stared, searched perfunctorily, pouted, then gave the devastating Gallic shrug which says more plainly than words, The matter is now out of my hands. His heart pounding, Renault forced him to search the platform. Again the shrug. Nothing.

In the driving-seat Alex grumbled, " Hanging about all this time . . . surely it's a simple enough matter to check out one suit-case."

" One suit-case," Renault said, holding on to his temper. " Apparently not two. We are in trouble, Alex, *mon ami*. The other suit-case is missing."

" So? "

" So we have our dispatches, but no means of warning London that the liaison is on. The transmitter has gone."

Now Alex and de Beaufort looked grave. They held a brief murmured consultation by the side of the car. Obviously the suit-case with the transmitter had been carried on past Henne-bont. If they could contact the official in charge of the baggage car at Lorient, there was still hope of contacting London, but if they were not on time and the train sped on towards the terminus at Quimper, there was then no hope at all. It was as simple as that.

Alex drove hard towards Baud. At Madame Le Crom-Hubert's villa he dropped Renault and Courtaud, then he and his assistant disappeared in a scurry of dust towards Lorient. For a moment the familiar miracle was reaffirmed, and Renault, holding Edith in his arms, hugging the children to him, remembered nothing at all. Then he pulled himself together. There was still a war. He must get his wife and children to England, but Girard's map and the other dispatches must get there too.

In their bedroom, away from the children, he told Edith, " *If* we can get the transmitter in time—and *if* we can raise London—a lot of ifs, my darling—I am taking you and the children with me to England. I have something here—something which I wanted little Paul to take—which makes it too dangerous for us to stay any longer." He waited, half-expecting her to say: I can't stand another move, before telling him what her life had been the last two years. She had never told him before, and Renault, half-ashamed, felt that he had always taken care to steer the conversation outside those channels. But she would be justified in telling him now.

Instead Edith only smiled. " You're here now," she said quietly. " It will be all right. I know that."

Renault said nothing more, but he wondered. In the car ride from Hennebont he had promised de Beaufort that he could journey with them on the *Deux Anges* to join de Gaulle. Seven passengers and a map of the Atlantic Wall . . . he doubted if the leaky old lobster-boat had ever embarked on a more dangerous voyage. Both Delattre and Mauger knew how the sea operations were scheduled, and if the Germans forced them to talk. . . . He almost wished he had talked Edith into a Lysander pick-up, but it would have needed at least two Lysanders to accomplish this mission. And " Guardian Angel " could no longer be used: the Germans had recently planted an observation post in the centre of it.

De Beaufort and Alex came back, dusty and dishevelled, but with the transmitter intact, and by midday they were all sitting down to lunch. Renault tried, for the children's sake, to be gay, but the good goose-liver *pâté* went almost untasted. Suddenly Courtaud got up and left the room. Renault glanced at his watch. Twelve fifty-five—the hour of " routines," when free London was on the look-out for messages on all the wavelengths used by Europe in chains. Renault helped the children to more *pâté*, and ten leaden minutes passed before Courtaud returned and calmly helped himself to enough *pâté* to stuff a squab chicken before giving him the most enormous wink he had ever seen. " Ten o'clock to-morrow," he said, " we'll have the answer."

Five hours later in London Dewavrin was sitting, tired and drawn, in his office at 10 Duke Street. Manuel, his deputy, was beside him, sorting out dispatches. Dewavrin had spent three hours that afternoon, on and off, consulting with the Commander; it had been a close thing, but the Admiralty had agreed. The trawler N 51 would rendezvous on Wednesday, 17th June at 4 p.m. G.M.T., again on the Thursday at 10 a.m. and, if that failed, again at 4 p.m. the same day. The trawler would wait an hour at each rendezvous.

Finally, they had asked for a code-name, and Lieutenant Mella,·one of Dewavrin's assistants, consulting the list of code-names available, came up with " Operation Marie-Louise."

Manuel asked Dewavrin, " Do you think they have a chance? "

" You want me to be frank? "

" Of course."

" Yes, I think they have a chance," said the implacable Dewavrin. " About one in five hundred. I wouldn't put it any higher than that." He knew nothing then of Girard's plan, but the odds would have lengthened considerably if he had.

At 8 a.m. on the Monday de Beaufort, Alex's assistant, arrived by car to collect Renault and his family. As they had to embark on the *Deux Anges* from the little river port of Pont-Aven, they were going to stay two nights in the village of Riec-sur-Belon, a mile and a half from the port, to avoid attracting attention, and Courtaud, the radio operator, was accompanying them to maintain liaison with London. With no inkling of what lay ahead, the children revelled in the ride, bouncing up and down on the springs—all except Michel, the baby, who, with the wisdom of eighteen months, slept soundly. Alex had booked three rooms for them at the Hotel Ostrea on the cobbled main square.

Early on the Tuesday Courtaud raised London again and the Wednesday meeting on the Lorient fishing bank was finally confirmed. Now there was nothing to do but wait. Once during the day Renault thought about their chances of escape, and they seemed slender, but if you examined the alternatives rationally they were bleak, too. The Gestapo wanted him too badly for him to remain at liberty for long, and on any count he violently rejected the idea of being captured. If he was going to die, he would die fighting.

That evening they left the children in charge of the hotel proprietress and clip-clopped away in an old horse-drawn carriage to the Moulin Rosmadec in Pont-Aven, a weather-beaten wistaria-covered inn with black old timbers sited by a thundering weir, which was—and is still—celebrated as a gourmet's paradise. Edith had the brief-case containing the dispatches, and Renault, who seemed doomed to spend his war struggling with parcels, was almost invisible beneath two enormous cardboard cartons of dispatches and the biscuit box holding Duchez's plan.

On the way an idea occurred to him that in the early morning a carriage might excite less suspicion than a car and he said to the sleepy young peasant who was driving: " Listen, my friend, I have some business for you. To-morrow I am taking my family for a seaside outing to Quimper. A car is picking us up in Pont-Aven, but we have no way of getting from Riec to Pont-Aven. What about picking us up at our hotel to-morrow and driving us to Pont-Aven? "

The peasant thought about it for so long that Renault thought he had fallen asleep, but finally he said placidly, " Ça va." Renault was so excited that he decided to cement the bargain by inviting the man to dinner, and soon they were all crowded along panelled linenfold benches in the long dimly-lit dining-room, with the white water of the weir drumming beneath the leaded window, laughing and chattering like any family party before the war: Renault and Edith, Courtaud, de Beaufort, Alex, wearing an old pea-jacket with a fore-and-aft cap jammed on his stubbly hair, and the driver, rather bewildered by these gay noisy compatriots.

Renault had left the cardboard cartons and the biscuit box with the map on a settee in the lounge outside, just inside the main doorway, where they were within eyesight but not attracting too much attention. As always, faced with a four-star menu, he had almost forgotten his troubles, and he was just advising a meal of Belon oysters followed by fat Breton crabs stuffed with herbs and m.u hrooms in brandy, and a bottle of cold dry Muscadet when Edith, putting on her best social smile for the driver's benefit, plucked his elbow and said, " Look, dear . . ."

Renault looked and for a moment his heart was knocking in his throat, because the hallway of the inn was suddenly packed with men in the neat navy-blue uniform of the German submarine service and two of them were standing right by the biscuit box. The four men exchanged quick glances, and Renault murmured, " We can only wait." Then a warm joy spread quietly through him, because the officers—six of them —were seating themselves boisterously round a table over-looking the garden, and the biscuit box on the settee was almost invisible beneath their peaked caps and their small arms. No one was going to touch it now.

It was not as dramatic as Duchez's ruse with " Albert " (Renault did not know about it then), but he said afterwards that it seemed as if the Germans were determined to help them with the map all the way. When the food came to the table and he said grace he added a brief prayer of thanks for deliverance.

At nine, when darkness curtained the river, they rescued the boxes from their load of caps and, leaving the carriage to wait for them, walked down the lane between white-plastered cottages to a tiny jetty beneath the trees. Even as Alex pointed out the *Deux Anges* lying at anchor, Renault knew something was wrong. Quietly, trying to keep the strain from her voice, Edith said: " We can't possibly get in there—not *all* of us."

" Oh, yes, we can," said Alex briskly, then, grasping all three boxes and the brief-case from Renault's arm, " Here, these'll be safer aboard. It's almost given me indigestion to see you fretting about them." He jumped quickly aboard, stowed the boxes in the forward hold, and clamped the hatch with a strong padlock.

Then he clambered back on the quay and said, " All right, this is your briefing. Be here at 6 a.m. to-morrow. Don't bring the carriage anywhere near the river bank. Pay him off and walk from the square, because you never know if he'll talk. But you *must not* be later than six. In that way we can join up at the river mouth with the boats going out from the other little ports. There won't be more than ten of them but if we all arrive at Port-Manech together, we shall stand a better chance."

" Port-Manech? " Edith was puzzled.

" That's about three miles away, at the mouth of the river. It's the German inspection point for fishing boats."

Renault felt his wife's grip squeezing on his arm as she said, " How is the inspection done? "

" There are about fifteen Germans on the strength. They board every other boat," Alex told her. There was nothing in his voice at all.

" And if they board the *Deux Anges* they will find us? "

" Of course," Alex acknowledged quietly. " We are all of us in God's hands now."

Renault climbed wearily from bed at 4 a.m. He had not closed his eyes all night, and now his mouth tasted thick and sour and every nerve in his body cried out for sleep. He saw Edith slowly open her eyes and felt a stab of pity, knowing that she had not slept either. He had felt her beside him in the night, her body shaking with silent grief. Slowly she climbed from bed and began to prepare the baby's bottle.

Renault went next door, to the room where the children slept, and in a moment they were sitting up in bed, squinting nervously under the harsh yellow light: Jean-Claude, staring uneasily at his father and moistening dry lips, Catherine, ready for anything, Cécile, smiling and full of confidence.

" Now, children," Renault said quietly, " listen and then get dressed. In an hour we are going to leave this house and take a boat and try to reach England." Suddenly he felt he loved them more than he had ever done, but this, too, had to be said: " We have not too much hope, but if we stay here we shall most probably be caught." The girls accepted it without question, but Jean-Claude asked uneasily how they were going to take the boat. Renault explained that the landlady, who believed they were making an early start for a day by the sea at Quimper, had promised to leave the main door unlocked. At five the driver of a horse-carriage was coming to take them to Pont-Aven.

Outside the door he paused a moment, thinking of the cold morning only six months ago when he had knelt beside the altar at Notre Dame, and again he prayed fervently: O Lady of Victories, we are in your hands now. At least grant the children a chance to know a better life than this.

Courtaud, who was to confirm their departure with London that morning, appeared on the landing in his pyjamas. Leaving him to cheer up the children, Renault stole silently downstairs to check the front door and stopped very still. The landlady had forgotten. The door was locked.

In sudden panic he ran from room to room, even invading the kitchen to try the outside doors. All locked.

Black despair seized him. Finished, finished, finished . . . and all because a fool of a woman, so typically, so casually French, had forgotten to unlock the door. He did not even know where she slept. He banged fitfully through the downstairs rooms, trying to make as much noise as possible, but the hotel slept on in the early sunshine: chairs piled high in the dining-room, shutters drawn. Five-fifteen had come and gone, still no sign of the landlady, but worse still, no sign of the carriage. When she appeared in dressing-gown and curlers at five-thirty, yawning and apologising profusely, Renault told her waspishly that it didn't matter at all. Finished. . . . Upstairs he found Edith, white and silent, with Courtaud and the children grouped round her like a disconsolate family group in a photographer's studio, the baby crowing jubilantly in her arms.

He told them quietly: " I am afraid that it is too late. You see, the carriage driver has forgotten as well." And the words were hardly out of his mouth when they heard a horse's hoofs, kock-kock-kock on the dusty cobbles outside. " He's here," Catherine shrieked.

Now everything blurred into a mad confusion. All of them knew that there was no chance of reaching Pont-Aven by six, but anything was better than staying and waiting to be caught. Hastily they shook hands with Courtaud and hugged him, piling en masse into the carriage, shouting down the driver's excuses that he had overslept and urging him to hurry. Renault thought he aged a little on that ride.

De Beaufort was waiting for them in the square at Pont-Aven, and they paid off the driver. They walked quickly, almost furtively, along the lane, under the thick grove of elms, hearing the shutters clatter back against whitewashed walls. Six-fifteen; the little town was waking up. The whole lane seemed full of eyes.

Down by the jetty the *Deux Anges* was ready to cast off; the outboard motor stuttered noisily on the misty air. Alex was on deck, his face impassive with anger, and it was now Renault's turn to blurt excuses (remembering Paul's face crumpling that day), but Alex cut him short: " No time for all that—just get on board, that's all I ask, and take up your positions." As they began to file aboard, Renault was struck suddenly by the incongruity of their attire: Edith in a dark half-length coat, wearing a turban, the girls in checked gingham dresses, himself in an old sports coat and pullover, with a beret and flannel trousers. To give authority to the story of the picnic their only luggage was a small suit-case and Edith's handbag. This is the strangest picnic party, Renault thought, that ever any family embarked on.

The *Deux Anges* was moving now, coughing out between high banks crested with pine trees, dotted thickly with out-croppings of rock and the yellow blaze of gorse. In the early morning light the water was like oiled grey-green silk; the wind came up from the Atlantic, salt and chill, and Renault, holding the baby, wondered incongruously whether it would take cold. Someone stumbled into him along the deck—it was Alex. " Everyone in their places," he said. " I'll show you where. Hurry now—we're at Port-Manech in ten minutes."

His mind still dazed with it all, Renault saw Alex bundle Edith and Cécile into the port stern locker and close the sliding-panel that sealed it off from the deck. Next Catherine and Jean-Claude in the starboard stern locker, and Renault shook his head in silent disbelief: the lockers were no more than six feet long by about three and a half feet high and two feet wide. No room to turn over or even to move. They would have to lie side by side, like the living tenants of a coffin. He heard Alex's voice: " Quick now! The hold in the bows for you." As he and de Beaufort stumbled along the deck, Renault, still with Michel, he caught the skipper's eye.

(The skipper, Louis Yequel, an imperturbable Breton, remembers thinking, If it wasn't for the kids I wouldn't have any part of this. With one agent we might stand a chance, but with every inch of the boat jammed with refugees . . . if the Germans so much as lift one hatch we're lost. . . .)

In the forward hold the old stale smell of fish and tar mingling with the petrol vapour from the engine caught Renault in the pit of the stomach. For a moment, easing himself gingerly forward with Michel in his arms, he almost vomited; the opening to the hold was about a foot wide but the hold itself was no more than two feet high and perhaps five feet square. Then his elbow coming hard against a petrol can took his mind to other things, and a moment later there was a muffled curse as de Beaufort did the same. The hatch swung back and a golden spoke of sunlight drove through the darkness. Alex's voice, furious: " Keep still—we're approaching Control."

There was only one thing to do, Renault thought, lie down and keep perfectly still. Beside him he was conscious of de Beaufort doing the same. The baby was on Renault's chest now, making no sound, but Renault was not a father for nothing. A prickling instinct told him that in the darkness his son was very wide awake and judiciously considering the moment when it might be appropriate to make a speech.

The engine had puttered into silence, and now, for what seemed like eternity, there was only a steady queasiness as the *Deux Anges* see-sawed on the choppy tidal water. In the starboard stern locker Jean-Claude and Catherine had struggled to turn away from one another, vomiting and vomiting again, a cruel mercy because as the acrid spasms wrenched them, they had ceased to think about being caught.

Fumbling in his raincoat pocket, Renault was trying to locate the bottle which Edith had filled before they left the hotel. He had planned this strategy well in advance: if Michel was feeding as they passed the Control point, everything would go smoothly. Soon, he judged, they would be in the line of boats, moving up to Control, and in the darkness he found the bottle and struggled to adjust the nipple. It was easier to plan than to achieve. Warm milk rained on his hand, and on the baby's face.

With sudden piercing clarity Michel laughed. For a moment Renault lay rigid with fear, holding the bottle, not moving. The boat was now nudging gently against something solid—a pier. Then his mind snapped back to urgent consciousness. Fatal to delay the feeding another second; he adjusted the nipple, urging the bottle forward, but Michel had other ideas. A chubby hand was pushing the bottle away, and in the darkness the baby began to crow delightedly.

God, Renault thought, the father in him supplanting the secret agent, why in the name of sanity did we succumb to habit and feed him at 4 a.m.? Of course he doesn't want milk now. A yard away the unmistakable sound of boots, nailed boots, was striking echoes from the stone of the jetty: German boots. Just then the baby cried again, and someone dropped the anchor chain on the worn wooden deck with a noise that seemed to burst inside Renault's brain. The phlegmatic Louis Yequel had presence of mind.

It was a good ruse, Renault thought frantically, but it would only work once. One more cry and they would be finished, all of them. The small hand fought stolidly against the bottle; Michel began to grunt with vexation. Suddenly Renault remembered a bag of chocolate drops that Madame Le Crom-Hubert had given him for the children two days ago. Where, *where*, could he have put it? Paper whispered dryly in his raincoat pocket: that was it. He popped a chocolate drop into the baby's mouth, praying that Michel would not choke and held his breath, waiting. Then a warm relief surged through him, because a steady sound of sucking had succeeded the grunting.

For what seemed like a long time Renault lay listening. Feet were sounding overhead, a lighter tread now, probably Yequel's. The engine began to pulse again, filling the hold with petrol fumes and drumming life. Now would be the worst time. Now they would be moving in the line of boats going up to inspection. The baby made an importunate glugging sound. Hastily Renault fed him another chocolate drop, and waited.

He was jerked violently forward against the petrol cans. Without warning the great hand of the sea had taken the *Deux Anges*, and tilted her violently upwards. Another wave, more gentle now, then another, the soft see-saw motion quickening and intensifying. They were moving at perhaps eight knots, two-thirds speed. They must be on the open sea.

" De Beaufort," Renault whispered, after a long moment. " Are we *out*? " And heard the other whisper back, " Yes, I think the inspection only lasted a minute."

" But why? "

" I suppose we were the other one. So they just looked at the list of the crew. Remember what Alex said—they only search every other one."

Now in the darkness Renault could not speak. Salt, not the salt of the sea, was in his eyes and in his mouth. He knew suddenly that he was crying as unashamedly as one of his own children, but he could not stop himself and he did not mind. He did not mind at all.

His wife and children were safe. Girard's plan was safe. Our Lady had heard the prayers he had uttered and in her mercy had granted them their freedom.

After that the time seemed to pass very slowly. Once Alex lifted the hatch to explain the full and fantastic extent of their luck: the *Deux Anges* had been the last boat in the line-up and the very next boat ahead of them, the last but one, had been searched. Michel, tired of being a paragon, began to wail bitterly, and Alex bore him hastily away, his mouth ringed with chocolate, to his mother in the forward stern locker. They could not risk other fishing boats suspecting their cargo. In the early morning, sound travels far over water, and all round, not more than a hundred yards away, the fishing fleet of that stretch of coastline, a score of little boats, rode on the swell, their nets spread, red sails ballooning in the breeze. A join in the hatch filtered a thin band of sunlight into the hold and Renault could see that the sky was intensely blue. There was no sound for miles, apart from the occasional thud of a landed conger thwacking heavily on bare boards.

The *Deux Anges* lay there for an hour, fished, then moved on again. Edith and the children were sleeping peacefully now, worn out by nausea and fear. Renault began to worry. The rendezvous was not until 4 p.m.; eight hours to go. Supposing something prevented the N 51 from keeping the first rendezvous? Then they would have to return to Pont-Aven, for boats of the *Deux Anges* class were not allowed to spend the night at sea—that was a privilege reserved for trawlers. At nightfall the boat was due back at Port-Manech for inspection, and their luck might not hold again. This time they might be searched.

Could they make a dash for England? But the boat's gas supply was not much more than six gallons, not enough to carry them more than thirty-five miles at the outside. Even if they risked it and stayed out all night, they would be picked up long before 10 a.m., the time of the second rendezvous. If they returned—even supposing they survived the inspection—there was no house in all Pont-Aven that could take the risk of sheltering them. All morning and afternoon the sky was filled with the whining anger of planes, Focke-Wulf 190s patrolling far overhead, and Renault crouched in the darkness with sweating palms, wondering.

Towards four o'clock Alex raised the hatch to announce that a two-masted trawler from Camaret which technically had no right on the Lorient fishing bank had been sighted some way ahead. But for the moment they could only wait: rigid security decreed that neither party must give the prearranged signal before the time agreed. The minutes ticked by, an eternity: peering through the tiny hatch, straining his ears to

Aboard the N.51. Left to right—Alain de Beaufort; Edith Renault; a sailor holding Michel, the baby; Gilbert Renault and Lieut. Daniel Lomenech, R.N.V.R.

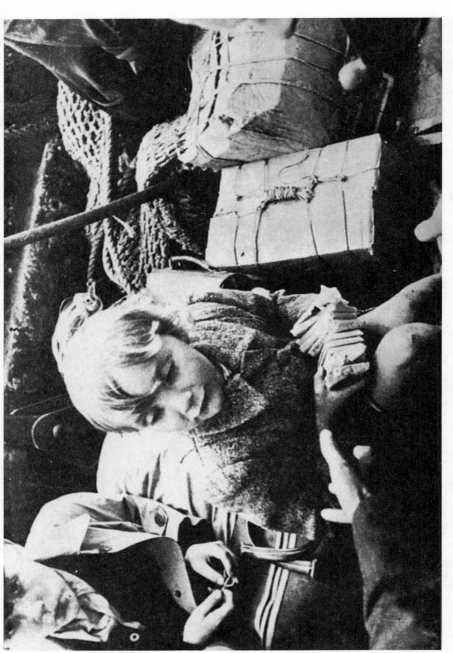

Aboard the N.51. Jean-Claude and Cécile Renault. Below the cardboard cartons containing Renault's despatches can be seen the biscuit box containing Duchez's plan of the Atlantic Wall.

catch Alex's sideline commentary, Renault could see nothing. Presently he heard Alex calling: " It's them all right—they're coming slowly towards us. Shall I give the signal? " But Renault, glancing at his watch, called up, " Better wait till the hour." A moment later he began to ease himself painfully through the hatch, and suddenly without warning, his ears were bursting with the sound of engines, and Alex was screaming at him, " Get in, you fool—get in! There's a German plane heading straight for us."

The hatch slammed shut; the humid darkness folded round him, and the overpowering stench of fish and petrol. He could hear nothing but the thin-edged snarl of the Focke-Wulf's engine coming closer, closer still, right overhead now. If it didn't stop his ears would split. Gradually it died away, the hatch creaked open again, and there was Alex, the sweat sliding down his face.

" Close," he kept saying. " Very close. They went over us at less than a hundred feet. What about that signal? "

" Give it," said Renault devoutly.

He could bear the stench no longer now; he squeezed through the hatch, followed by de Beaufort and rolled sideways on to the deck. God, but the air smelt sweet. Alex was close to the mast, pretending to arrange a rope, while the jib flapped in the wind. Three hundred yards away, on the deck of the trawler, a man in a blue fisherman's jersey was going through the same motions. The N51 moved slowly towards its rendezvous.

In the wheelhouse of the trawler Lt. Daniel Lomenech, R.N.V.R., saw the *Deux Anges* breasting the waves at the same moment as he checked his position by the small purple dot on the chart—Latitude 47.37, Longitude 4.2. " Slow-slow ahead," he ordered the helmsman, and quietly, skilfully, the N51 eased bows on to the wind until the lines were made fast fore and aft and the trawler's silhouette masked the tiny bobbing craft from the shore. It was a perfect spot for a rendezvous. Not a sail or a smudge of smoke stained the horizon.

With the map still foremost in his mind, Renault ran to Alex, taking the boxes and the brief-case of dispatches from his outstretched hands. Clutching them, he stumbled to the bows, raising his arms above his head, and calloused brown hands stretched down from the trawler to receive them. Next went Michel, followed one by one by the family. His heart bursting with thankfulness, Renault shook hands with Alex, Yequel and the Bihan brothers, who made up the rest of the crew. He said, " God bless each one of you, my friends, and thank you all." Then he stretched upwards, hung for a second above the swell and clambered aboard the N51.

Sailors were crouched beside the gunwale, with Sten guns in readiness, and Renault could see more arms glinting in the innocent tangle of nets. He felt a sudden atavistic surge of joy at the thought that they would not be taken alive. Other sailors were craning to shower gifts on the deck of the *Deux Anges*: packets of tea, packets of Gold Flake, loaves of tawny crusted bread. There were shouts, waves, as the *Deux Anges* moved away, and for the first time in his life Renault saw Alex smiling.

" Au revoir! See you soon! "

" Good luck—and God bless you."

Soon Renault could see nothing but a small red sail on the iridescent blue of the sea: the *Deux Anges* that he had doubted and despised going back alone to Pont-Aven.

All that evening, as the darkness thickened across the water, the N51 slipped quietly north at about eight knots. That night they slept on mattresses spread on cabin floors and in alleyways, but the sea still rocked gently, and of the children only Michel was in good appetite. The others waved away the china mugs of hot tea and thick bread and butter, groaning instead for basins. Next morning—18th June—the patrols were still not far distant and Lomenech, the young Breton skipper, warned Renault and the others to keep below. By six that evening they were off the race of Seine, and there was one nasty spine-chilling moment when it seemed that two small German war-ships were going to hail them. But suddenly the two ships veered north for Brest and the tension passed.

On the Friday they were in home waters and the N51 suddenly showed herself in her true colours, with the white

ensign fluttering at the masthead, and twin Lewis gun mount-
ings gleaming fore and aft. At eight in the morning two twin-
engined fighters roared close towards them, not 150 feet above
the sea, sweeping in over them, circling and wheeling like gulls
for the rest of that day. (They were Beaufighters that Dewavrin
and the Commander had arranged for the ship's protection.)
At just after ten on the Saturday they anchored at Tresco, in
the Scilly Isles. An M.T.B. stuttered across the shining bay to
collect them, and the skipper, the tall red-bearded Lieutenant
D. M. Curtis, who had distinguished himself in the St. Nazaire
raid, took them to his cabin. With him were another naval
officer and a British Intelligence man.

Cécile and Catherine and Jean-Claude, by special permission, had been allowed on the bridge, where they were
bouncing up and down in an ecstasy of freedom, and Edith,
also by special permission, was putting Michel to bed in
Curtis's bunk! Then Curtis and Renault and the Intelligence
man repaired to the day-cabin, and quietly, so as not to disturb
the baby, the Intelligence man said: " Well, now, Colonel
Rémy, what have you brought us, apart from your wife and
family? "

Renault answered, " Maps." But when the Intelligence
man countered, " What maps? " all that Renault could do was
open up the biscuit box and produce the plan that Duchez had
stolen. Both Curtis and Renault swore thereafter that the map
was so long that it more than extended the full length of
Curtis's cabin, and since it was almost ten feet long and two and
quarter feet wide, that is not surprising.

" My God," Curtis said, " I've never seen anything like
this before. How on earth did you get hold of this? " And
Renault had to reply truthfully then that he did not know.
(Nor did he find out the story at all until after the war.) As
for the Intelligence man, he only looked wise and said nothing
at all.

Presently Renault recovered himself sufficiently from the
daze of events to ask where they were going, and Curtis
explained that they were heading for Dartmouth at a speed
of eighteen knots, and that before proceeding to London

Renault and his family would all be spending the night aboard a yacht as guests of the Commander.

" You'll be able to get a decent bath aboard," Curtis said reassuringly. " Perhaps we might have a pink gin before dinner if you're agreeable? " And Renault knew that he was back in a free world.

Chapter Ten

BLUEPRINT FOR CENTURY

ON THE Monday following, 22nd June, Dewavrin's tables and office floor were inches deep in maps and reports. Frowning, his lips pursed, that implacable young man was sorting through Renault's post-bag, aided by Manuel, his bald bespectacled deputy.

Renault had exulted earlier that day about a map of the Atlantic Wall, but there had been fifty solid pounds of reports to sift through first. When he came to it, Dewavrin stopped short and whistled soundlessly. Then he lifted a red " Most Secret " phone, moved the indicator to " Scramble," and called Sir Claude Dansey to say, " I'm sending something over that I'd like you to have a look at urgently." There was very little Dewavrin did not know about the progress of defences along the coastline. This, he divined correctly, " was something of more than routine interest."

Just how many people were destined to evince a burning interest in the map during the next few weeks even he could not have foreseen.

The focal point of the interest was a bleak basement called the " Martian Room " in Storey's Gate, St. James's Park, where a few self-taught Intelligence experts had unwittingly become Britain's greatest authorities on what was going on across the Channel. (Martian was the code-name for anything bearing on a far-distant invasion plan.) Headed by a tall bespectacled Oxford don named John L. Austin, the " Martians " or Theatre Intelligence Section G.H.Q., Home Forces, had been set up to sift the networks' dispatches for the benefit of interested Air, Military and Naval departments.

Duchez's plan, as Austin recalled later, " scored a very great hit—it was the first genuine home-produced information about German defences that Britain received."

First there were the troop dispositions shown. Enough intelligence had flowed in from other sources to show that north of the Seine the concentration of troops was almost three times heavier than the little divisional flags on Duchez's map indicated for the Normandy sector. Even weaker than the garrisoning were the guns; for various highly technical reasons, artillery experts calculated that some of them were so sited as to be unable to hit any kind of ship. It was obvious too, that bunkers and blockhouses were adhering rigidly to the old Siegfried Line-West Wall specifications. Later they found tha even a few already built had not been spotted by air re- connaissance.

With the help of some friendly R.E.s, the Martians over- printed all these details on to a watered-down contour map, and in the first week of July, Duchez's plan became the star item of the " Martian Report " circulating weekly to planners and inter-services committees. " It turned their attention sharply to this weakly-defended sector," said Austin later, " showing that many earlier estimates of the strength had been alarmist and that a good deal of photographic interpretation had been in error."

Meantime Dewavrin very urgently wanted his map back. It had dawned on him that there *might* be a sporting chance of producing a convincing enough fake to be smuggled across the Channel to Caen before the theft was discovered. Trying to call in a top-secret map from interested Services departments, however, was more easily said than done, and for some days he chafed in vain. Then, in the second week of July, a bleak note arrived from Max Petit, Renault's deputy in Paris. Decoded, it read: " SEARCH FOR MISSING PLAN IS PROCEEDING IN CAEN AREA."

It looked, then, as if it had all been for nothing.

In Caen, until the end of June, things had been deceptively quiet. Then, one morning, Leblond, the young police inspector, got a routine call from an informer which made him reach abruptly for his telephone. Among others he called Meslin, the government engineer, and Torres, the massive security officer, saying merely, " They're rounding up the draughts-men," before he disconnected.

The full story may never be known, but looking back it seems to have been the machinations of bureaucracy that saved the day. Drawing up blueprints for the Normandy coastline was the job of *Oberbaudirektor* Weiss, Todt Organisation's chief engineer at the Paris H.Q. of *Einsatzgruppe* West (area control sector of Holland, Belgium and France). Each fresh set that Weiss drew up had first to be approved by Berlin before coming back to Paris for distribution to area H.Q. and sub-sectors; it was lucky for Duchez that the map he abstracted had been one of twelve duplicates which had already passed through " Out " trays in Paris, Berlin and St. Malo. Thus, when *Bauleiter* Keller, in Caen, discovered that his set was one short, he at first assumed that another department had retained it for study. The chief of Caen's Todt Organisation, *Bauleiter Ingenieur* Ött, seems to have assumed the same. For several days various departments were engaged in the age-old pastime of passing the buck. But at last it became painfully obvious that the map was now a long way from the Avenue Bagatelle.

But both Keller and Ött trod very warily. For obvious reasons they made no attempt to contact Bürger, the St. Malo chief, much less the fearsome Weiss in Paris. Neither von Rundstedt, the defender of the Wall, nor *Generalfeldmarschall* Wilhelm Keitel, head of the Armed Forces High Command, became party to the secret. Todt Organisation, Caen, which had a vested interest in keeping the story quiet, also had their own mechanism for carrying out a search without even troubling Helmut Bernard's Caen Gestapo. Their security detachment, an S.S. squad under *Sturmbannfuehrer* (S.S. Major) Friedrich Riekert, held direct responsibility for the well-being of all secret documents; it was in Riekert's interests, too, to find that map without making it obvious what had really been lost.

Riekert launched a series of hit-and-run raids. At the

Café des Touristes Paul watched in bewilderment while the S.S., on what he took to be a routine search, poked long spikes down the stuffing of his benches. (Not being in the secret, he was worried that the broken-down boiler would receive a going-over, but the Germans never gave that a second glance.) In other cafés, grumbling customers were forced to unbutton their shirts, and Meslin, reading *Le Figaro* over a coffee, had the newspaper torn from his hands, held against the light and examined page by page. As Leblond had warned, the draughts-men in all Government departments were called in for questioning. It occurred to Riekert that local talent might have been employed in making a copy of the map.

Lodging-house keepers stumbled through long question-naires as to every guest they had harboured in the past six weeks. A score of completely innocent citizens had the chilling experience of being cross-questioned by Riekert's thugs, ultimately to be released for lack of evidence.

Except Duchez. The painter's boast seems to have held good, for incredible as it seemed to the men of his network there is no evidence that he was ever suspected, and he was certainly never searched. His air of benign idiocy had paid dividends. But, so the story goes, an electrician who had done some work at the Todt Organisation some weeks previously was not so lucky. He was held prisoner and questioned for three days, in sweating terror, never even knowing, until after the war, what he was supposed to have done. (When he finally did discover his comments were understandable but unprintable.)

Later a rumour arose, even reaching Dewavrin in London, that Duchez had gained possession of the map with the help of a collaborator who was later shot for his part in the theft. But the story was never substantiated, and as Girard says, " Indisputably he got hold of one of the most important maps of the war—and very likely in the way he said he did. There was this about Duchez—he could get away with things with the Germans that no other man stood a chance of doing."

Other people were finding the map a puzzle. Renault

called on Dewavrin looking rather like a small boy who has brought home a good end-of-term report and now awaits the customary half-crown. He said, " Did you see the map? "

Dewavrin's sixth sense recalled a three-month-old conversation on the need for faith. " I saw a lot of maps. Which one? "

Renault's face fell. " Why—the map of the Atlantic Wall, of course. . . ."

" Oh, yes," said Dewavrin coolly, " very interesting. What about lunch? "

Renault said wrathfully later: " That Passy! I had to wait six months before finding out I hadn't risked my life for nothing! "

In his enthusiasm to see France freed Renault was a bit ahead of schedule. The talk at this time was all of invasion, but as a basic principle, not as a stern reality, and neither American nor British planning teams then contemplated an assault in the area covered by Duchez's map. The British pondered an assault west and east of Le Havre, on beaches from Deauville to Dieppe. The Americans talked of a push in the spring of 1943, seizing bridgeheads that could be consolidated and expanded between Le Havre and Boulogne.

Duchez had done better than he knew, but like many a good man before him, he had done it a little too early. For a little while yet the map remained with " the Martians " for further study.

In Paris, Girard sought the guidance of Colonel Touny and Berthelot, the precise ex-diplomat, on the future of the new network (London had provisionally christened it " Century " and by a regrouping of existing O.C.M. agents it now had branches all over northern France). Touny, whose military brain was perhaps the most incisive in the whole Resistance, had drawn inspiration from his view of Duchez's map. " In future," he announced after some discussion, " that is the field on which we should concentrate."

Girard was not the kind of subordinate who enjoys differing with a chief, but he doubted—and said so—if the same coup could be pulled off twice.

Touny explained. " It would be useless if it could. Remember, above all, that the Germans are not fools and that they have such a thing as the *Abwehr*. What this agent did may have been valuable, because it possessed the element of surprise. It was in the nature of a shock-punch. Now they may do one of two things. They may make it easy for us to remove maps—maps they would be delighted for the Allies to see. Or, assuming that those fortifications don't yet exist, they may revise their entire building programme. In either case an independent check is necessary, isn't it? "

Girard was not slow on the uptake. " In other words, *mon colonel*, we make our own? "

The colonel inclined his silvered head, like the diplomat he was. " Precisely, we make our own."

For some days Girard hugged the new problem to himself. His network had little experience of anything, let alone maps. There was, of course, Douin's map, but there were few agents who could legitimately penetrate a belfry and jot down their findings. Yet it was elementary military strategy that maps produced on French soil by the trusted agents of de Gaulle were, in the long run, worth more than any number of stolen maps of doubtful pedigree. There was precedent for this. In ports like Lorient and St. Nazaire, Renault's agents had been busily sketching scale diagrams of locks and torpedo-nets and the dimensions of basins for the last two years.

Stolidly, not rushing any of the logical processes, Girard thought of the maps the Caen cell *had* done. On Dewavrin's instructions, every network in France had at least produced maps of suitable dropping-grounds and landing-fields in their own area. Agents like Duchez and Arsène, on their daily rounds, kept a weather-eye open for the flat terrain 600 yards square that the Air Ministry had stipulated before pacing them out by night and feeding the details to Douin or anyone else who knew the feel of a mapping-pen. The scale was that of the Michelin road maps—one in a quarter of a million or four miles to the inch. Hatchings in blue or yellow marked the dropping ground, and a legend of coloured symbols spot-lit any drawbacks or advantages—high tension wires that could transform a low-flying Lysander into a crumpled aluminium ball, wheat fields where parachute containers could be peacefully interred.

Douin, the implacable Royalist, had done a number, consoling himself that if the planes were British their cargo *was* destined for the French. But for more intensive mapping Girard found himself thinking of a map done for the Bayeux area by young Robert Thomas.

That had been a good map, neatly enough executed to stir Girard's methodical soul—and, moreover, as a potato controller the lad had freedom of passage. . . .

There was a strong sympathy between Girard and Thomas. Neither was a demonstrative man; both took understanding. When Girard stumped into a room, barking out orders, sweeping aside objections with the familiar gesture of his right arm, those closest to him—Meslin, Torres, Harivel, the insurance agent—looked beyond the scowling determination to the hint of the smile, cynical, kindly, in the hot brown eyes. Thomas was a different physical type, the visionary who seems always younger than his years, with fine sensitive features and fair hair cut *en brosse*. In the students' cafés of every city in the world you would find Thomas, his woollen muffler wound loosely round his neck, descending to earth with a bump when directly appealed to, swallowing his sentences as if they embarrassed him.

" Robert," said an agent close to him, " is of the world, but never seems part of it." And perhaps as a corrective to this it was to the most down-to-earth men in the movement— Girard, Meslin, Arsène, the one-eyed plumber—that Thomas gave his loyalties.

The idea cropped up first on a June evening in Caen. The scene was a small apartment on the old winding rue St. Jean, the headquarters of Girard's Caen Resistance; though his parents had a small villa in the University Quarter he would not involve them in a danger that could only increase as the war against the Wall gathered impetus. (The café was never used for top-secret discussions.) Duchez and others were present that day, and Girard as usual dropped his ultimatum like a man dropping a stone into a well: " What we want from you, young Thomas, is all the information that we can get on the Atlantic Wall in map form."

Thomas, conscious that everyone was looking at him, smiled his shy rather charming smile, then blushed and mumbled: " To want it is one thing, to get it is another."

At the same time, he was pleased. Although he had been a Caen garage mechanic until war came, his secret ambition had always been to work with maps. If Robert grew fractious as a youngster his father, who worked under Meslin as an Inspector of Roads and Bridges, was always able to restore order by drawing him a map. Thomas, a frustrated cartographer, saw himself in luck.

But—the Atlantic Wall in map form! For a moment the words stuck in his throat, then, rather shakily, he asked, " But what about depth—and area? "

Girard was brisk. " It should not be too difficult. You will do them to a depth of one kilometre inland only." The literal Girard, then, was seeing the Atlantic Wall purely as a matter of beach defences. He added: " Technically, you will be covering the area between St. Malo and Le Havre but "—the slow smile lit up the room, then was gone—" as we have no one in St. Malo or Le Havre at this moment, which is much to be regretted, you will concentrate your attention between Cherbourg and Trouville."

Thomas knew the kind of map that Girard had in mind. Duchez was explaining it now, with his irritatingly shameless grin. In France they are called Cartes Etat-Major—literally General Staff maps—and although primarily cadastral they serve the Government and the Army in much the same way as the Ordnance Survey does in England. A dedicated cartographer would see France as 1,060 of those maps, on the same scale that Douin had employed in his belfry—one-in-fifty-thousand, a little more than one inch to the mile. Maps like this are more detailed than the English Ordnance Survey;

every copse and barn and straggling cow track shows up as if in a mirror.

Thomas cycled home wrapped in thought. How, in the first place, to get the maps? In peacetime you could buy them at any stationers; the road maps were available even now and to map out dropping grounds Century had already bought several from a friendly bookseller named Henri Marigny. General survey maps, having more strategic possibilities, were a tougher proposition. The Germans, with pigeon-hole efficiency, had called in every one.

But even if you got the maps, how would you get the information? Through the same channels as it had come up to now, the few agents who could travel, scraps of information in letter-boxes, the once-weekly collection by Gille or Harivel? It struck him that this arrangement had drawbacks. To present a true picture in map form you needed more agents circulating though that only increased the risk—for themselves and for others. As few people circulating as possible, that was Girard's golden rule.

Now, somewhere in his brain, a cell awoke and an idea began to stir, but when he tried to pin it down it evaded him: he could not give it words. Several times that night he tried to isolate it, but it sneaked away capriciously, as palpable yet as elusive as gossamer. With mounting frustration he put it aside and went in to supper.

The Thomases' family life would have done an outsider good to see. It was an inviolate unit, adhering to its own unwritten code, clinging jealously to its own corporate loyalties. It was hospitable and kindly to strangers, but even a thick-skinned outsider must have sensed the " family " atmosphere, the warmth of their unity. Papa Louis was its nominal head, a gentle modest old man blinking kindly behind gold-rimmed spectacles, but the real polarising force of the family was Mama —tiny and birdlike with enough energy for ten, never far from her stone-flagged kitchen with its bundles of leeks and tall green bottles of rough cider and her iron pots of stew and soup bubbling on the range.

Mama knew that every day in that war was an enemy that

you could allow no quarter, that her husband and son were good Resistants, that her daughter, Jeanne, who worked in Meslin's department, was in it too, to say nothing of the tall outspoken Madeleine, who worked for the Chief of Police in Trouville, and Marthe, the plump and vivacious one, who worked at the Prefecture in Caen. But she would not have had it otherwise. (And when I asked the indomitable old lady how it had felt to be part of it, she answered with fire: " How should it have felt? A fine thing if my children had been part of the Resistance and I had known nothing of it!")

Thomas knew from the first that the only safe way to get maps was from his father, but he had no qualms above " involving " his family. The difficulty would have been to keep them out of it.

He broached the subject that evening, saying, " Look, Papa, I need some of the maps you use at work—as many sections of the Cartes Etat-Major as you can get me." And the mild old man merely looked slightly surprised before saying, " What for? No, I mustn't ask what for, I suppose, no, of course not. All right, Robert, my son, I'll do the best for you that I can."

The next night he was back with four tucked under his coat. Century was in the mapping business.

It was a good start, but much more would be needed. The general survey maps used by Meslin's department only covered the coastal area for which the government engineer was responsible—from the fishing port of Honfleur, thirty-five miles north-east of Caen, to Isigny, forty miles west, at the mouth of the River Vire. The general survey maps show this area in four sections—seventy miles of coastline, compressed into six feet. For the rest of Normandy and the Cotentin peninsula, which holds out the great port of Cherbourg invitingly towards England, Meslin's department held no maps at all.

" Another thing," said Papa Louis anxiously, " you'll have to be quick with them. In these days you never know when the Germans may not make a surprise check of the maps in use."

All one hot week Thomas worked at the maps. He worked

from just after dinner until the cocks crowed, shrill and imperative, from the backyard across the street. In the airless night, the ragged orange flame of the candle was shadowy and uneven, but he could risk no brighter light. The Gestapo kept an eye open for lights burning late. At dawn, with the candle a grey mess of wrinkled grease, he crawled into bed, awaking two hours later drugged and unrefreshed.

At the week-end he knew a quiet incommunicable triumph. The work was done. Each map was traced and inked in, the grid references checked, each landmark as clear as in an aerial view—the beach at Le Hamel, a sixteenth of an inch wide but plain enough, the Church at Asnelles-sur-Mer, and Ouistreham lighthouse, visible even though scaled down to the size of pinheads.

Nobody said much at breakfast but there was a quivering sense of excitement. Papa had to return the maps to the office without arousing suspicion. Jeanne was to take Robert's tracings and somehow make enough mimeographed copies for the heads of the network to begin operations.

It turned out to be easy. When Jeanne arrived at the office that morning it was as busy as an ant's nest, clerks scurrying everywhere with slide rules and rolls of tracing paper. Obviously something big was afoot.

She buttonholed a passing clerk. " What's the panic? "

" Oh, the usual—extra work, but no extra rations for doing it. The Port Commandant wants tracings of every map in our area."

Century was in luck. Late the previous afternoon the urbane Karl Hoëfa had called on Meslin and explained that the *Kreigsmarine Wehr* were making a new survey of defence along the wall. He called for several dozen maps of each sector to be traced and mimeographed within twenty-four hours. Meslin had told his assistant Alex Jourdan, whose section, the Service Maritime, held all dossiers on local ports, to get busy.

As Jourdan turned to go, Meslin said quietly: " You'll make sure these tracings are delivered to the right quarters, won't you? "

Jourdan, a taciturn young man with a habit of sucking profoundly on a meerschaum pipe before speaking and then, most often, saying nothing, grinned slightly and nodded.

Had Meslin done what seems obvious—ordered tracings on his own initiative and passed them on to Girard—there was always the risk of a stool pigeon in the building noting and reporting it. Meslin knew nothing then about Robert Thomas, nor, oddly enough, did he know that Papa Thomas and his daughter Jeanne, who were on his staff, were also in his network and doubly under his orders! Such tortuous security called for patience and circumvention but it paid dividends in the Resistance.

Events moved faster than Girard had anticipated. In the general confusion of executing Hoëfa's rush order, Jeanne Thomas ran off half a dozen copies of each map and delivered them to her brother. Then, two days later, Thomas was working late at the potato controller's office when Jourdan dropped in. Thomas was surprised and pleased. He had known Jourdan for eight years, ever since they had done their military service together, but lately they had lost touch.

After a bit Jourdan said rather abruptly, that if by chance Thomas was engaged on active Resistance work there were certain plans he might find useful. He unfolded the tracings from his breast pocket, and Thomas, after surveying them for a long moment, roared with laughter.

" What's so funny? " asked Jourdan suspiciously.

" The funny thing is that any time you don't feel like walking round here—not that I shan't always be delighted to see you—I can save you a lot of trouble. Just give them to my sister."

Jourdan saw the joke then, and after that it was a good deal easier; Meslin knew about Thomas, though he vetoed his ever visiting the office and Jourdan became Thomas's No. 2 in Century's new cartographic service, with Douin helping out. Each time the *Kriegsmarine Wehr* erected a new fortification in a port they notified Jourdan's department, and Jourdan was already aware that they planned an intensive programme at Ouistreham. (Ouistreham was the small fishing port nine miles upstream which could take cargo ships up to 6,000 tons. Through the freight link of the canal it connected Caen with the sea.)

" It's part of my job to note locations on our charts for reference," Jourdan said virtuously. " Each time I do I'll bring you a tracing. Save *you* a lot of trouble."

Thomas shook his head admiringly. Jourdan was the first member of the network officially classed as a P-1—or part-time agent—who really pursued his Resistance from his office stool with German sanction.

By mid-July, when the first map was ready for transmission to London, they all felt vaguely pleased with themselves, though compared with the results they later achieved the system was amateurish. True, the general survey maps for Meslin's area covered only seventy miles, but Century's intelligence covered barely twelve—between Le Hamel, on the eastern flank of what was later known as " Gold Beach," and Luc-sur-Mer.

Even most of this was filled in by Meslin and Jourdan, who held a secret session one afternoon to pool the information they had gathered on official visits. Meslin, for example, knew that mines had been sown somewhere in the two and a half miles between Ver-sur-Mer and Graye-sur-Mer. There were mines again on the sea front at Luc; he had driven past with Hoëfa one afternoon in the Port Commandant's armoured car, with a German tommy-gunner as bodyguard squatting dourly in the front seat, past the bricked-up boarding-houses and deserted beaches, and there had been black skull and cross-bones signs " *Achtung Minen* " grinning the whole length of the promenade.

But what about the details Girard had pressed for, the length of the minefields, the depth inland, the type of mine? Meslin didn't know.

" We must just show the area as mined," he told Jourdan quietly, hiding his disappointment. " It's a beginning, any-way."

The same difficulty cropped up over every defence they knew about. The Germans had an underground tunnel behind the sea front at Luc, but for what purpose? Nobody knew. Here and there it was easy enough to pinpoint heavy earthworks, strange embrasures in the cliffs, but the finer points of detail—the thickness of the concrete, the calibre of the guns— defeated them.

Before drawing the final map, Thomas held a brief consultation with Duchez, but again he drew a blank.

A few more summer days dawdled by, then Thomas had his brainwave. It came so suddenly and so logically that he lay awake all one night thinking about it, and it is curious to note that quite independently he had hit upon what was really an extension of Dewavrin's original idea.

At the next meeting he took his courage in both hands and raised it with Girard. Girard's idea, he knew, was that more agents entailed greater risk, but Thomas was convinced that with a few more agents the network could produce maps of the whole coast—*and* without risk.

Only agents who lived *on* the coast, Thomas argued, would have a chance of studying the fortifications in detail. Casual visitors, unless they kept moving, were at once suspect. Then why not appoint agents on the coast to hold a permanent watching brief? The liaison agent's sole responsibility would be to collect the information and do a quick visual check.

Girard believed in the efficiency of small units and said so with force. To have hundreds of agents keeping written information all over their houses, and the liaison agent risking his neck once a week to bring it back to Caen would be, he thought, the rankest kind of folly.

" No, no, no." Thomas was so excited that he was swallowing almost all his words. " Each one of them will have a map —a map of *their* area." On fire with conviction, he rattled on. From now on, the Cartes Etat-Major would serve as control maps at base. Each agent would have a section of map showing his own area, on a scale about one and a half times larger than the control maps. That left him with no more than thirteen square miles to cover, and almost every man had permission to travel that widely in his own district. Supposing a man saw a blockhouse or a battery going up? Over a period of months he would have the chance to spy out details which no traveller could ever unearth. Those details could be noted on cigarette paper, and familiar landmarks could help him pin-point the grid reference on his own map at home. Apart from that, his one concern was to find somewhere in his house where he could hide a square of mapping paper roughly eight inches by six.

Thomas finished triumphantly: " In that way, without risk, we can make a map of Normandy—a living map."

And, yes, Girard thought, it was possible, though it was his policy to doubt in public before reflecting at length in private. Girard was a loyal and courageous Frenchman, with the kind of dynamism that marks the great leader, but he knew the exuberance of his countrymen, their itch to close with the enemy regardless of risk. If his seeming insensitivity sometimes ruffled people, that was deliberate policy. He liked to keep them down to earth as often as he could.

There were many discussions before Girard decided that the idea was at least feasible. But the basic problem—circulation—remained the same. To scout for new blood along the coast, liaison agents needed more than a pass permitting them to travel through. They would need reasons to linger and make contacts—reasons valid enough to hoodwink the little core of collaborators that poisoned every community.

Duchez went to see Caillet about it at the *Mairie* and that nervous and amiable man went almost rigid with fear as the painter cheerfully stated his needs within a few yards of the genial *Hauptmann* Kramm, not at all reassured by Duchez's repeated cry of " It's all right, *mon vieux*, they don't mind me— I'm a fool and a drunkard, they take no notice." But the upshot was that Caillet agreed to provide not only identity cards but complete sets of papers, false ration cards, permission to own a bicycle and signed permission to be in the zone—not issued unless the applicant possessed a bicycle. Caillet began carrying these permits home at lunch-time, while his wife Alice, who worked in another department, marched beside him carrying the *Mairie's* official stamp in her powder compact.

After lunch Duchez collected them and Odette, his wife, got busy inventing false names and appending bogus but official-looking signatures.

The crowning triumph came one evening when Arsène, the argumentative plumber, paid a conspiratorial visit to Thomas. He began by tiptoeing dramatically into the kitchen, finger to his lips, then to the astonishment of old Madame Thomas, who was busy at the range, began to take off his shoes and socks. From one sock, with an air of mystery, he produced a strip of purple rubber.

" *Voilà!* " he proclaimed, his one eye glinting triumph behind the steel spectacles. " Our passport to the *zone interdite*."

It was the official stamp of *Feldkommandatur* 723, and no set of passes into the coastal zone was complete without its frank.

Arsène said modestly that it had been easy to get though the Thomas family had the feeling that, aside from Duchez, only he could have worked it. That afternoon, overhauling the central heating at the *Kommandatur*, in the commandeered Hotel Malherbe, Arsène had seen the stamp lying on a desk. Stripping off the rubber, he hid it in his sock and threw the mount into the wastepaper basket. Trouble arrived shortly in the shape of an energetic *Hauptmann* who wanted the stamp. Arsène and his three mates turned to and helped him, and soon, Arsène related, joyously acting every part in turn, the room was ankle-deep in litter as they upended all the wastepaper baskets in sight.

The cleaners had gone home, but Arsène conveniently found the wooden mount, pointing out that the stamp had probably been swept up with the day's dust. The *Hauptmann* wasn't quite satisfied. He called in soldiers to search the four but without result.

When he had finished the Thomases drew a concerted breath. Finally Robert said: " Well, now we can go ahead, but if they searched you I can't understand why they let you go without making you take off your socks? "

Arsène gave a diabolical grin. " I don't think they suspected us too seriously," he said, " and, in any case, the Boches are fastidious. I hadn't changed my socks in weeks."

Chapter Eleven

MAPPING THE PORTS

By July, Century was planning more extensive action. Armed with Arsène's malodorous stamp, Thomas and Odette were now producing as many as a dozen batches of fake identity papers a week. Not to be outdone, Madeleine Thomas, Robert's tall good-looking elder sister, who worked for the lackadaisical Chief of Police at Trouville, stole *his* official stamp, and a sample of his signature for good measure. Thomas soon claimed they could dispense with the sample because he inscribed the signature with so much more distinction than the Chief.

Soon other stamps rolled in, so many that it would be hard for a liaison agent visiting the zone to remember whether he was that day representing the Prefecture at Trouville, the repair depot at Caen Station, the Caen tramways board or the gasworks at Deauville. Thomas in time collected 150 of them, hiding them along with his maps in the big wicker laundry hamper in Mama Thomas's kitchen. Experience had taught him that the hygienic Germans fought shy of rifling through mounds of soiled linen.

Now all of them were ready to learn the worst about the Wall.

In Paris, while making the motions appropriate to a busy cement executive, Girard was concentrating on strategy. He was always on the go now: from his own apartment to Touny's office or Berthelot's, to the headquarters of Renault's C.N.D., which Max Petit was still running on the Boulevard de la Chapelle. Wherever he went the lovely Dany went also,

keeping a watchful eye open for the men wearing the mack-
intoshes and green felt hats which were almost the badge of the
Gestapo.

Either ahead of her boss or trailing him, she accompanied
Girard almost every day to the Ministry of War. Oddly
enough it was the one Government building that the Germans
had not taken over and Colonel Touny had found temporary
sanctuary in it for the experts checking O.C.M.'s dispatches.
The Germans thought the building too old and decrepit to be
worth commandeering.

A suite of rooms on the ground floor was appropriately the
Paris headquarters of Century's war against the Wall, and of
the five heads of O.C.M., who planned to use the twin weapons
of maps and resident agents to maximum advantage. Touny
had also brought in two long-standing members of O.C.M.
for chair-borne Intelligence work—Richard Rivalin, a young
medical student, whose father owned this " grace and favour "
apartment, and " Colonel Personne."

" Colonel Personne" whose name was French for "nobody,"
was in reality a bland moon-faced young politician named
Jacques Piette, who had chosen his cover-name from the
famous episode in the *Odyssey* when Ulysses, shipwrecked with
his companions on the island of the one-eyed Polyphemus,
persuades the giant that his name is " Nobody " before
blinding him with a red-hot stake. " Remember how Polyphemus raved and screamed to the other giants that Nobody's
treachery had undone him, and they thought he was talking
nonsense? " the imaginative Piette would recall. " That's
like the Underground's war with the Germans—silent, savage,
anonymous."

On one factor all the experts were agreed: the priority area
for mapping was the Cotentin peninsula, which Duchez's
map had shown as most strongly defended. (It was mainly
left to the Navy, whose sectors of the Wall were sounder than
anything produced by the Todt Organisation.) The north
coast, from Cap de la Hague to Pointe de Barfleur, covered
only fifty miles, but that alone held twenty-six medium or

heavy batteries. It seemed to add up to a formidable defence.

To crack the Cherbourg nut, Girard appointed his lieutenant, Jacques Bertin, Comte de la Hautière, better known by his cover-name, Jacques Moulines. Moulines, six feet two, fair and carelessly good looking, was perhaps as insanely fearless as Duchez, with all the Frenchman's traditional instincts towards beautiful women. A restless and tortured idealist who wanted the Resistance to achieve if not a new heaven, at least a new earth, he was also the only live aristocrat the network ever had, and his first impact on women was often devastating. After he had first breezed into Meslin's office at Caen, it was weeks before little Jeanne Verinaud really got it in perspective.

In a way Moulines's life was typical of most field organisers, though of all Century's departmental chiefs probably he had the hardest task. The port of Cherbourg and the fifty square miles around was tough not only in terms of fortifications but in terms of troops and of vigilance. Moulines, the peacetime aviator who went everywhere hatless, in an old leather flying-jacket, riding a spavined bicycle that Girard called a digrace to the aristocracy, had to move warily.

There were 37,000 Germans in Cherbourg alone, which shows the weakness of his position, but many of the citizens had seen them goose-stepping arrogantly through the streets—*their* streets—two years earlier, and that paradoxically was his strength.

"And we shall need more agents than I'd thought," Moulines reported after taking stock and when Girard asked why, he explained: "Because there's such a restriction on circulation, *patron*—you've no idea. You need permission to move even from one canton to another." (A canton is an administrative sub-division of many square miles and the Department of the Manche, in which Cherbourg stood, had eleven.)

Girard sighed wearily, resigned to yet more agents, and told him to do his best.

Moulines did rather better. Using Touny's military contacts, who were geared to an armed uprising rather than to routine intelligence, he first sought agents as close as possible to the A.A. batteries marked on Duchez's map. Above and beyond the port of Carentan there were five heavy batteries ringing the navigable canal, but there was also a plumber named Roger Foineau detailed for watch on the defences. As head of the Cherbourg cell, Moulines recruited a wholesale grocer named Yves Gresselin, whose 120 agents were concentrating on troop movements and shipping as well as defences. Both these last appointments were a better plant than Moulines then knew.

With the zeal of a chain-store boss intent on expansion, the young count opened branches everywhere. Wherever he could, he went right to the top. In St. Lô, an important railhead twenty-five miles from the coast, he was lucky to find Adolphe Franck, a heavily-built schoolmaster from Lorraine, speaking faultless German, with big surprised eyes blinking like an owl's behind horn-rimmed spectacles. He persuaded Franck to apply for a job as interpreter at the Prefecture, and put him in charge of the whole St. Lô area. Franck gathered a team of more than one hundred men around him, three of them colleagues at the Prefecture; within weeks they were sending a steady flow of information on rail traffic and fortifications. One triumph was securing the plan of the locks at La Barquette, which controlled the tidal flow for twenty miles up the nearby Douvre River. When U.S. parachutists seized them before D-Day to stop the Germans flooding the eastern half of the peninsula, there was very little they did not know about how the locks worked.

They used an old tried method of Renault's to pipe-line Franck's dispatches to Caen. One of his men, a railway guard called Bonnel, took the bulky package in his van and left it behind the bar at the Hotel de Rouen, with Mayoraz, the big impassive Swiss proprietor. Together with the Cherbourg dispatches these went on to Meslin's office for typing and transcription, though many of the scraps of paper came now to Thomas and Jourdan and two other cartographers Girard had appointed, Jouvel and Menguy. The Manche was on its way to becoming the living map of Thomas's dreams.

Thomas was red-eyed now from lack of sleep; he set himself

the heavy target of completing one sector map each week. He ate without appetite, his brain on fire with details of grid references and " heavy earthworks 100 metres north of church," and " Farmer reports battery of 155s due north of farm house," using his work with the potato controller to check them whenever he could, and the one reward that sweetened the hardship was Girard's great bearlike paw on his shoulder every ten days or so. " Ah, Thomas, *mon vieux*, a wonderful batch of maps you sent to Paris last week."

About this time Girard and Thomas had a long discussion about maps. For some weeks now they had been mapping sectors as far as six miles inland, but Girard explained that the Wall could no longer be reckoned in terms of a line of block-houses on the seashore. Nor did the resources that could bring it into blazing life be said to stop short at six miles.

He said, " What about it? Can you manage farther inland as well? " He was diffident because Thomas had grown pale lately; the rims of his eyes were sore and inflamed through constant use of the powerful magnifying glasses he needed for mapping.

Thomas was cautious. " How much farther? Even with five of us it sounds like a job."

" About forty miles."

" Forty——? Why, that's as far as Vire. Well, now, wait a minute——"

" I know, *mon petit*, I know, but don't you see that we must find out too what the Germans are doing *behind* the Wall. Any Wall is only as good as the troops and the munitions and the resources to defend it. We want to know about munitions dumps and barracks and factories—particularly factories."

" Ah, well," said Thomas resignedly, " it'll mean more travelling, but I can but try."

Each night, at the risk of being stopped by a road-block, Thomas had been cycling three miles or more, clearing " letter-boxes " for the information that went to make the maps. From the Hotel de Rouen he collected dispatches from Cherbourg and St. Lô, while the house of Jean Chateau, the big florid electricity-board inspector, on the Bayeux road and the boiler of the Touristes served his needs for the Caen district. Now most of Sunday, too, was taken up in travelling to new letter-boxes: the box-office of a cinema in Flers, the sacristy of a church in Alençon. Four times on his way to letter-boxes he was arrested, but the rich cream of the jest was that within an hour he was always free again, having proved his bona-fides by one of his own faked cards. The Germans never suspected the real purpose of his mission. They had arrested him because with his fair cropped hair and pink and white complexion they were convinced that he was a British airman on the run!

The tough and hard-bitten Girard, the gay well-born Moulines and the sensitive Thomas were a notable combination, each in his way contributing an individual value to the kind of team that Dewavrin had envisaged in operation. It was characteristic that each saw the next man's job as tougher than his own. Despite the never-ending strain, Thomas counted his own lot as enviable beside Moulines's. He and Duchez and the others were among their own kin, but Moulines had no permanent place to lay his head, and for the eternal stranger like himself, the Gestapo set traps. In Cherbourg and St. Lô he was careful not to take a drink before checking with a local contact: overnight the Gestapo would decree that no bar could serve red wine on Tuesday or Friday afternoons, and bartenders had to report anyone ordering it. He always entered a town wheeling his boneshaker; on some days riding two abreast was arbitrarily prohibited.

And sometimes, beating up the west coast towards Cherbourg, the wind thrashing at his old leather jacket, he would see through the poplars the graceful eighteenth-century pile of the Château la Brisette, where his parents still lived, remembering the smell of wood fires and the banging of guns on an autumn afternoon and the high echoing rooms that smelt of linseed polish. But the Comte de la Hautière saw death as an ever-present certainty; he rarely went home to endanger his family until the war was over.

He slept like a fugitive, often in his clothes, carrying only a razor and toothbrush. One agent's wife remembers: " Sometimes the poor boy would arrive drenched with rain and looking like a beaten dog, and just creep upstairs and sleep as if he was going to die." Always his faith was invincible. Once the same woman, momentarily cynical, asked him whether he really believed that the Resistance was worth it, and the tall fair young man went quite white, and said: " It is, you know. It must be, because it's got to be. It's the greatest chance that France has ever had for spiritual regeneration." In Caen where he slept mostly at the Hotel de Rouen, Mayoraz recalls him as a man without fear. Once Moulines slept undisturbed in a small back room on the ground floor while outside in the bar, five yards away, a dozen Germans whooped it up over calvados until the small hours.

Girard, forced to spend much time in Paris, found his lieutenant's movements a shade unpredictable. Moulines, he knew, was all too susceptible, and when, on an average of once a month, he fell in love, one district would receive meticulous attention to the exclusion of others until the passion cooled. Once, at this time, Moulines was a week overdue. Beneath Girard's rigid no-nonsense exterior was a man of intense feelings; believing that Moulines had been caught and tortured, he was suffering the agonies of the damned.

At five one afternoon a knock came at the second door of the three-in-one flat. Dany felt that her heart stopped at the same moment—hardened Resistants called it " door-bell psychosis "—but she went to open it and there was Moulines shifting from one foot to the other. The conversation was uneasy too.

" Oh; hallo, Dany. *Ça va?* "

" Ah, *oui, oui, ça va bien.* And you? "

" Oh, I'm fine, just fine—in fact, couldn't be better." Too casually: " I was—well, rather wondering if the chief was in."

" No, he's out," said Dany hastily, hoping that she could shoo Moulines away before Girard got wind of anything, then more severely: " He's been worried to death about you. Where have you been? "

" Oh, that's a pity," said Moulines unhappily, fingering his cheek and staring at the ceiling. " That *is* a pity. I didn't want him to be worried. If I'd just seen *him*, you know, I could have explained everything. . . ."

Dany was just urging him to come back when she had paved the way, when the inner door opened and Girard called: " Who *is* that ? " And then there was no hope for it. Dany waited outside quaking; she did hear Moulines say, " I can explain everything, chief. . . . You'd understand if you'd seen her—she was *so* pretty." Then there was a sudden explosion and for a time she heard only Girard's voice reverberating like a summer storm.

Presently, in an attempt at appeasement, she heard Moulines explain that he had managed to install another transmitter in the Manche (smaller, more portable sets had now replaced the cumbersome 60-lb. affairs of 1941), and that the agent who had charge of it would now be able to radio all troop movements in his area direct to Dewavrin's operators in London.

" Well, that's one good thing," said Girard mollified. " How did you get it down there ? "

" I took it on the carrier of my bicycle," Moulines said, and Dany, guessing what was coming, winced.

Another explosion, much louder. " YOUR BICYCLE ? Are you stark raving mad ? Don't you realise it might have been inspected at a barrier ? Do you *want* to be tortured and jeopardise the lives of everyone else in the network including all your own agents up there, however many you've got ? . . ." There was much more in the same vein before Girard said suspiciously, " By the way—how many *have* you got ? "

" Two hundred, chief."

" Two——? " Girard looked into Moulines's eyes, which were clear and blue and always extraordinarily free from guile when he was justifying an *affaire de coeur*. " I don't know," said Girard at last, gratingly, his heavy brows wrinkling until they almost met. " You've been working, anyway. But you're incorrigible. There's only one thing I can think of doing with you that's any good "—he paused angrily, then suddenly grinned, the storm was over—" and that is to forgive you."

At the best times it was always like that. Between Girard

and Dany and Moulines there was an easy comradeship, born of Resistance, that readily spilled over into laughter and a sense of warmth engendered by the value of the friendship—like the first glow of good cognac, only more durable. In the evenings they sometimes went to the *Pourquoi Pas?* a little restaurant known to all men of the Resistance, and there would be much music and laughter. One subject always good for a laugh was Girard's weight, which turned the scales at around 200 lb.; lately he had taken to using a bicycle to keep his Paris appointments and Dany and Moulines would warn " Monsieur Le Mince " (Mr. Slim) as they had christened him, that his repair bills were likely to be heavy.

Off-duty Girard was a charming and lively table companion with a rich fund of humour, telling them about his stay with a Wandsworth family as a fourteen-year-old learning English, and of how he had fallen in love with Lucy, the daughter of the house, engaging in bitter rivalry for her favours at Clapham Roller Skating Rink with a German lad named Schulz. To win the upper hand, Girard had learned a poem for her which he recited in a fascinating Maurice Chevalier English: " Lu-cee you are the joy of my 'eart and the sunshine of my ex-ees-tence."

Then they would go back happily, arm in arm, to the three-in-one flat and Moulines would feel briefly that he had a home again.

There was a sense of urgency in the friendship too, an urgency that kept step with the calendar of war. One such date was 19th August, 1942. That afternoon, 1,000 Canadians, British and Americans died on the beaches of Dieppe, and of the 6,100 men who embarked on that expedition, only 2,500 returned. It is history now that Dieppe was planned as a miniature invasion, involving the full use of combined arms and mass landings of infantry and armour, with the object of seizing (though not holding) a beachhead. Whether it was a tactical success or a tactical failure is a question still exercising military brains, but from Century's view-point it had one immediate result. Allied planners were impressed with the toughness of the Wall, the need to concentrate the maximum weight in the first assault in order to breach it, and Dewavrin, too, became increasingly anxious to learn more of the Wall's secrets.

At the end of August, Colonel Touny summoned Girard to the " Red Cross " branch office. Renault's Centrale had passed on instructions from London that all networks must concentrate maximum efforts on the ports.

Girard thought. " I think Moulines has as many men in Cherbourg as it can safely stand," he said; " but I'll go to Caen and have a word with Meslin."

Meantime, in Berlin, the Germans were revising *their* conception of the Wall. Any Allied invasion, it seemed, would first have to aim at the seizure of key ports. On 29th September Hitler called a three-hour conference, attended among others by Goering, Reich Minister Albert Speer, Chief of the Todt Organisation, and *General-leutnant* Rudolf Schmetzer, Inspector of Land Fortresses for the Western Front, in the Reich Chancellery. Apparently Hitler was fully convinced that Dieppe was a major landing attempt that had failed, but he warned against any delusions that further amphibious assaults were thus ruled out. The British, he said, could only try again, and when they did they might enjoy air and naval supremacy.

To this pretty problem he saw one answer: Concrete.

The new Atlantic Wall would now consist of 15,000 concrete strong points to be defended by at least 300,000 men, a minimum of twenty men to each strongpoint. The goal was an impervious and permanent defence ring, so strong that the enemy could be smashed at the water's edge in their weakest moment—the moment of landing. U-Boat bases would rate first priority, then harbours suitable for coastal traffic, followed by harbours suitable for enemy landings and the Channel Islands. Lastly, a long way behind, came landing places on the open coast. The target date for completion was May, 1943.

The canny Speer kept most of his thoughts to himself, but in private he hinted that his Todt Organisation would be lucky to get 40 per cent completed by that date.

Apart from Cherbourg and Le Havre, France's greatest Channel ports, the most vital ports in Girard's area were Carentan, Ouistreham and Port-en-Bessein. Big ports presented

158

big problems, but Girard thought that Ouistreham and Port-en-Bessein, being closer to the main headquarters at Caen, might be more easily handled.

At first glance there is nothing to mark out Port-en-Bessein from a hundred forgotten coastal ports. The sea wind carries the good, exciting smells of seaweed and mackerel and ships' tar along its cobbled streets, and the bistros are full of men wearing blue rough-knit jerseys and fore-and-aft caps, playing belotte. The harbour is sheltered by two long breakwaters like curved concrete arms, and at the mouth of the Drome river lies the port itself, in a deep cleft between two high hills. In wartime fishing was allowed infrequently; the port was dead, sullen, apathetic. Now as a result of Girard's instructions, Port-en-Bessein began to come to life.

From his headquarters two miles away, the head of Century's Bayeux cell, a dark perpetually-smiling bicycle merchant named Georges Mercader, set his agents to work. Shipping movements were divided up between Henri de Saint-Denis, a ruddy-faced ironmonger, and a boat-builder named Joseph Poitevin. That was the first step. Each day they reported the movements of Bessein's minesweepers and six patrol boats to Mercader; there were two lighter speed boats as well for inshore patrols, 70-tonners, about 65 feet long, armed with two machine-guns and anti-aircraft pompoms. Each day Mercader signalled their movements to Dewavrin's operators in London from the small Phillips transmitter below his bicycle shop. It was cached in a hole in the wall, behind the second row of bottles in his wine cellar.

In time Mercader got a fixation, trying to remember whether *both* rows of bottles would look convincingly dusty to a search party and was always slipping down to make sure.

The Caen cell, too, was planting its own agents; one of the Bessein fishermen, Georges Thomine, was already feeding details to the redoubtable Madame Vauclin, the tiler's wife. They were verbal reports and no papers changed hands, but it was noticeable that on the Bessein bus, a rattle-trap local service crammed with farmers' wives and live geese and sacks of potatoes, Madame Vauclin was always knitting. On her knee was a pattern book and from time to time she noted numbers in the margin—45—63—19. These represented neither numbers of rows or stitches but items such as the distance between the customs post and the path at the foot of the cliffs. Back at Caen, Duchez received them with undisguised delight.

Thus, piecemeal, a picture was building up of Port-en-Bessein. From the seaward side the agents reported the port to be very heavily defended: the Todt Organisation had done their work well. The defences were disposed roughly in the form of a triangle, with powerful strongpoints on the heights to the east and the west. The problem was to approach closely enough on the landward side to glean the microscopic detail needed, and it threatened to beat them altogether until François Guerin, a young student from Bayeux, had an idea. Guerin was not much above sixteen then, a handsome boy with steady blue eyes and a mop of dark curly hair, but one of his closest friends was a man thirteen years his senior, Joseph Poitevin's cousin Arthur. All the Poitevins were good Resistants, heavily-built men with glinting eyes; it was said that there had been Poitevins in the Port-en-Bessein district since the time William the Conqueror's fleet, massing in the tiny harbour, marked the prelude to the Norman Conquest.

Now Arthur Poitevin, a music teacher, sturdily built and as blond as a Saxon, was a good Resistant too, but no one, least of all the Germans, cared how near to any fortifications he approached. For Poitevin was blind.

A common feeling for music had brought the master close to the pupil, close enough to be on Christian-name terms, and often, to reach other pupils, Poitevin would accept a pillion ride to outlying districts on the boy's noisy velo-cycle. Sometimes, passing through Port-en-Bessein, it was natural to stop for a breath of sea air, and what could be more innocent then than a boy guiding the footsteps of a blind man? The harbour offered a limited choice of strolls, and most often their steps led them along the breakwater, above the black jagged teeth of the rocks capped with seaweed, below the yawning concrete mouth of the casemate that marked the western strong point.

"The wind's good," Poitevin would say. "Even if you're blind, young François, it's good to feel the sea wind on your face. It's coming from the west to-day. Tell me quickly, François, what can you see?"

"I can see a casemate," the boy said eagerly. "That's just above us. And a gun—a really tremendous one. I just don't know its calibre."

"Never mind, the Germans will talk about it in the cafés. When they have drunk, they always do." The blind man always spoke with the biting distaste of the ascetic revolted by excess. "I will find out the calibre of the guns, but look at the casemate, François. In which direction is it sited?"

The boy stared across the harbour to the grey needle spire of the church, computing by means of the weather vane. Always he had the uncanny feeling that the blind man saw more of this than he himself. Two hundred yards away, on the jetty, some officers of the *Kriegsmarine* were gathered, yet they had glanced only fleetingly at the big blond man with the white stick. He said finally: "The casemate seems to face north-north-east. There's a path leading up to it quite near where we're standing. It must be almost 150 feet from here up to the strongpoint. It's a chalk foundation, jolly slippery, I should think, in wet weather." He took the blind man's arm. "Now we're turning back, Arthur, and I'm going to start counting. We'll see how many paces it is from the breakwater wall to the cliff path. Then I'll count again and we'll see how far the path is from the main jetty. Will you honestly be able to remember all that?"

Poitevin's reply was sombre and always the same: "When you're blind you've got time to remember, François."

Back in the neat little studio in Bayeux, where for convenience everything seemed on top of everything else, the boy found even his brain, accustomed to the daily grind of dates and facts, reeling with those measurements. He was glad enough to grasp a wafer of cigarette paper and scribble down the details which came effortlessly from Poitevin's lips. It is no secret to physicians that blindness, by a process of compensation, sharpens the faculties, particularly the memory, but

Guerin was only a boy; he marvelled at the sensitised accuracy of his teacher's mind.

Sometimes Dewavrin's staff in London raised a query and a few weeks later the whole walk would have to be done again, but Poitevin's memory was rarely at fault. The boy had found the right man.

After sounding out contacts in Bayeux, Jean Chateau, the Caen electricity-board inspector, also had found the right man: a blond, barrel-chested giant named Léon Cardron, former skipper of the trawler *Ave Maria*. Another agent, summing up Cardron, said, " He was tough—really tough—a man who could make his point without raising his voice." When, after Dunkirk, the *Kriegsmarine* had offered to rent the *Ave Maria* for patrol work, Cardron's answer was to take an iron bar and wreck the trawler's engine. Strangely, the Germans neither shot him nor punished him. Fishing was rarely permitted more than once a week; they may have thought that scraping a living with a twenty-foot job called *Le Maseu* was punishment enough.

The check that the *Kriegsmarine* kept on Bessein's fishermen never varied. What they searched for most diligently at the control point were transmitters: they tooth-combed the lockers, even testing for loose boards in the decking that might be used as a hiding-place, but Cardron had no need of a transmitter. Instead, tangled in his 40-foot herring net were four eight-by-six plans of the coastline west of Bessein, prepared by Thomas's cartographic service.

Time out was limited—sometimes four hours, usually two —and he had to stay in sight of the shore, but none of this bothered Cardron much. Like hundreds of Girard's other agents, he was the man Dewavrin had envisaged long ago in St. Stephen's House, when he doodled on scratch-pads and feverishly consulted maps. Cardron knew every inch of the crumbling chalky coastline. As a boy he had scrambled on the shelving cliffs in search of gull's eggs. Each landmark carried a meaning which was sometimes poignant. Before the war, in the good days, coming back from Havre with the herring catch sold and the knowledge of gold in the bank, the cliffs there at Longues had told him that soon he would be back in his warm, dimly-lit cottage with its religious emblems and carved clipper models and all the family gathered round the long dining-table.

Now there was a mighty battery at Longues, four 155s, roughly equivalent to 6-inch guns, mounted in a reinforced concrete casemate and a seemingly endless minefield surrounding it. Barbed wire clearly marked the seaward perimeter. In the calm autumn weather Cardron anchored 500 yards from the shore and dropped his net. Calculating distance in terms of sailing time he could mark the position of the battery on Thomas's maps correct to a few feet.

Cardron was not a man of words; he had a surer way of registering the physical details that Century needed. The nets had also camouflaged a pre-war box camera; squatting down in the bows, pretending to adjust the trawl, he squinted through the view-finder. *Pik* went the shutter. He wound the roll, fished a while, moved on again.

Presently he was moored off another town—not really a town or a port at all, but a summer resort, with a long desolate beach, the châlets sand-bagged and shuttered now, like blind eyes. But Chateau had asked for details of everything along the coastline so he lifted the camera and registered the scene. Again the shutter went *pik* and in the same casual way his mind registered the name without any sense of its importance. He had known Arromanches for forty years, ever since he was a boy.

On 21st October, Renault returned to France. The C.N.D. was still functioning, effectively though with great risk, under Max Petit's guidance, assuring weekly liaison with London from new headquarters in the rue Dufrenoy. One of the first things Renault did was send for Girard, and the big man was shaken by his first sight of him. His back was hunched like an old-age pensioner's, a scrubby reddish-brown moustache covered his upper lip, his skin was as wrinkled as a prune. All summer he had badgered Dewavrin and the Commander to let him take up the reins of his network, which had grown to number 1,000 men and this had been the price: a nightmare session in the hands of a make-up man from Denham Film Studios, which had ensured that neither Edith nor the children, let alone the Gestapo, could have recognised him.

At least, Renault thought, it had softened the pang of parting. Edith and the children, safe in the English countryside, were still rocking at the thought of it, and even the austere Dewavrin, in the midst of conferences, would suddenly choke with helpless laughter.

" I can't even enjoy good food any more," said Renault mournfully. " They've given me a kind of false paunch and it's interfering with my digestion." Then, getting down to business, " Just before I left I saw General de Gaulle. He asked me to convey his personal congratulations to the man who took the plan which you gave me in June. He did a fine job of work and the General has since told me that the High Command have found it of enormous value." Girard glowed. His inner core of scepticism had always kept him wondering whether the plan was of use or not.

During the next month Renault saw Girard and Colonel Touny many times. The suave and polished Colonel came to his headquarters almost every day, and Renault became more and more convinced that the ultimate organisation of the whole of French Resistance must use Touny's movement as the hard core. On one occasion Renault said: " I am particularly pleased with this Intelligence network, Century, that Berthelot and Girard are running. At first, in London, we regarded it as one more C.N.D. agency, but they're sending through so much stuff that we're becoming overloaded. We shall have to think about separate transmission facilities."

That was almost the last time that Renault saw Touny. When he left for England again, on 12th December, this time stifling in the manhole of the *Deux Anges*, his idea was to return almost immediately. But after that Dewavrin ruled that the personal danger was now too great. He had been a pioneer in the struggle to unearth the secrets of the Wall, but like so many pioneers Renault was forced to step aside and watch rather wistfully while others fought and died in a battle he had planned.

All along the Wall, that autumn, the network signalled a new activity from the ports. Gresselin, the Cherbourg grocer, reported that the great mountain of Fort du Roule, 180 feet high, was honeycombed with subterranean galleries and casual travellers like Gilbert Michel, who still went there weekly as a hostage, brought rumours of a formidable stockpile of torpedoes and munitions. Many of the guns guarding the port, including the 6-gun heavy A.A. battery on the quay, could be brought to bear against shipping. The same with the heavy battery at the Torpedo Storage Depot. The batteries covering the harbours and the quay where the famous *Normandie* had once come alongside were all under concrete now, linked by underground tunnels, and an intercom system of zinc voice-pipes.

Le Havre, too, was stoutly defended. Roughly 11,000 German troops, including 2,000 of the *Kriegsmarine*, were in possession. On 15th December, 1942, after a meeting in Paris, Girard appointed an old colleague, a cement executive named Lucien Jacquemin, as head of the Havre cell. Almost at once Jacquemin, a sharp-eyed meticulous little man like a family lawyer, had a stroke of luck.

Ostensibly he had become friendly with a German named Döttlin, one of the heads of the Berlin-based Polensky and Zöllner Construction Company that had built the submarine base in the Darse Sud. The base was never, in fact, used for submarines but its neat little pens served as anchorage for the 150 E-boats of the 5th Torpedo Boat Flotilla.

But Jacquemin's firm had supplied some of the cement, which gave him a good excuse for showing more than passing interest in the construction when he chatted with Döttlin. The chance came one day when Döttlin revealed that his firm had also constructed the submarine base at Dieppe. " Then why," Jacquemin asked, " did you use waterproof cement there, but not here? " Döttlin assumed the superior smile of one technician about to amaze another. There was a piece of paper lying near—Jacquemin said afterwards that it cost him ten sweating minutes to manoeuvre it into position—and on it Döttlin began to sketch a blueprint of the great iron girders that had been driven into the ocean bed to form a skeleton for the reinforced concrete structure.

Jacquemin began to talk idly of tides. The continual ebb and flow of the tide, he said, must have made it hard to ensure that the foundations would support such an enormous weight of concrete. By the time he had finished Döttlin had supplied him with the exact thickness of the concrete used to support the load. He left the office without destroying the sketch and Jacquemin often wondered afterwards if he had *wanted* the Allies to know.

Inevitably a lot of the information passing through Caen to Colonel Nobody and his checkers in the Ministry of War suite was a duplication, though that was useful, serving as confirmation. Seven agents alone, for example, were working Port-en-Bessein, all unknown to one another! Inevitably, too, some information conflicted and for the agents on the spot there was the wearisome and risky job of going back to check again; the cautious Jacquemin, in Le Havre, drove his sixteen agents quietly crazy by his unwillingness to transmit any information until he had received three confirmations. Thomas and his map-makers never paused for breath because 60 per cent of all the information filtered through now was designed to be translated into map form.

In London, Dewavrin's staff had an even bigger headache, because by this time other networks had created cells working in the area, although none but Century had achieved a complete coverage of the whole coast.

Chapter Twelve

SECRET ARMY

DUCHEZ SPENT much of the winter of 1942 as the spearhead of the forces mapping out the port of Ouistreham. As usual, procuring maps had been the main problem. The defences were too thickly clustered in one area of the port to register more than an unintelligible blur on a general survey map, but Meslin's office possessed no large-scale plan. Jourdan, his assistant, had to make some studiously disinterested inquiries in Caen before a Government office—he has forgotten which—came up with something which gave him a quiet thrill of joy.

It was a complete town plan of Ouistreham on the scale of one-in-a-thousand, which the tourist publicity office had issued before the war. Not only was every street and boulevard marked in but a legend for visitors picked out all the landmarks which ensured a happy holiday—the Casino, the Turkish Baths, the miniature golf course, even the chemists who would help keep the liver in shape.

" We'd better make a plan on a larger scale and divide it into sections," Meslin decided. " Each section will show so many yards of sidewalks and we'll show the pill-box defences and barriers for every street. In that way we can give London the full picture of what's going on."

Later Thomas and Jourdan agreed that among all those they produced, the Ouistreham map was the biggest headache. With fresh details trickling in every few days, most sector maps took an average of three months to complete: Ouistreham took six. The *Kriegsmarine Wehr* only kept Jourdan's department posted on new defences that affected the running of the port, and the port and the gare-maritime, on the east side of the town, were only a small part of Ouistreham. Fashionable Ouistreham, with its memories of Spanish-style week-end villas and lovely girls in one-piece bathing suits lay west of the River Orne, running along the Boulevard Aristide Briand, and this sector was sealed off completely. It was, as Meslin told Girard, " a forbidden zone within a forbidden zone "—what the Germans called a *Stuetzpunkt* (strong point).

Lacking knowledge of the defences, Thomas, his father and Jourdan divided the cartographic side of Ouistreham between them, picturing the town in three mammoth plans—roughly twenty-three yards of pavement to every inch. These were the trickiest plans that an agent had so far handled, since their size did not make for easy concealment. One set, luckily, was apportioned to Duchez, who always seemed to revel in the idea of taking risks.

The painter had found the months since his great coup dragging interminably. Under half a dozen aliases he had been pressuring agents in the Caen area, feeding a constant stream of information to Meslin's office, but to Duchez this was disappointingly work-a-day stuff. As stimulus he needed the constant excitement of tangling with the enemy, of bearding them in their own den—*sous la barbe de Monsieur*, as he put it. An advertisement in the local paper, *Le Bonhomme Normand*, gave him a fresh chance. In view of the accursed Anglo-American air-raids on Ouistreham and Caen, it announced, volunteers were urgently needed for Civil Defence service. Duchez approached Henri Marigny, the bookseller, who months ago had supplied the network with their road maps for parachutage. Marigny, a dark solid man with horn-rimmed spectacles and a clipped moustache, had begged to be employed more fully.

" If you really want to play a more active part in the Resistance," Duchez told him, "here's your chance." Marigny's home was at Ouistreham and Duchez could plead that work took him frequently to the area. Within days they had been accepted as air-raid wardens for Ouistreham.

The quest for detail was now launched. Twice a week, as part of a roster, the devil-may-care Duchez and the prudent

Marigny, equipped with the white helmets and blue arm-bands of the French Civil Defence, stood a dusk-to-dawn vigil in Ouistreham. On their night patrols, their footsteps ringing hollow on the deserted sidewalks, the Boulevard Aristide Briand lay open to them, and when they saw it they stopped amazed.

Bauleiter Ingenieur Ött had done his work well. From the eastern end of the promenade to the Casino, a clear 300 yards, hotels, châlets and beach-huts had been wiped away—bulldozed into nothingness. In the darkness blockhouses and casemates loomed from the sand like the concrete tunnellings of mole-men and the squat wicked barrels of the guns poked forbiddingly at the skyline—155s, 75s, 230s. The strong point was sealed off from the streets running parallel by barbed wire unwinding like an endless watch spring across the torn scarred ground.

Some of their most significant discoveries were made as the bombs came howling from the sky. Once, dashing for cover, they dived into what they at first took to be a slit-trench—until they identified it as an anti-tank ditch, more than two feet wide, which had been scooped from the *pavé* of the Boulevard Daladier. Then there was the ack-ack. Close to the old Casino, on the beach, the Germans had posted two flak batteries to protect the immediate area of the port. During the alerts, which came often that winter, it was easy for air-raid wardens to pace out their exact position as the glowing balls went hammering upwards, drowning the silken rustle of sea on sand.

In time they picked out the one small quarter of the fortified zone still occupied by French civilians from the larger area made up of German barracks. " Easy to tell," chuckled Duchez, who had a Frenchman's aversion to restraint. " As usual our countrymen have the worst blackout discipline in the world."

Within six weeks they had gathered together a general picture, enough for Thomas to begin filling in small black crosses on the virgin spaces of the street plan. But the detailed overall picture which eighteen months later was to be of invaluable aid to Captain Philip Kieffer of No. 4 Commando called for careful prospecting. More time needed to be spent in Ouistreham, especially in daylight hours.

Duchez found the solution. Several times that winter judiciously aimed sticks of bombs put the locks of the canal out of action for days. In Caen the *Mairie* called for volunteers to drive lorries loaded with vegetables up to Ouistreham and bring back the meagre supplies of fresh fish. Among the volunteers were Duchez and Marigny. The turn-around period was employed profitably in gleaning more information—about the two munitions depots sited at either end of the west quay, about those roads which were screened by mines and those which were blocked only by machine-guns and pill-boxes.

Waging this kind of war, Duchez was in his seventh heaven. Marigny was an impassive man who kept his fears pretty much to himself, but Duchez really exulted in the risks. Driving the lorry loads of fish back from Ouistreham—always in the centre of the road, to the despair of the German traffic patrols—he would sing abominably through his nose, happy in the knowledge that he had perceived one more chink in the German armour. What did it matter if, as he was bound to be, he was searched as a matter of routine? The salient points were noted down in cider on wafers of cigarette paper, which remains invisible until treated by heat.

His conviviality became a by-word in the bistros of the port. As in Caen he joked and clowned and missed nothing. At the eastern end of the promenade, for example, the Germans had installed a battery of flame throwers. More precise details were hard to come by. But in the cafés where the workmen gathered the talk was all of the Wall, and a few had seen the tests. They believed the flame-throwers were operated by remote control and that their flare could shrivel a target to nothingness sixty-five yards away—right by the water's edge. The roaring orange jet operated in high-pressure bursts, lasting from five to ten seconds.

Duchez found there were even ways of sabotaging Hitler's Wall in advance. In one café he and Marigny met a man named Chrêtien, a contractor from St. Aubin, whose firm was supplying much of the cement for the Ouistreham defences.

Duchez leant across the table, his eyes glinting. " Take my tip," he hissed. " Don't give them your very best cement. For that kind of construction, one part cement and two parts sand is a much better mixture."

The painter was right. Eighteen months later, under heavy bombardment from the U.S. 9th Air Force, some of the blockhouses tilted crazily sideways and their German defenders had to retreat hastily.

Jourdan, too, was working on the town. Early in July he had obtained permission to visit relations in the area, though it was noticeable that he spent more time drinking and smoking his meerschaum pipe in a small café on the Boulevard Boivin Champeaux. He knew the ritual of his countrymen: the café bore the legend: " *On peut apporter son manger* " and from midday until almost three the workmen would be drifting in, in ones and twos, bringing their lunch-packs of bread and garlic sausage, to be washed down with harsh red wine. They, like most of the town's available labour, were engaged on sections of the Wall.

" That's a mighty-looking blockhouse you're working on beyond the barrier," Jourdan would say. " The concrete looks pretty thick."

" Thick enough," a man grunted, after masticating a chunk of sausage and surveying him for a minute. " The Boche don't leave much to chance."

" I can believe that," Jourdan would rejoin. " I'm an engineer myself and I know concrete two feet thick when I see it."

The approach was childishly simple. A skilled agent could have seen the question coming minutes before it landed. But the workman was not a skilled agent, and Jourdan had counted correctly on the passionate desire of his countrymen to prove that they are in the know.

" Two feet, you say? Engineer or not, monsieur, your eyes deceive you. We've had special instructions to build the walls four feet thick on all the blockhouses I've worked on to date. . . ."

Later they had a drink or two and presently, Jourdan,

seemingly in friendship, followed the man into the street and watched him past the barrier, walking with the short fumbling paces of the *ouvrier* who rarely sheds his clogs, towards the site where his workmates were busy. It was a crisp sunlit afternoon, with no sea-mists and Jourdan, puffing doggedly at his pipe, leaned against the door post of the café, watching him. Thirty-five . . . thirty-seven . . . thirty-nine paces exactly, from barrier to blockhouse.

He went back to Caen to tell Thomas about it.

That was the last week of February, when the heads of the movement in Paris suddenly received electrifying news. " Colonel Passy " had arrived in France.

Only Dewavrin's implacable obstinacy had got him there at all. At the end of January his visit had been all set and the clever sardonic Brossolette, now his deputy, had gone ahead by Lysander to make preparations. Then, on 15th February, had come the sudden and peremptory news that the War Cabinet had vetoed the trip. It took a few minutes to sink in, then all his old mulishness was stung into life again. By phone call and minute and personal visit he began to bombard officials as zealously as he had once done over the precious concept of the networks. In vain did his old friend and ally Sir Claude Dansey point out that Churchill himself was against the mission, on the understandable grounds that if the Gestapo got him there were very few secrets of the Resistance that he didn't know. He even reminded Dewavrin that, a year back, he had been formally sentenced to death, by Vichy, but the young man did not seem to mind at all.

Dewavrin's next port of call was de Gaulle himself. First, he pointed out, Brossolette had already gone, and the journalist had quite as much detail at *his* finger-tips. Secondly, in case of capture by the Gestapo, he had armed himself with a hollowed-out signet ring, with a swivel top, containing a cyanide pill. De Gaulle took one look at his implacable young Intelligence chief, who was always willing to die for an idea to prove it was right, then rang Churchill. Two days later the ban was lifted.

So at approximately 3 a.m. on Friday, 27th February,

Dewavrin parachuted from the hatch of a Halifax bomber that had brought him from Tempsford aerodrome, England, and billowed gently down in a cornfield near Lyons-la-Forêt, twenty miles from Rouen. Accompanying him was a British officer, Wing-Commander Frederick Forrest Yeo-Thomas of " F " Section, Special Operations Executive, the British-operated section which undertook to supply the arms and equipment to Dewavrin's networks. Yeo-Thomas, who became known to the whole of French Resistance as " Shelley " or " The White Rabbit," had come to make his own independent summing-up of the task in hand.

The task was a mammoth one, and Dewavrin had no very clear idea of how to set about it. But before the conferences began, there was the risky problem of reaching Paris in safety. From the darkness of the dropping-ground loomed the imperturbable Olivier Courtaud, the radio operator, who had aided Renault's escape to England nine months earlier; he had headed the reception team which guided their Halifax to the target. To Dewavrin, at least, the next twenty-four hours were like the slow awakening from an anaesthetic. The odd purposeful silence as they trudged from the cornfields; the lurching uncomfortable bicycle ride through the icy darkness; the sudden painful sense of being home again when they arrived stealthily in the small hours at the house of the local C.N.D. agent to find a meal of Bayonne ham and rough cider awaiting them in a brightly-lit kitchen.

Next morning there was Rouen, black, medieval and unfriendly, in the pre-dawn cold, with troops of S.S. swaggering everywhere, then the long stuffy bus ride to Paris, to find yet more Germans, Germans in rough grey uniforms pressing against you in the Metro, staring stolidly ahead of them like pink well-drilled animals. As Courtaud led them out of the Porte Dauphine Metro into the frosty night, Dewavrin knew already that Paris was different. The Metro smelt the same, the rough smell of *caporal* tobacco was the same, and in the parks the full moon lent a theatrical black-and-silver beauty to the formal vistas of the chestnut trees. Yet everywhere Dewavrin, a Parisian, could feel the unhappiness of his native

173

city. It was as if the bleak winter of 1942 had turned its heart to stone.

Their first rendezvous was with Brossolette in Berthelot's flat on the Boulevard Flandrin. (Renault had urged that Colonel Touny and his deputies deserved closer study, and this was to be a decisive factor in the future of Girard and his men.) The dark volatile journalist, who had thoughtfully dyed the white streak in his hair to escape recognition, had found a safe flat for them on the rue Marcel-Renaud, a ground-floor apartment overlooking a courtyard. Now their work began.

Dewavrin had been awaiting this moment for almost a year. In London, all through 1942, there had been many conferences, and the upshot had been unanimous agreement on one point. The time had come to organise the entire French Resistance, not only in the coastal zone, but far behind the Wall, under one top authority. Up to now its weakness had been that every movement worked independently of all the others—not only because, as secret organisations, they lacked communications, but because their political views were poles apart. The task of Passy, Brossolette and Yeo-Thomas was this: to unify and finance ten large rambling inexperienced groups and a dozen smaller ones under General Charles de Gaulle.

If they could achieve it—and it was a big if—the first step was for the leaders to form a committee responsible to de Gaulle —the National Council of Resistance. But this was to be only the beginning. Their next task was to create ? Secret Army, under direct command of General Delestraint (Vidal to the Underground), a frank and fearless Regular officer appointed by de Gaulle in London. The Army was to be organised on a regional basis with local commanders appointed for air and military liaison. It was a plan which looked to the eventual co-operation of the French Underground with the Allied armies on D-Day, and one worthy of Dewavrin's fertile and patriotic imagination.

Their first step was to sound out the leaders of the principal Resistance movements. Now the conferences began. Sometimes they were held hurriedly in small " safe " apartments, which were only " safe " for twenty-four hours, sometimes in cellars; at other times in O.C.M.'s suite at the Ministry of War, or in the small restaurant called the *Pourquoi Pas?* (the Why Not?) in the crowded rue de Lille. Here Brossolette, who had already met Girard and Touny, laid the groundwork. In his cold logical way he told Dewavrin: "You know Renault was right—this Organisation Civile et Militaire can offer both troops *and* discipline. Any Secret Army will have to be built round them."

That was the beginning of it. On 2nd March, after a previous meeting with Berthelot, Dewavrin and Brossolette met up with Colonel Touny in that elegant flat in the rue du Général Langlois. The head of O.C.M. was inclined to be stiff with strangers, and all were cautious, a little on their guard. Only at their second meeting did Dewavrin lay his cards on the table. He explained the concept of the Secret Army, which on D-Day would be given specific tasks designed to harass the Germans in the rear behind the Wall.

Out of months of fevered discussion—Duclos, the stock-broker, now back in London running B.C.R.A.'s "Action" section, had helped too—had emerged three key plans. Most ambitious was the "Green Plan," which aimed, by means of 1,000 rail cuts, at slicing the critical military railroads on D-Day. Aligned to this was "Operation Turtle," a plan for the strategic stalling of all German road traffic. The "Red Plan" was designed to confuse and harass the enemy by free-for-all guerrilla action, and the cutting of military telephone lines.

Touny was intrigued. He promised, by 10th April at latest, to render a complete return of his strengths in all the regions between Bordeaux and the Belgian frontier.

Meantime there were more journeys, more conferences. The leaders of four other movements similar to Touny's—Ceux de la Resistance, Ceux de la Libération, Libération, and the Front National—had to be met and wooed. Brossolette journeyed along the Wall itself and in Caen held earnest conference with Meslin the Government engineer, and Duchez, who impressed him particularly. Yeo-Thomas went south to inspect Touny's units in the river valleys of the Nièvre, the Cher, and the Allier.

Dewavrin went north beyond the Somme to the desolate region round Calais.

In these weeks Dewavrin knew too many tumbling emotions for anything as uncomplicated as fear or satisfaction. The one emotion that seemed to transcend all others was loneliness. He no longer had the sense of belonging in this cold smoky garrison town. For security reasons he could not contact his mother, who was still living in Paris and neither he nor his colleagues ate in restaurants more than they could help. To his proud introverted nature it seemed that when he travelled by Metro people moved unobtrusively away from him. It was as if they *felt* he was different.

He had never felt so alone and Renault's words came back to him vividly: " Is it any wonder the networks sometimes ask themselves whether London makes any use of the information they get or whether they're even interested? "

The world knows now that the joint-mission of Passy and Brossolette and Yeo-Thomas was initially successful. On 26th March the leaders of the five principal Resistance movements, together with their assistants, arrived secretly and severally at an apartment in the suburb of Neuilly to announce that they accepted de Gaulle as their leader. Besides Touny there was Monsieur Lecompte-Boynet, the scholarly head of Ceux de la Resistance, then 1,000 strong, but able to command between 25,000 and 30,000 men in the Champagne, Vendée and Contentin areas by D–Day; Coquoin, head of Ceux de la Libération with a potential of 35,000 agents among the police and transport drivers; Monsieur Perigny, head of Libération, an Intelligence movement with a strong trade-union background, and Ginsburger, head of the 30,000 strong Front National, the Resistance organisation of the Communist Party.

All of them solemnly signed an agreement to carry out the instructions of the Allies as transmitted by General de Gaulle. The National Council of the Resistance was formed.

So far as the war against the Wall went, it was not this meeting, but one arising out of it that really tipped the scales in the battle.

Two days before General Delestraint arrived in Paris, with
Jean Moulin, de Gaulle's political representative for the unified
Resistance, Dewavrin met Touny again, and out of a chance
remark came a bold scheme designed to increase the efficiency
of Girard's network thirty-fold. As Dewavrin entered, Touny
looked up from a sheaf of strength returns.

"As I promised, my figures are complete," Touny announced. "I can offer you 32,000 men."

It was a moment before it registered. Then incredulously,
"These are the men you expect to have in position by the date
of the Allied invasion, not the men you have in position now?"
But, politely, Touny disagreed. The men were in position at
that moment—thirty times the number that any organisation,
aside from the Communists, could then offer.

Dewavrin, who had a lithe and adaptable mind, thought
furiously. Much of the old fire and obstinacy still smouldered
within him but three years as de Gaulle's Intelligence chief had
taught him something of the value of compromise, and in the
light of experience he was never afraid to change his ideas.

He had seen enough now to convince him that he could
make an old dream come true. There were close to forty
Intelligence networks now, and you could form as many as you
liked, all over France—but to what point? Networks meant
radios, radios meant regional transmission agencies and in
London there was a crying shortage of the technicians who
could be sent to supervise them, men like Courtaud and Julitte.
There were even fewer men of Renault's calibre, men who
could organise the networks and appoint local heads. Why not,
then, concentrate on the Secret Army and turn *its* members
into part-time agents?

"What I propose is this," he told Touny. "For security
reasons you should keep your Intelligence agents and shock
troops separate. But as the troops must come across so much
information that they never pass on we'll issue both agents
and fighters with a standard questionnaire listing the points
on which to concentrate—the scale on which to draw rough
maps, the details which we regard as important. From now on,
I shall split the Confrérie Notre Dame into two for security and

to cope with the volume of traffic." One of Renault's deputies, Jean Tillier, would take charge of one branch, handling the intelligence from the agents, while Olivier Courtaud would take charge of all information coming in from shock troops.

Until further notice it was agreed that maps and dispatches would be routed to England by the method which then held good—by twice monthly pick-up from a ground near Arras during the moon period and, on the dark side of the moon, by the *Deux Anges* out of Pont-Aven. Renault's system was a year old now and still working well.

There was a little more discussion before Touny said: " Colonel Passy, this is something I should not ask perhaps, but *when* may we expect an Allied landing? And where? "

Dewavrin thought like lightning. Some of the other Resistance leaders had asked him that question when he first arrived in Paris. Dewavrin had no official intimations but he was an intelligent man who had studied not only the maps of many defences but the strength returns of every German unit between Belgium and Spain. Some of these leaders are still alive to testify that he first guessed with uncanny accuracy: " Somewhere between St. Brieuc and the bay of the Somme— in the spring of 1944." But the response had been only a grave silence, and in every man's eyes he could see the thoughts unspoken: Twelve more months—a year to wait. You can go back, safe and secure to London, leaving us to twelve more months of this.

So now he shook his head positively. " I have no idea," he told Touny, thinking *It's still as I told Renault. They've got to have faith.*

Nor was his faith in them misplaced. Four days afterwards, late on the night of 16th April, a Lysander touched down between the glowworms of light on the field near Lyons-la-Forêt and carried Dewavrin, Brossolette and Yeo-Thomas safely back to London. Six days after, on 22nd April, Thomas completed the last map of Ouistreham—a perfect one-in-a-thousand blueprint of all defences from east to west. A week later it was on Dewavrin's desk.

Chapter Thirteen

THE WHISPERING MAP

TRUE TO tradition, it was an outsider—and a woman at that —who saw most of the game that followed. From her ringside seat in the Government engineer's office at Caen, little Jeanne Verinaud recalls it vividly: " About the middle of May, 1943, London became insatiable. Each fortnight M. Meslin would send reams of typed reports on an area, with maps and photographs, but suddenly, a few weeks later, they'd ask so many supplementary questions we might never have sent them a line."

The job had been hard enough before, but it was now a hundred times more complex. The first impact of Dewavrin's scheme had been to almost double everyone's responsibility. On de Gaulle's behalf, Brossolette had appointed Girard commander of Region " M " of the Secret Army, which was soon to give him charge of 7,000 shock troops in fourteen departments of Normandy, Brittany, Poitou, Anjou and Maine, as well as being an O.C.M. chief and western regional organiser for Century. For the Caen-Cherbourg region, Meslin took command of all Secret Army troops and Century agents. The unit chiefs who were his subordinates, all along the Wall— Mercader, Franck, Gresselin—had much the same task. When they were not organising reception teams for parachutage, arms dumps and the training of para-military units, they were sifting Intelligence reports and routing them on to H.Q. at Caen. Watching over it all was Girard, who moved them hither and thither like pawns in a gigantic game of chess.

Viewed dispassionately, it seems a gloriously embroiled

chain of command, but boiled down to its simplest terms it meant that some men watched the Wall for information that only the Allies could use, some watched lesser targets behind the Wall that local shock troops could tackle on D-Day, and a few men, chiefs like Meslin and Duchez, did both at once.

Whatever the information an agent turned up now, there was a departmental head who could find a use for it. Duchez, Deuxième Bureau, now held sway over all part-timers for an area of 9,000 square miles. A spry grey-haired man named Pierre Faure headed the Premier Bureau, which screened personnel. As head of the Troisième Bureau, Girard had Lt.-Col. Gaston Corbasson, a fine, classically handsome ex-artillery officer, with a young man named Robert Kaskoreff as his assistant. Their job, corresponding roughly to a G-3 Ops department, was to liaise with Post Office and railway officials, selecting local sabotage targets like factories and transformers for final approval by Duclos's " Action " Bureau in London. The Quatrième Bureau was headed by Emmanuel Robineau, a shambling, fair-haired youngster, whom time was to prove brave to the point of foolhardiness. His job was to concentrate on aerial liaison, mapping out dropping-grounds and arranging the stockpiling of arms, munitions and medical supplies for D-Day.

For now, as a result of " Colonel Passy's " inspiration, the Normandy countryside swarmed with busy men. Sometimes they were men in belfries, or men trawling their nets in the blue water, but more often they were men ploughing the red earth or pruning the old dead wood from the hazel hedges, or staring not too interestedly, like Arsène, from the driving cabin of a camionet. Brave unobtrusive men in patched denims who listened in cafés, sometimes prompting, offering a drink at the right moment, going quietly home to transcribe their discoveries on to the small sector plan that was hidden where prudence prompted.

Whatever the information they gleaned, it took shape ultimately in the form of a map. No longer confined to fortifications alone, Thomas and his cartographers now drew maps of telegraph lines along the Wall, of the permanent way system at the Gare Centrale, street plans that showed German barracks and billets. They laboured long hours over plans of docks and quays, on airfield plans, blown up five times larger than the general survey maps, showing the oil supplies and bomb storage dumps behind the Wall. " They're doing marvels," Girard said once, with true humility. " It's the greatest thing this network has ever achieved."

For it was as Thomas had predicted. Normandy had become a living map.

It was appropriate that Duchez should have been in the thick of it all. For to all intents and purposes the invasion area had been decided, and Duchez, in his own individual way, had helped crystallise that decision.

Planning of a sort had gone on, in London, all through 1942, and it had become clear that geographical chance was going to scale down the possibilities to two feasible assault areas. One was the Caen region, and the other was the Pas de Calais. The chief attraction of the Pas de Calais was its closeness to England, and Lt.-General Sir Frederick Morgan, who was co-ordinating Cross-Channel operation plans for the Combined Commanders, set a British planning staff of COSSAC (Chief of Staff to the Supreme Allied Commander) to study it in detail.

But air reconnaissance and agents' reports effectively ruled it out. In the Pas de Calais area Hitler's Atlantic Wall *was* too strong. It is no secret now that the Germans always saw it as the first invasion area and some of the concrete there was 20 feet thick. (In 1942 the area was allotted four times more concrete than all Normandy and Brittany.) Then, too, the region lacked ports, its beaches were unsheltered and the terrain altogether ruled out the defence and exploitation of the bridgehead. Now the beaches between Vierville and Colleville (later called Omaha) and those eastwards, around Ouistreham and the mouth of the Orne, came under active consideration. The planners had to count on favourable winds and tides, and assume resources in the drawing-board stage, like Mulberry

Harbour, but some of Century's earlier objectives became of first priority.

Of course, there were drawbacks to the plan. Caen would have to be seized to avoid defeat in the early stages. Those vicious coastal batteries at Ouistreham that Duchez had dogged so assiduously would have to be neutralised. But from other viewpoints the area was tempting. The sheltered Bessein beaches offered good anchorage. The area was near enough to ensure fighter cover from British bases, the soil was right for quick airfield development, and only eighty miles from Caen was a first-class port, Cherbourg.

There were the clues offered by Duchez's map, too. Twelve months had passed since that audacious coup, but incredibly, against all the planners' logical convictions, the position in the Caen-Cherbourg region remained unchanged. To Austin's "Martians," now an Anglo-U.S. unit on the top floor of Peter Robinson's store, Oxford Street, it seemed that the Todt Organisation were building their Wall as if Duchez had never existed, and Thomas's maps confirmed it. As, one by one, the blockhouses sprang up in the expected places, the R.A.F. flew over and photographed them, and the maps offered valuable clues when they came to interpret the results. The holding strength of troops remained about constant, but the Russian front was proving a hungry front. In quality and mobility they were declining monthly.

Summing up later, Austin said, " I think that whatever the defences, we should ultimately have landed where we did—the beaches decided that. But this plan, certainly one of the most memorable ever furnished by the Resistance, gave enormous confidence by showing the fixity and weakness of the defence system well in advance." The final decision was still many months away but from now on (as Renault, back in Duke Street, proudly noted) the pressure by many interested Allied departments to pump more and yet more information out of Century became relentless.

It is only fair to add that for security reasons scores of other networks from Norway to the Pyrenees took equal risks to send information which their masters knew sadly in advance could be of little use. If it is lucky to win military glory, Girard's men were lucky to be in the front line.

The first interest of all Girard's departments was to plug existing gaps along the Wall scientifically. One of these took in the sector known later as " Juno Beach," from the mouth of the Seulles river to St. Aubin-sur-Mer—roughly three and a half miles. The tactics evolved by Thomas and Duchez began to pay off. Through Kaskoreff of the Third Bureau, Century now found itself an agent right on the spot in the seaside village of Luc-sur-Mer. His name was Jacques Sustendal, and he was the village doctor.

For as long as anyone could remember, Sustendal had been the doctor at Luc. He was a heavily-built stoop-shouldered man with a straggling moustache, disconcertingly brusque unless you knew him well. Patients haunting his surgery with imaginary ailments were apt to be greeted with the damning remark " That's not very complicated," and when Kaskoreff briefed him for the job, it was almost the only response he offered. But no patient who stood in need of his skill ever thought him brusque.

The country doctor had as much need of Century as they had of him. He was a God-fearing man and a good doctor, and it was hard for a man who was both to remain unembittered by the war. The conditions he saw on his daily rounds told him something was horribly wrong. The rich complained that the Germans were bleeding the country white, that they were racked by hunger pains, but they still advertised in the columns of *Le Bonhomme Normand* for " parlourmaids accustomed to good service " and in Paris they sought restaurants specialising in black market steaks under a soft green camouflage of lettuce. The old and the crippled and the very poor, with neither the agility nor the means to barter, existed in rooms where the walls sweated water, suffering with the dumb tragedy of animals. A cut finger would not heal for months. Teeth grew black and carious and rotted away. If you broke a bone it knitted badly and with agonising slowness.

Sustendal thought it was good for a doctor to be in the

Underground heart and soul. For the time being it was something positive, an antidote for the sickness of the age at a point where medicine fell short.

Coldly, clinically, he planned his Resistance. His practice would give him access to the entire area where agents were lacking, but he must think always as a doctor, not as an agent. (It was Girard's dictum: " Keep it normal.") He would not risk visiting any sector of the coast unless a professional call provided him with an alibi. The call would be logged in advance in his day-book, and the pharmacist's records would serve as a double check that he had called and prescribed medicine. The immunity of the battered black Gladstone-bag holding instruments and stethoscope would be a useful cover for his sector map.

At first the system seemed to work well. That underground tunnel at Luc that had so puzzled Meslin, for instance. Local inquiry by Sustendal now revealed it as a cunningly-camouflaged petrol dump. Once, when Kaskoreff congratulated him on clearing up such problems, Sustendal grunted: " After all, it's fairly simple. They're so frightened of anyone seeing the fortifications that they have a seven o'clock curfew. The only man in Luc who can travel after that is the doctor, yet so far as I'm aware the doctor is the only agent here."

One factor that stood him in good stead was the hated S.T.O. Short for *Service Travail Obligatoire* or compulsory labour service, it had been instituted by the Germans, with Laval's blessing, in October, 1942, to ensure that all Frenchmen between nineteen and thirty-two registered for work with the Germans. In Paris 20,000 of them were being rounded up every week. Those who had stamina and the worst of luck were shipped to Germany or to the Russian front, those with both stamina and resolution fled to the new " Maquis " bands that were springing up, and those with little stamina and more luck stayed to dig trenches or to work on the Wall in France. One such was Jo-jo, a frail sallow lad in his twenties, who walked into Sustendal's cold little surgery one spring night and complained of severe shooting pains in the chest.

Sustendal did the routine tests, growing gradually puzzled

184

and all the time the boy with the scared eyes was talking, never once stopping, about the rigours of the work, the pain he suffered each time he lifted a pick-axe or hod. Presently Sustendal murmured softly: " Ah, I know—they've been talking about sending some of your lot to the Western Front, haven't they? Replacements or something."

The patient nodded, swallowed but did not answer. Sustendal was conscious of a screaming tension in the ether-scented air. There was something this boy wanted to say. Physically, at least, there seemed nothing wrong. Outside in the waiting-room he could hear the patients coughing and scraping their feet and riffling the pages of old newspapers. Playing for time, he said: " I don't quite know what to say about your condition. It requires—consideration."

Almost at once the boy blurted out: " If I *didn't* go—away, I mean—if I wasn't fit . . . I could help someone who wanted to know about the work we have to do . . . things like fortifications."

So it was out, plain, like a straight flush spread on the table, and Sustendal knew that if he answered directly his life might be forfeit. There was a good chance that the boy was what the Resistants called a *mouton*—a stool-pigeon—a raw and un-fledged one, of course, to account for his fright. The Gestapo might have promised him immunity from deportation if he undertook to betray patriots: a stinking bargain, though there were Frenchmen not averse to keeping them if their own skins were in the balance.

He said abstractedly: " I don't know what you're talking about, lad—why should I be interested in fortifications? I'm a doctor, not an engineer. But I'm none too sure about your condition, you know—I shall want to make a further examina-tion. Meanwhile, you get this prescription made up and come back and see me next week."

That was all. Each week Jo-jo came back and the ritual was repeated: the sounding of the chest, the non-committal diagnosis, the steady trickle of information. Sustendal took no notes at the time, he retained it in his head to be noted later before checking it for himself. Mostly it turned out to be true.

How had Jo-jo sought him out? Sustendal never knew and in the spring and summer of 1943 he was too busy and too desperate to care. Other agents along the Wall—Jean Marion, the Mayor of Grandcamp-les-Bains, Jules Picot, the farmer at Neuilly-la-Forêt—had much the same contacts, took much the same risks with each dispensation of trust, but got the information through, and a few of them—the ones with luck—survived.

Century were plugging other gaps along the Wall, too, only sometimes it called for more ingenuity. One worried them for a long time; it lay between Ver-sur-Mer and Graye-sur-Mer, where 50th British Infantry Division (30 Corps) later came ashore. Then one of the network, Pierre Comby, a stockily-built Caen coal merchant, came up with an idea born incidentally of his own business problems. German troops stationed in Caen had as much coal as they wanted sent from the Fatherland, but only 50 kilos a month—roughly 112 lb.—were doled out to civilians. Comby told Meslin that with a little nudging the Germans might agree to his prospecting for peat on the coastline, as an alternative source of fuel power. Not being a geologist Meslin looked blank.

"There are several deposits on the Norman coastline," Comby enthused. "The temperature's just about right and the soil retains water pretty near the surface. Offhand, I remember some near Cherbourg and some just by Mont St. Michel, but more particularly at Ver-sur-Mer." Meslin chuckled then. He understood.

Feldkommandatur 723 approved Comby's application, and the coal merchant, doing things in style, founded a limited company styled *Société des Tourbières de Normandie* (Normandy Peat-Cutters Incorporated) setting up office in an old creeper-covered mansion on the Place St. Sauveur. The process of winning peat for fuel is not complex: the peat is deposited on the shore in tidal drifts, cut into sections with long shovels, and then dried out before being transported. But to chart the most likely sectors to find the deposits, Comby and his assistants had to visit the coast many times. And each time they went, a whole sheaf of geologic maps went with them.

Although the Germans watched them closely, there were then few fortifications at Ver-sur-Mer, but they were within gunshot of the two pill-boxes on the rocky spit of land called Les Roquettes and the anti-tank batteries of 75s that covered the beach from Le Hamel. All these defences, as well as several areas near Bayeux useful for parachutages, were shaded in as " strata " calling for urgent attention. For reasons that later emerge, Comby never removed much peat from the shore, but he left enough of it there, as a War Diary recorded sourly, to bog down many of the tanks of the Second British Army.

In Paris, late that May, the sixteen-man National Council of the Resistance had held its first meeting and the Underground's war seemed to be progressing steadily if slowly. The heads of the Resistance movements were thinking more in terms of persuading local organisers to send in monthly strength returns on time—which Dewavrin had insisted on, as an earnest of French intentions—rather than of disaster. Until 9th June, 1943.

The actual events of that day are still a shade confused. But it was a day which neither Dewavrin, nor Renault, nor Girard would ever forget. Girard got the news from Berthelot and afterwards, on that still June morning, he sat in his apartment for a long time, thinking. General Delestraint and Jean Moulin had been arrested within hours of one another. Two months after formation the Secret Army had been decapitated.

Scarcely a day passed then without further body blows. "Operation Grand Duke," the brain-child of Colonel Relling of *Abwehr III,* had been launched from the Lutetia Hotel on the Left Bank with one object—to smash all French Resistance. On 28th June the Gestapo trapped the radio operator, Olivier Courtaud, head of the newly-formed operations branch of C.N.D., and scores of others with him. Luckily, few important archives were captured and Dewavrin sent instructions for another operator, Robert Bacque, to carry on with three assistants and keep the radio link open. C.N.D.'s other radio link was unaffected, but the Secret Army was leaderless.

Among the Paris underground, morale was at its lowest ebb.

Again Girard had that uneasy sense that the Gestapo were close to him.

One day in the last week of June an afternoon meeting was being held in the flat of Jacques-Henri Simon of O.C.M.'s economic and political research department. The morning had been warm and sunny, and Simon, returning for lunch at midday to his flat in the rue de la Pompe, felt at peace with the world. A short cherubic lawyer with a lisp and a Charlie Chaplin moustache, Simon angered many by his abrupt downright manner, but events were to prove him a brave razorwitted Resistant.

He had just parked his bicycle in the entry hall of the white shining modern flat-block when the concierge came out of the lodge and stopped him. Not looking behind her, almost whispering, she said: " You must leave at once, Monsieur Simon. The Germans are in your flat and I've got two of them waiting for you in my lodge."

Simon said nothing but, turning, pretended to adjust the handlebars of his bicycle. Then, with a little run, he had gained the saddle and was off. He rode a hundred yards, sweating in the June sunlight, until he reached the Chaussée de la Meutte Metro station near the Bois de Boulogne before stopping short. For the first time he remembered that Girard and many of his colleagues were due at the flat after lunch. Unless he could find them and warn them, half a dozen of Century's leaders would fall unsuspecting into the trap.

Simon parked his bicycle and sat down heavily, a plump desperate man, under the green-striped awning of the Café de la Muette. He ordered himself a bock and thought fast. For civilised reasons that all who have done business in France will understand, he could not telephone: it was the " lunchhour," the sacred three-hour interval when no Frenchman whose digestion remains intact will be found near his office phone.

The meeting was timed for two-thirty. Simon thought that the bulk of those attending would be travelling to the Metro station direct from their favourite restaurant.

He knew that he had to sit tight. The extreme left-hand table where he sat was exactly opposite the Metro's exit. He could see the steps, framed by a green frieze of plane branches. For more than two and a half hours, while the Gestapo waited for him with mounting impatience only a hundred yards away, he stuck it out under the awning with the sweat pouring down him. To make matters worse, the café stood by a crossroads with traffic lights and every few minutes velo-taxis, bicycles and German Army wagons came to a halt, blinding his view for throbbing, sputtering minutes before grinding forward again. Simon thought that he aged a little that afternoon.

Then punctually at two-thirty the well-groomed figure of Lamoureux de la Saussaye, the gaunt scholarly head of Century for the Le Mans district, breasted the steps. Only by frantic signals did Simon manage to attract his attention, then rose to grasp his bicycle. He muttered " Gestapo in my flat. Tell the others. I'm off." Then he pedalled off into the afternoon sunshine to seek the first of many temporary refuges before he reached England and safety. So the chain proceeded. Saussaye waited until Girard stumped into view, then he, too, vanished. Girard eased his bulk into a wicker chair until he had warned Colonel Touny; Touny stayed to warn " Colonel Personne." An hour later, uneasy, but still marvellously alive, they were all gathered in what by previous arrangement was their alternative meeting place: Berthelot's office, camouflaged as a freight-carriage service in the Place Madeleine.

All except Moulines. The meeting had only just started when they realised the young aristocrat was missing and Girard felt a constriction of the heart. But while they were still discussing whether to send out scouts Moulines strolled in. Instead of taking the Metro, he had as usual come on his battered old bicycle and run clean into the Gestapo on the staircase. He had been seized and searched, only escaping arrest by explaining that he knew a blonde in the building.

Someone remarked that it wasn't a bad alibi, but might have gone badly awry if the Gestapo had checked up, and Moulines, looking a shade self-conscious, cut in: " Yes, but you don't see the point. *They* did and *I* did—and actually I'd known her for years." All of them just looked at him, and the meeting proceeded according to plan.

In London, Dewavrin had word of the disasters, and was forced to harden his heart. Bitter experience was teaching him that one day you could know men like Moulin and Delestraint and then suddenly, by an abrupt and inexorable process, the Gestapo struck and if you wanted to sleep you no longer thought of them at all, in case you pictured not the friends you had loved but men whose physical appearance was now an outrage before God. B.C.R.A. had statistics on it now: if a man was arrested, 55 per cent of all those he had known were also swept into the net. Dewavrin was now forced to the bitter logic that much of the Secret Army and many of the agents would be expendable but he could not waver. At least the communications network was still intact. Two substitutes, Captain Serreulles, de Gaulle's former A.D.C., and Bingen were smuggled across the Channel as temporary replacements for Moulin and General Delestraint. At the same time the men who made up the living map were urged to concentrate on certain specific factors.

Back in February the German propaganda mouthpiece had trumpeted throughout Normandy, " The installations on the sea front and inland together constitute an impregnable fortress! " As source they quoted Field Marshal von Rundstedt, who was then engaged on an inspection of the Wall, though von Rundstedt had made no such claims. Instead he had warned that the Wall was valuable for fighting as well as propaganda purposes but " it must not be believed that the Wall cannot be overcome."

To him the Wall had little surface and no depth; it was depth of defence that he wanted, above all, so that even if the enemy broke through the outer crust, there would be fire-power to hold him long enough for a decisive massed counter-attack. When Hitler assigned priority to those parts of the Wall defending rocket-launching sites, he urged the same point in a report to the Fuehrer. Hitler did not listen. He had ordered an impregnable wall to be built and if it was impregnable enough the enemy could be stopped at the water's edge. That ended the matter.

What interested Dewavrin more than concrete (" as an ex-professor of fortifications," he told Renault, " I don't believe in them! ") was radar. The German's radar had advanced a long way from the early days and Girard found himself pressed to furnish up-to-date details. The chance came late that summer, when Gilbert Michel, the cement contractor, no longer travelling to Cherbourg as a hostage but now Todt-appointed liaison man on *Service Social des Chantiers de Travaux* (social service at work-sites), found himself in an enviable position that Dewavrin had long foreseen. He was told to help build a radar station.

German radar coverage for shipping and aircraft detection had been adequate, if limited, at the end of 1941. Now several new types of detectors were being brought in, of greater range and accuracy: the giant Wuerzburg (like a big inverted electric-bowl fire), the chimneys (like steel versions of that useful item) and the big latticed hoardings. Some of these could pick up aircraft at a range of forty miles. Warships approaching the coasts of north France would register blips on the screen twenty-five miles away. Girard and Michel thought that the three powerful posts the Germans were siting, one mile inland from the Wall on a high triangle of ground near the village called La Délivrande, were likely to prove a thorn in the Allied flesh.

As things turned out, the keynote of the La Délivrande project was glorious lethargy. Officially, Michel was interpreter and liaison man for the French labour corps, whose total strength was 120. But of these only twenty—never the same twenty—reported for work each day. And each day, up on the site at La Délivrande, where the salt wind streaking from the Channel bends the hawthorns into lyre-shapes, Michel apologised endlessly to the Germans for the shiftlessness of his compatriots. He would like to see strong measures taken against these idle Frenchmen, who did not realise that Germany was their best friend. The man in charge, a slow-spoken, thick-witted *Schachtmeister* (Todt foreman), listened wearily, rarely noticing—or past caring—that Michel timed his apologies to coincide with the arrival of the lorries.

The lorries were supposed to unload their ten-ton cargo of Belgian cement before returning to the base near Carpiquet for more, and Michel talking, shrugging and apologising like a stage Frenchman, neatly hid the fact that three lorry loads of sand were being dumped for every one of cement.

What should have been a three-months' job was thus not entirely complete in the spring of 1944. This suited Michel. He wanted to observe each stage of the construction at leisure: the plotting-rooms, on the top floor of the two-storey building, sunk partly in the ground with concrete walls four feet thick, the operating cabin (armoured at the front, he noted, but not at the sides), the intelligence that 150 personnel were slated to man this post.

Piece by piece he fed these observations to the letter-boxes; week by week Jeanne Verinaud's fingers flew over the keyboard of the old Underwood typewriter, blending them into a report. Girard and Meslin were delighted. Such chances might come too rarely.

Along the Wall, other agents took up the tale. The Germans were setting up similar radar installations on an average of one every $4\frac{1}{4}$ miles (outside the ultimate invasion area, between Cap Blanc and Boulogne, it was thicker, an average of 1 every $1\frac{1}{4}$ miles). Cardron, the trawler skipper, reported one on the cliffs east of Arromanches; Franck's men reported another three miles north-east of St. Lô at the village of Bourg d'Enfer. The north coast of the Cotentin where Moulines had his men planted was a nearly continuous chain of them. In addition the coastal chain was being strengthened by new stations at interior towns like Vire and Bernay, an extension of the inland G.C.I. system.

These were the eyes and ears of the Wall, able to spark both coastal and flak defences into angry life against airborne and seaborne forces, and it would be hard, if not impossible, to neutralise them by jamming.

No matter how small the crumb of information, the risks were greater. Michel's radar station, for example. By day it was guarded by sentries, without road barriers, but the ruddy-cheeked contractor had no knowledge of the night defences. Then, before many weeks were out, Dr. Sustendal at Luc heard about the site and decided to make his own inspection. Such is the human element that had he known Michel was building it he would have left it alone, but he did not even know Michel, and it was not Girard's job to discourage one agent from unwittingly cross-checking and amplifying another's work.

As usual Sustendal had taken precautions: earlier that evening he had lanced an abscess in a farm cottage in the village of Fontaine-Henry. It was an airless August night, the cold pure light of the harvest moon bathing the white shocked corn. Thunder grumbled faintly in the west. Sustendal drove steadily, heading for the crossroads that connected the villages of La Délivrande, Beny-sur-Mer and Basly. On the high ground formed by the triangle he knew he would find the radar and that his road home lay right past it.

Suddenly a storm lantern flickered ahead: a barrier gleamed in the headlights. Careful now—he was almost there. The sentry of the *Schutzkommando* (camp security guard) came alongside, and the command slurred out: " Your *ausweis*." In the lantern light the man's forehead gleamed with sweat. The doctor's papers were scarcely out before the man gestured muzzily: " Go on, get out of it." And he realised for the first time that the sentry was ingloriously drunk.

He drove slowly north-east, not quite believing his luck, his mind tabulating impressions. The headlights washed briefly over man-made dunes of red earth—they were digging deep air-raid trenches, then, in the shelter of the hedges. Come to think of it, the barrier had been unusual—a heavy affair, like a steel gate on wheels, interlaced with triple-dennert barbed wire. That was worth studying! Would there be another one like it at the other entry to the camp? It would be like the Germans, so meticulous in some instances, not to bother. . . .

" *Halten!* "

He had nearly hit the second barrier head on! Another sentry stumbled towards him, waving a lantern. A thick porcine face and little glinting eyes thrust through the window.

A harsh liquid voice promising no quarter. "*Aush-weish*—don't try any tricks now. . . ."

"But I already showed them at the——"

The eyes narrowed. "*Aush-weish*, I said. . . . I know you tricky Frenchmen. . . ."

Sustendal, in one second of time, realised two things, which hit him like small successive shock waves. This sentry was, if anything, even more drunk than the first—but the worst, the most terrifying thing, was that the trigger of his Schmeisser machine-pistol had somehow become wedged against the lowered window. The man was slumped there, sneering, with all his weight on it, the trigger quivering and the muzzle trained at the doctor's heart.

He was sweating and dry-mouthed, his fingers no longer obeying the promptings of his brain, but somehow he managed to locate his papers and shove them through the window. Grasping them the sentry swayed backwards, taking the barrel of the gun with him. He was still mumbling to himself, the garbled insults of the gutter: "Stinking Frenchmen . . . don't even appreciate the benefits we've brought you . . . people who can't even keep your streets clean." Then again the clatter and the doctor's heart was stifling him: the gun was at the window again and slowly, slowly, the trigger was squeezing. . . .

He came to from an oblivion of prayer, and suddenly from three feet away there was a thundering of sound. "Go on! Get out of it before I hold you on suspicion . . . stinking Frenchman."

The sentry was so drunk that he had stumbled away, carrying the gun with him and now he stood swaying, making dry retching sounds as if he was going to vomit. Sustendal let in the clutch with a jerk and the old car moved away, going fast between the flat green acres of turnip fields.

When he was near Douvres he took stock and it seemed to him that out of that night's work one factor had emerged: the Germans had a new kind of mobile barrier across the camp, and the site was doubly blocked as well as guarded by night. The information, passed to Kaskoreff, would supplement

Michel's own and would find its place on a map drawn by
Douin, the Royalist (scale three inches to the mile), but
Sustendal did not know that and could take no comfort in it.
He drove on sweating with more than the August heat.

Duchez, too, was having trouble on his night journeys, and
the way he wriggled clear of it had the network's heads alarmed.
Both Girard and Meslin heard rumours that he was in the
habit of repeating his first success at the Todt Organisation,
and that sometimes, painting or papering at the Municipal
Museum, he would tuck maps or dispatches behind the pictures
in the art gallery until he had finished for the day.

Caillet, too, had a nasty shock one morning as he and
Duchez were passing the leaden equestrian statute of General
du Guesclin, which still commands the Place St. Martin.
Pointing upwards, Duchez chuckled: " Well, that's a horse
who's been well fed this morning."

Caillet tittered dutifully, then the sentence really registered
and he noticed that Duchez was looking like the cat who has
swallowed the canary. He said acidly: " Exactly what do you
mean by that? "

Duchez leered. " I was coming back after curfew last night
with some plans and it suddenly struck me I was going to hit
a control point before I got home. So I shinned up and hid
the plans in the horse's mouth, but I can get them after it's
dark to-night. Climb up and see if you don't believe me."

Caillet, outraged, declined to do any such thing.

Since April, Duchez had been taking great pains to perfect
another system that Century had been called upon to tackle—
organising an escape route for aviators. Several Century agents
now dedicated much of their time to sheltering airmen, or
acting as a spotter system during air battles: the doughty
Madame Vauclin, Janine Boitard, a tall and devastatingly
attractive girl with a husky voice and corn-gold hair, the
daughter of a local wine merchant, Léonard Gille, the advocate,
big Jean Chateau, and his bubbling little wife, Albertine,
Leblond, the police inspector, who sometimes got airmen
through road blocks by handcuffing them as " suspects," and

inevitably the Thomas family, who would have felt quite hurt if Duchez had left *them* out of it. Each took it in turn to shelter R.A.F. or American fliers for a few days, while others got busy collecting false identity cards, money and the right clothes for the journey. From Caen the escape route led through Paris to the Haute Savoie, where the Maquis led by the famous Colonel Roman-Petit gave them safe conduct to the Swiss border.

Only Duchez, however, had the bright idea that there was one place the Germans would not think of looking for aviators —inside a maternity home. The matron of the home at Benouville, a formidable old lady named Lea Vion, had become one of his most faithful allies.

All the same, the network was worried about Duchez. He was doing too much, organising too much, being seen in too many places. The patient and placid Odette, without revealing what she really felt, worried herself sick, as only a wife can. And she knew what others didn't: the invoices that were piling up in Duchez's dusty office at the back of the house, for the painter was too absorbed to send out bills unless she did it for him.

Time and again only Duchez's resourcefulness saved his neck from the executioner's block. On one occasion, after collecting two Polish flyers from Benouville, the painter was driving the maternity ambulance towards another refuge when he ran into trouble. A long line of cars jammed the road ahead. The *Sicherheitsdienst* had set up a temporary road-block and were checking all occupants.

His mind working overtime, Duchez slipped from the driving seat, and doubled round to the back. Five minutes later the ambulance drew abreast of the barrier. Duchez showed his pass but to no avail: two jack-booted sentries jostled past and flung open the door of the ambulance. Flung it open, and as suddenly recoiled.

In the back the Poles lay trussed as helpless as chickens, their hands behind them. Thick gags of towelling were wadded between their parted teeth. Their eyes bulged insanely.

" *Achtung!* " bawled Duchez. " Dangerous lunatics! "

196

In record time they had raised the barrier, and Duchez was on his way.

After that, so far as Century was concerned, the name " Duchez " had outlived its usefulness. To them, for ever after, he was " Third Fool."

When Meslin, as head of the Caen cell, heard of this and other palpable indiscretions, he sent for Duchez. There followed a long and painful lecture on the importance of prudence and discretion, which the seemingly chastened " Third Fool " heard out in silence. His eyes were fixed at a point on the wall, about a foot above and to the left of the Government engineer's head, and suddenly the old mischief was dancing in his eyes. His lips twitched with repressed laughter.

Meslin said crossly: " What are you grinning about now? It's no laughing matter and if only you paid more attention to what I've been saying . . ."

Duchez opened his eyes very wide. " But I have, Meslin, *mon vieux*. I heard every word. I'm not very discreet and I talk too much in cafés and I run stupid risks." He beamed. " And yet, you know, I'm not really such a fool. For example, I know where you keep the network's secret papers."

Meslin started as if he had been stung. " What? That's impossible."

" But not at all—merely a matter of professional observation. You keep them in this office, the third shelf of your big card-index cupboard, second drawer from the left. . . ."

Meslin had gone quite pale. " Duchez, I sometimes wonder if you aren't the devil incarnate. How could you know that? "

" Simple, *mon ami*. I'm a painter, and when I see roughly a hundred drawers and one above all where the paint on the knob shows constant signs of fingering, I might know what to expect."

Crossly Meslin told him to get out, but that night, Jeanne Verinaud remembers, he removed the papers from the office, took them home and hid them in his rabbit hutch. There was something about Duchez . . .

Danger was closer to all of them, though, than he and the

others suspected. Perhaps it was Odette who had the first inkling. It was a hot still morning, Duchez had been gone some hours and Odette, in the living-room, was busy with house-work. Through the open window there drifted the voices of children at play. Her daughter was among them. It was good, she thought, to have them off one's hands for an hour or two at least.

Then she stopped short. Outside she heard her little girl's voice and no words of hers can ever describe the cold agony of fear that seemed to shrivel her heart, as the three-year-old Monique's piping came treacherously shrill and insistent, from the sunny pavement.

" Your house hasn't got a name like our house," Monique was calling. " *Our* house is called the Deuxième Bureau."

Chapter Fourteen

A WALL HAS EYES

For a moment Odette stood appalled. Then, forcing herself to be calm, she opened the street door, and descended the worn stone steps to the pavement. She called, " Monique! Come here a moment, *chérie.*"

Half a dozen pairs of childish eyes watched her with the polite hostility reserved for adults who intrude unwanted into a world of make-believe. Among them, with a sinking heart, Odette recognised the little girl who lived along the street— in the house next door to the Gestapo officers' billet.

Odette said, " Come inside a moment, *chérie*. I want you to help Mama." Then, smiling with what she knew was false brightness, she took the plunge. " What sort of game have you been playing this morning? "

" We've been playing houses. Our house is the Deuxième Bureau. I heard Papa say so."

Now was her chance. " *Mais non, ma petite,* you didn't understand properly." She turned to the other children, sharing the secret: " At home, you see, we have a game—each room is a different bureau. The living-room is the Premier Bureau, the kitchen is the Deuxième Bureau, the bedroom is the Troisième Bureau. Each room, you see . . . a different bureau . . ." Her voice faltered and died; the children stood and stared, saying nothing. They were not fooled that easily. The deadly significance escaped them, but it was imprinted on their minds now, and they would wonder why Madame Duchez was anxious to pretend that her house wasn't called the Deuxième Bureau when so obviously it was. Children like to know the reason for things. They might ask their parents. . . .

And Monique was still repeating stubbornly, vexed at being

made to look foolish: " But, Mama, our house *is* the Deuxième Bureau. . . ."

Hastily, inventing some excuse, Odette let the child indoors. For the rest of the day she took care to keep her well within earshot. But the worry obsessed her: for how long? They could not keep her indoors for ever. You could not explain to a little girl of three that the lives of her father and mother hung on her weighing every word she let slip in play.

When Odette confessed her fears, Duchez did not assure her breezily, as he so often had done, that everything would work out right. He, too, saw the need to watch his words, even in front of his children, and from that moment he began to like himself less.

Whichever way you looked at it security was a problem. Some of the part-timers, like André Masseron, the big phlegmatic pork butcher, from Bretteville-sur-Laize, preferred to commit nothing to paper, and almost every day Masseron called with fresh information on the bomb stores or the petrol tanks at heavily-guarded air bases like Carpiquet and Fontenay-le-Marmion. (One of the first requirements of the invasion planners was to neutralise all airfields within 150 miles of the Normandy coast, so that the Germans were operating from air bases as far back from the Wall as the English bases used by Allied planes.) Masseron, who held the contract to smoke the Germans' pork, was the most popular man on these airfields, and no one awaited his verbal bulletins more eagerly than Duchez.

But now Duchez told Masseron and other agents like him: " Don't come to my house more often than you can help. Look for me in the Café des Touristes and if I'm not there, leave a message with Paul in the boiler."

Maurice Himbert, the courier, was still bringing the weekly questionnaire down from Paris and the queries were piling up on Meslin's desk. It was hard to observe more than average caution in gleaning the information, too, because Dewavrin's questions had an urgent hurry-up quality that brooked neither delay nor argument. For instance, in the last week of August, 1943:

TOP PRIORITY

Information is urgently required on the following defensive positions which you have already reported in the coastal zone:

1. The exact emplacement, and details of the blockhouses at HONFLEUR, particularly surrounding the railway station, the Chamber of Commerce and the Central Quay.

2. What is the limit of the minefields on the beach west of HONFLEUR? Are they anti-tank or anti-personnel?

3. State exactly the calibre of the battery situated at the entry of the harbour at DIVES.

4. Is Mount Canisy only fortified near BARNEVILLE, or near TOUQUES and south of DEAUVILLE as well?

5. South of MORSALINES you have signalled 7 blockhouses. Are these not rather platforms for artillery? Give corrections and precise details.

There were other questions, too, fourteen in all and for Meslin to issue instructions to his departmental heads, for them in turn to prod local agents, was a tedious nerve-stretching business. The Todt Organisation was building feverishly now: between the Bay of Biscay and North Cape, Norway, Hitler had 300,000 slaves working like beavers on his impregnable Wall—in one year they had shifted almost two million cubic yards of earth! But Dewavrin's scheme to enrol the Secret Army as agents had turned the scales in Century's battle to glean more and yet more detail.

Guns had ever-increasing priority in these questionnaires. To the Allies they counted more than solid concrete: each coastal battery covering the sea approaches held from two to six guns, and some could fire 12-inch shells by radar prediction, with a 360-degree range of fire. Moulines had his agents well planted in the Cotentin peninsula, where the concentration was thickest: the schoolmaster of St. Croix, Monsieur Richard, was reporting on the heavy batteries in the north, round Cap de la Hague, and another schoolmaster, an Alsatian named Unterreiner, kept watch on the batteries at Couville, south of Cherbourg. But all these men reported greater difficulty now in spotting the real thing. The Germans were beginning to camouflage them cannily, tunnelling strong points from the soft chalk of the bluffs, masking the telltale embrasures with pine branches and turf.

One that they knew a little about—and what they knew they feared—was in the wild heath country at St. Martin-de-Varreville, guarding the seaward approaches to what was later called " Utah Beach." Moulines badly needed more details on that battery, and in the nearby village of Ste. Mère-Église he singled out an electrician named Antonin Maury, a pink scrubbed-looking little man, full of old-world courtesy, who seemed more like the dean of a provincial university. Maury still recalls the afternoon he looked up because a shadow had barred his work bench, and there was Moulines, in his old leather jacket, standing in the doorway and announcing rather dramatically: " I am looking for a man loyal to General de Gaulle."

Maury replied with feeling: " Who isn't? " But in a few days he was an accredited Century agent, haunting the road that ran past the gun-sites near the tiny village of Ste. Mère-Église. Using Thomas's maps, it would not have been difficult for anyone to work out the actual co-ordinates of the sites, but Maury achieved what, even for Century, was a unique thing. He plotted the distance between each site of the six-gun battery without ever leaving his bicycle.

There was never time to linger: pedalling hard, he would pass one battery, two hundred yards distant across the rolling heath, and there were armed *Schutzkommandos* everywhere, waving him on, but he had no need to stop. He kept pedalling grimly on up the sheer twisting road, between the gorse and the pines, a pink perspiring Frenchman in a beret who could feel his thigh muscles knotting with the strain of the uphill grind.

Maury was checking every revolution of the pedals, to achieve the same effect of pacing as if he had walked.

Once, when Moulines dropped in for the night, as he so often did, to find a bed and check results, Madame Maury challenged him mock-severely: "Are you trying to turn my husband into a madman? Whenever I see him now he's rushing into the house muttering numbers to himself and scribbling them down on bits of cigarette paper."

What always presented a bigger problem was discovering the calibre of the guns: even a man on the spot needed luck for that if the sites were some way off the public highway. Usually Girard confined his men to finding out the artillery regiment, before unearthing the kind of guns they used from sources close to the Germans. But Maury managed it all on his own at Varreville, pausing for breath on his bicycle to say: "Big guns," appreciatively, every time they checked his pass. He employed this ruse a good many times without success, until an unusually dim-witted sentry, prompted by patriotic pride, answered: "*Ja, ja, gut*—155s—Tommies *kaput.*" After that he may have wondered what became of his little friend, the electrician, whose rides became noticeably fewer.

For the record Maury was in the train on the way to the office of Harivel, the insurance agent, on the Place St. Sauveur, Caen, wearing a disreputable belted leather jacket whose lapels were frayed beyond repair. Tucked securely inside the rents were rolled wafers of cigarette paper inscribed with the battery co-ordinates and the relative distances.

Where one man asking too many questions in the district would have quickly aroused suspicions, the presence of Girard's Secret Army troops in the Manche spread the risk evenly. Few except Colonel Nobody and his checkers in Paris could see the final picture building. At Varreville another agent, unknown to Maury, reported that the 150 men manning the battery were housed in a stone building on the east of the village of Mesières; a third, working on the site, helped distinguish the battery dining-room from the iron equipment hut.

The checking was so precise that when Dewavrin in London pressed impatiently for details on a small sinister

concrete structure that had sprung up on site, Moulines's men
had the answer within days. It turned out to be a shower
bath!

Just east of the village of Grandcamp-les-Bains, perched on
the rocky spur of Pointe du Hoe, the Todt Organisation had got
busy on what later proved to be the most lethally-sited battery
in the whole Normandy sector of the Wall. Obviously something would have to be done about those guns, perhaps even
a task-force raid in advance, so that what mattered most, as
urgent questionnaires informed Century's organiser, André
Farine, were the defences surrounding the defence on this
isolated bluff. Farine got to work with a team of forty men—
twenty Century agents, twenty Secret Army men—but the
first results were disappointing.

A strange man, Farine, and a contradiction in terms. Close
to forty, an ex-sailor with a brick-red face and a clipped
moustache who still walked with a nautical roll, he took a
perverse pride in being totally unamenable to discipline. " I,
André Farine," he would growl, " have seen the inside of the
lock-up in every port in the world. The Navy could do
nothing with me! " The discipline and patience he exercised
to plumb the secrets of the Pointe du Hoe battery earned him
the Croix de Guerre, though Farine would have knocked down
the man who laboured that point unduly.

Near Grandcamp, Farine kept the Café de l'Étanville, a
cheerful crowded brasserie that could accommodate a hundred
covers. Holding this trump card, he began to use his ingenuity.
First he applied for a licence for baking bread; then for
permission to travel inland and buy wood to fire his bread ovens.
Presumably nobody lost sleep over why he bought all his wood
from one farmer named Fouché, but it was more than coincidence that Fouché's farm was perched on the top of a high
hill called La Perruque (The Wig). From here, with the aid of
binoculars, Farine had a perfect view of the orchards and the
gentle green fields sloping up to Pointe du Hoe.

Now, using maps and binoculars and compass, cross-
checking with the church spire at St. Pierre-du-Mont, he could
work out the co-ordinates of the six-gun battery—but not the

calibre of the guns, they were too far away. There was a double network of barbed wire, too, superficially camouflaged to resemble hedges. The ghost of a smile creased Farine's brick-red face as he knelt in the coarse grass. A fine hedge that glittered like tinsel when the autumn sun caught it! The local gossip had it that those " hedges " were mined. The gun emplacements were very close to the cliff-edge, seeming to crouch above the naked rock, and Farine shook his head, troubled. He knew that beneath the cliffs the smooth tan sand stretched a long way, almost fourteen miles from Port-en-Bessein to the Iles St. Marcouf. If these guns were like some others of which he had heard tell, all those beaches would lie well within their range.

The questionnaires gave Farine no clue as to *why* the guns were important. No one, in any case, had yet christened those beaches " Omaha " or " Utah." With him, as with the others, it was a question of faith, and although he got the information that counted, after six months' patient inquiry, it would have covered no more than a page of typescript. Like Dr. Sustendal, he had to win the confidence of the reluctant young labourers of the S.T.O. On Sunday nights his café grew crowded and noisy, with a big iron stove in the centre of the room glowing almost red-hot, an accordion squealing jauntily from the bandstand as the labour corps youths and the village girls shuffled cheek-to-cheek in the murky twilight of the dance floor. German edicts forbade dancing, but there were few Germans in the area to enforce them, so Farine defied them cheerfully—to prove himself " beyond discipline " and to win the confidence of his customers.

Sometimes they formed a group round the shirt-sleeved proprietor and fed him information. It was as bad as he had feared—the guns were 155s with a blasting 25,000-yard range. Rumour had it that the batteries were to be stoutly manned—a guard of 125 shock troops and 85 gunners. As for the distance from the water's edge to the cliff base, that was easy, they had walked it many times—twenty yards—but what troops could scale cliffs over a hundred feet high, as high as a nine-storey building? The batteries and cliffs had been photographed many times, confirming this intelligence, before the 50th U.S. Rangers settled down to solving that problem on similar cliffs at Swanage in the Isle of Wight.

What caused Century even greater concern were the mobile guns. Behind the coast the Germans were building up a force of ultra-mobile 170s, with a range that even out-distanced the 155s—32,370 yards. Eight of them were spotted by Moulines's agents in the Cotentin peninsula and Jean Chateau reported a whole concentration of them not far from Caen, east of the Orne. One of which the Germans were particularly proud lived on a truck mounting in a railway tunnel behind Houlgate. It took malicious pleasure in sneaking in again whenever the R.A.F. came over to look for it.

In cafés the Germans boasted that these guns handled so easily that they need fire no more than two rounds from the same position. Two rounds! This was Duchez's area, and the painter knew enough gunnery to realise that this made effective counter-battery fire almost impossible. Eventually, after he had thought about the problem, he came up with a partial solution smacking strongly of psychological warfare. Long observation had taught him that one of the noisiest bees in the German bonnet was fitness—above all, the fitness of youth.

Doling out faked passes and papers he and Odette began recruiting large mixed parties of youngsters in their 'teens, owning cycles. At week-ends, when they put on track-suits and pedalled rhythmically along the sheltered lanes east of the Orne, the sentries tended to eye them benevolently and not ask too many questions. The sections of control-map hidden inside their handlebars helped them check weekly changes of position, the news being transmitted from the one permanent radio set that Century then possessed in Caen. Post Office workers had made it secretly to " Third Fool's " specifications and so far it had escaped detection in a unique hiding-place: the chimney stack on Arsène the plumber's roof.

Nobody, least of all Duchez, was getting much sleep now. For one thing Dewavrin was asking too many questions, and Girard, who received the questionnaires first, added some of his own. Troops were coming more and more to occupy his attention, for, given that " Third Fool's " map *was* the German defence plan, the location and quality of troops was the factor deciding any Allied estimate of strength. No sooner was there a hint of fresh troops being drafted to the coast than no cell along the Wall received any peace. What village were they in? How many were there, and what branch of the service? What transport did they have available and what kind of arms? What was the size of the unit and where had they fought? How, above all, was morale?

Century already knew the answers to many of these questions. They reflected the big problem haunting von Rundstedt, who also knew that the combat value of most Atlantic Wall units was non-existent. No matter what priority the Wall rated on paper, in practice trained and eligible men were needed on the Russian and Mediterranean fronts. The bulk of those left were a mixed batch of Mongols, Czechs, Poles and Austrians who had little stomach for the defence of *Festung Europa*. Most of the Germans were throw-outs from the Russian campaign with third-degree frost-bite—sixteen plus or hovering on fifty—and Mercader, who sold bicycles to them in Bayeux, estimated that there were no more than 1500 of these in the twenty-five miles of coast between Courseulles and Grandcamp.

To the observant French, small signs, viewed from a national standpoint, provided big clues. At Grandcamp, the " undisciplined " Farine watched a small group sipping their apéritifs in sombre silence while his wife cooked Sunday dinner in the kitchen. That afternoon he submitted a classic report: " The morale of the troops is low. They are *not* well-fed, reacting almost with anguish to the smell of kidneys stewing in cream."

The steadiest and most valuable information on troop dispositions and movements was coming from Aloyse Schultz. A big gangling man with prominent eyes, Schultz spoke French and German with equal fluency in the harsh accents of Alsace. The proprietor of a small radio shop in Vaucelles, a working-class suburb south of the Gare Centrale at Caen, he had been recruited by Chateau, the electricity-board inspector, because his basement seemed a likely place for a transmitting post. After a few weeks, Chateau asked Schultz how he got along with the Germans. Schultz said he got along so well that they came in parties to his basement to listen to the radio.

Chateau said incredulously: " To the radio? Can't they listen to the radio in their barracks? " And the big ungainly man replied seriously: " Well, yes, old friend, put that way, no doubt they can, but I don't suppose they can listen to the B.B.C."

Many Germans passed through Caen on leave. Some came from as far afield as Cherbourg—to see girl-friends, to look up old comrades in other units, or merely on their way to the fleshpots of Paris. Now, by word of mouth it was spread that a Frenchmen in Caen who spoke German " like one of us," did a marvellously cheap and efficient job of repairs on portable radios.

Of course you had to wait your turn, so many other Germans went there, and the cursed Anglo-American raids meant that delivery of spare parts was slow but all the same . . .

" I'd like to promise it'll be ready by the time your leave's up," Schultz was saying a dozen times a day, " but if you're only here another two days . . . Tell you what, why don't you let me send it? Give me more time and I can do a better job."

" Well . . . yes . . . all right, I will. I can rely on you? "

" Never yet, *mein Herr*, have I let a German officer down. Now let's see, it's Leutnant Keppel, of course, and you're at——? "

" La Rivière, just up the coast."

" La Rivière, of course. And I'd better have the unit, Herr Leutnant, just in case . . ."

" Why, yes. Stupid of me to overlook it. 441st Ost Battalion will find me, Monsieur."

In this way Schultz was able to deliver a score of radio sets each week—and a score of unit locations for onward transmission to London. Franck, the Alsatian schoolmaster, secure in his job as interpreter at the Prefecture in St. Lô, or Jean Augé, the bald dapper little stationmaster at Caen, did their bit too, but with greater difficulty. Augé, for instance, knew how many wagons were taken up by a division of infantry, but with forty troop trains rattling through Caen daily, he was bound to miss a good deal. Movements orders were one check but later, to create a false show of strength, the Germans issued false movement orders for the benefit of railway Resistants.

But in such humble cases as Leutnant Keppel's radio, Century had the surest check of all. Either he gave Schultz the right address or he never saw his radio again.

No one could quite explain it, but despite the triumphs there was fear in the air. The fear was infectious, though hard to analyse. A man afraid for his life finds many fears blending violently into one. The fear of the knock at the door, a daily fear, prompting the unspoken racing questions. The milkman? The leather inspector, calling to check how many shoes you had? Or the men you feared more than death, who wore neither black nor field-grey, but gentlemanly raincoats and green pork-pie hats.

Often enough they searched your home, defiling it systematically in the process. You were too numb, too sick with hatred, to know fear then, but if they found nothing, the fear worsened. They could so easily have stumbled on it—so now you feared the next time. There would *be* a next time. You knew that. When it came, you feared the torture, but supposing you survived the torture, bleeding and outraged, the worst fear mocked you in the cattle trucks on the journey to the concentration camp. The hollow twisting fear that it had all been for nothing, that you would never survive to share in the better life which had made the shock and the agony endurable.

No doubting now, in the autumn of 1943, that the Gestapo suspected something. They were putting out feelers. Three times they came to Sustendal's little surgery behind the windswept promenade at Luc-sur-Mer. Each time the interrogation, conducted by the infamous Einst, dragged on for hours. Sustendal, startled, found they remembered more of his journeys than he could. For instance:

" Four times between the 1st and the 5th September you visited Courseulles-sur-Mer, Doctor. Why? "

And Sustendal would look vague, tugging his scrubby moustache. " Well, gentlemen, you know more than I do. I shall have to check. . . ." He had been gauging the length and depth of the minefield along the seashore, of course, but luckily the alibi was there in the big leather day-book: an old lady with suspected bronchial complications.

Einst knew all about that, and knew, too, that the prescription had been delivered to the pharmacy on the evening of the first visit. So why three further visits? And why such frequent visits to Colleville-sur-Mer.

Always the day-book was the staunch friend, cloaking the real motive; always, too, the Gestapo had checked the prescription at the pharmacy. By a stroke of luck they did not search the house, but the questions were too near the bone to reassure. " You're up to something, Doctor," said Einst unpleasantly, when they left. " I wish I knew what."

Within days Arsène, the argumentative plumber, was searched—perhaps because an officer at the *Kommandatur* unwisely asked his views on current events. With the Germans Arsène rarely smiled like Duchez or feigned camaraderie. His hate was violent and uncompromising. The lank black hair flopping across his forehead, that unsubmissive man answered: " If every Frenchman thought like me, there'd be one German hanging for every cider apple ripening in Normandy." A long shocked silence followed his words. Next day the Gestapo searched his house.

They searched three times in as many weeks. They tore up the parquet with chisels and almost wrenched apart the lavatory cistern. His wife and children were terrified. But Arsène stood there smiling maliciously, unafraid. He despised the " thoroughness " of their searches because they stopped short of real intelligence. They tore up his parquet but left his roof alone; their pigeon-hole minds could not envisage a man transmitting from behind a chimney pot. They knew so little plumbing that they never spotted the false compartment close to the spigot in which he hid his maps.

In those days the burly Torres, Century's security officer, was coming often to Meslin's office. To make Century's security watertight, they held long dicussions. Agents were warned afresh to use the dictionary system of memorising names. Fierce ingenuity went into plotting new hiding places for control maps. Roger Deschambres, the melancholy red-haired plumber, packed his into a lead pipe and sealed it, before attaching it to a windlass and letting it down into his well. Maury, the electrician of Ste. Mère Église, scraped the cement bindings from the stones in his rockery, lining it with maps instead; Gresselin, the Cherbourg grocer, buried his in flower-pots. From police headquarters Leblond, the young inspector, supplied a list of collaborators for guidance. It was guaranteed authentic, since the Gestapo themselves had compiled it.

If some on the list died suddenly and violently after making contact with Century they had themselves to blame for picking a risky profession.

Torres issued fresh instructions: beware of using any new cafés as rendezvous. The Gestapo were wiring some with concealed microphones. Distrust friendly " priests " who claimed to shelter Allied aviators: this, too, was a favourite way of infiltrating a stool-pigeon into a group. Beyond a certain point, trust of anyone was at a premium.

Torres's security was good on his own account, so good that Meslin offered his congratulations. That morning, talking to another of the network, Pierre Faure, head of the Premier Bureau, responsible for screening personnel, Meslin had asked: " What do you think about Torres? " Faure, a neat greying little man like a well-groomed mole, hedged, " What do you mean, what do I think of him? " " Well, where do you think his interests lie? "

Faure knew Torres only slightly, but his girth and gar-gantuan appetite were a local source of wonder. (The Germans' greatest drawback, he complained, was that they ate too many vegetables and not enough meat.) " Apart from eating and talking," said Faure frankly, " I don't imagine his interests lie anywhere at all."

Meslin never forgot it. But so complex is the mind of man

that Torres was torn between pride in his own camouflage and indignation at the slight on his war effort.

From London Dewavrin had urged the whole of the French Resistance to concentrate on planned decentralisation. The arrests of General Delestraint and Jean Moulin had made that need plain, and there was no sign of " Operation Grand-Duke " slackening up. Early September had seen a heavy wave of arrests in Paris, and the overall morale of the Resistance was perilously low. If Century's Intelligence work, backed by the Secret Army, was going smoothly, this was because the agents along the coast were not yet compromised. Brossolette, that dark dynamic man, was sent back to Paris with Yeo-Thomas to put the whole organisation on a business footing. Central control would remain vested in Paris, but sabotage and shock· troop organisation would now be controlled regionally, and have independent contact with London.

As yet there had been few arrests in Caen, but Girard was worried. In the first week of September the Gestapo unearthed an arms dump at Falaise, twenty miles away, and twenty-two members of the Secret Army were arrested. Then, at Lisieux, too, an arms dump was discovered, and the arrests snowballed. Comby, the coal merchant, reported that the office on the Place Saint-Sauveur was being watched: Normandy Peat Cutters Inc. was under suspicion. Through Meslin, Girard sent instructions that Comby and Robineau, the rather rash young man who had charge of the arms dumps, should disappear.

To plan the decentralisation scientifically, Girard held long discussions with Brossolette, Berthelot and Colonel Touny. The work that Century alone was performing—the mountains of maps, papers, and weekly reports on morale—was now awesome to contemplate. Colonel Personne estimated that Himbert, the courier, brought him about 7 lb. of papers—a pile three and a half inches high—from Caen each week.

Through his contact with the Post Office, a man named Ernst Prouvost, Touny arranged that after checking by Personne and his aides, Century's reports should now merely be passed to the C.N.D. for addition to their dispatches and collected by a Post Office van. Travelling under the blameless cover of Post Office sacks they would be routed as ordinary mail to an agent called Troalen, at Concarneau in Brittany. There, under the supervision of the gruff Alex Tanguy, they were loaded aboard the *Deux Anges*, and brought in the manhole of the fishing boat to its rendezvous with the N51.

The despised little *Deux Anges*, which began her war service with Renault, had now completed about seventeen voyages for Century.

There was urgent need to revise more than the courier service. So much information filtered through Caen that if Meslin's headquarters was hard hit Century and Secret Army work would suffer badly. Touny gave Girard urgent instructions to create new Secret Army cells at Rennes, Angers and Le Mans which could not only recruit local agents but serve as alternate transmission centres between the Wall and Paris. The headquarters would be sited if possible at Le Mans. The gay Moulines was to take charge of all Intelligence work in these areas, with Dany acting as a liaison agent between Girard and the local heads. Meslin would continue as head of the Caen cell, with Gille as his deputy on military matters and " Third Fool " Duchez handling Intelligence.

On Wednesday, 8th September, Girard and Dany were booked to depart for Le Mans and set this ambitious programme in motion. But at the last minute a conference was called in Paris with two Secret Army delegates who had just arrived from London, Abeille and Kemerer. Touny had arranged the meeting in the " safe " apartment of Madame Wastel, an imperious old lady who was also one of Farine's agents at Grandcamp.

At two that afternoon, on the fifth floor of No. 29 rue Claude-Bernard, the meeting began. Touny was presiding and Girard, Berthelot and Moulines had also been called to the discussion. The subject under review was D-Day; all of them were convinced now that next spring must bring positive results, but a close observer might have detected that on this mellow afternoon Girard seemed to have little interest in " The Green

Plan " or " Operation Turtle." At intervals his eyes half-closed and his thick fingers beat a slow, soft tattoo on the arm of his chair—a sure sign that he was ill at ease or bored or angry.

Watching him, Moulines wondered idly which. Suddenly, almost rudely, Girard's voice cut harshly across Touny's words. " Moulines! Get downstairs and check with Dany. I have a hunch that something odd is going on."

The young count felt faintly rebellious. Between Madame Wastel's apartment and the street level where Dany was keeping watch were five flights of steep dark stairway and the building had, moreover, no lift. Hazarding that Girard would scorn premonitions, he tried to laugh him out of it. He said: " Come on, *patron*—you've never believed in hunches before." Then, with a shrug of the shoulders, " I still don't."

Girard rasped, " Young man, I am not asking your advice. I am giving you an order. Check with Dany. You'll find her on the street somewhere."

It was an odd trait in the prosaic Girard, one he rarely discussed, but he *knew* when something was wrong. Call it a gift, call it sixth sense, but often, like a dog, he could sense the footfall of danger long before a human ear could register the sound. Time and again, in war and peace, it had saved his life: this sense that everyone in the room or street had receded, and all time had ground to a halt, waiting. . . . Like the afternoon in 1917, when the battlefield was quiet and the trenches were full of small relaxed jokes, but something kept urging him, move, find cover, the shell landing three minutes later, just where he stood, and it was not him but a man he had known well who was now a pulp of blood and bone and hair.

But Moulines had never known of this and a score of other incidents. Cheeks burning, he strode from the apartment, and all the way down the steep stairway, he smouldered. *Mon Dieu!* But he'd have a word with the chief later—calling him to order like that in front of strangers. Since when had *he* taken to believing in hunches? From the doorway he surveyed the wide sombre street which linked the Latin Quarter with the working-class district of Gobelins, but nothing strange was in sight. Only Dany would be loitering somewhere.

He set off briskly up the pavement, arms swinging, and suddenly there was a light patter of heels and seemingly from nowhere Dany came running.

The encounter was not quite what he had expected. Suddenly her arms were round his neck, the cool grey eyes were looking into his, and as she kissed him, the delicious subtle scent of her perfume was in his nostrils. " Darling," he heard her cry. " Oh, but you were naughty to keep me waiting so long." And the susceptible Moulines felt his blood stirring. For a moment he thought, Why, I'd never thought of Dany in *that* way before. . . .

But only for a moment, because the level sympathetic voice he knew better murmured, " Thank God you've come. Any moment now something's going to happen. Walk, but don't look behind."

Chapter Fifteen

A NETWORK IS BETRAYED

HER WORDS registered then, and dazedly Moulines was walking beside her, fighting a gnawing curiosity to peer over his shoulder. The full implication was still hard to grasp: Dany still snuggling against his arm, talking loudly and (he thought) convincingly of how much she had missed him. Suddenly she tugged at his sleeve.

" Darling, look! I've tried all over Paris, but that's the one I want you to buy me."

Moulines looked and as he did so the panic gushed through him and the reality of the danger took on paralysing shape. They had stopped in front of the electricity showrooms at No. 45, and Dany was pointing and he was looking at the glossy refrigerator in the window, but across the street, mirrored in the window glass like an image in water, was the sight that really held him. A thick-set man in a raincoat and a green pork-pie hat with a small feather tucked jauntily in its brim, leaning in the optician's doorway, paying no attention, face half-screened by a copy of *Paris-Soir*. Too studiedly careless, too still.

Moulines felt his knees turn to jelly, but to give credence to the charade he bent to examine the price-tag. As loudly as possible, hoping there was some way out, he said, " Forty thousand francs is a lot of money," and then, " How long has he been there? " Her reply was so soft he could scarcely catch it: " About half an hour. I was worried to death; there was no way to make contact." The drawback of the meeting place, as both knew, was that it lacked a phone, but Resistants could not afford to quibble over the shortcomings of gift apartments.

" But how, Dany—*how*?" Still bending to the shop window.

" It was the chief. The man was waiting for him outside the Cluny Metro station. He tracked him all the way here. He would have gone for reinforcements long ago, but he's been hoping I'd give him a lead."

Moulines straightened up. Ostentatiously he checked the money in his wallet: a newly-wed husband half-persuaded by the little woman's blandishments. " We'd better split up," he said. " Somehow you must lead him off and give him the slip while I get back and warn the others."

But Dany was more practical. " How do we know which one of us he'd follow? If he follows you, the others'll be worse off than they are now." The Gestapo agent had tried so hard to escape notice, she explained, that he had walked ahead of Girard. When he turned around, Girard had disappeared. Unless the man had seen Moulines leave the building he was still uncertain where Girard had gone to ground.

" All right," Moulines decided wryly. " We'll go to the bank and draw out our savings for that refrigerator. Somehow we've both got to draw him away from here."

Arm in arm, strolling like lovers, they ambled along the rue Claude-Bernard. Several times, woman-like, Dany evinced a desire to peer into shop windows and make sounds indicative of feminine cupidity. Each window told the same tale: the strategy was working.

The man in the green hat was following, only now the distance separating them was growing less. He was not losing the advantage.

They turned left into the long slatternly rue Gay Lussac. At mid-afternoon the queues were still sluggish outside the food shops, shuffling in voiceless apathy for a stale haunch of rabbit or a withered lettuce. This was too slow, Moulines decided; stepping from the pavement he began urging Dany along the gutter, past the silent crowds.

He glanced back. A hundred paces behind, the Gestapo man was in the gutter too, stepping out doggedly, keeping pace.

They walked more quickly now, fear mounting. Once,

taking advantage of a sudden shining stream of cycles, they dodged across the pavement into the Boulevard St. Michel. Outside the Capoulade and the Luxembourg crowds of students argued passionately over bocks and the *commis* whisked the first leaves of autumn from the green painted iron tables. Green Hat crossed the street, too, negotiating the bicycles without difficulty.

For the first time there was anxiety in Dany's voice: " How are we going to get rid of him? "

" We'll have to head for a quiet neighbourhood where there aren't crowds," Moulines said. " Then he'll fall back."

By common instinct they turned right along the rue Soufflot, making for the grey mushroom dome of the Pantheon. From the quiet square surrounding the temple, the poor cobbled streets of the rue St. Jacques quarter, with the little tainted *bals* and the one-night hotels, drop between high houses to the river. In these narrow streets they would have a chance.

They began to hurry, half-running. The agent was only a few yards behind now; there was no more pretence. They turned into the great square under the lee of the Pantheon, and the thought jumped into Moulines's mind: it's a trap.

Fifty yards ahead a large black covered wagon was drawn up by the kerb. Looking back, they saw that Green Hat was no longer hurrying. As they watched he stopped short, pulled a whistle from his pocket and blew. The shock was like a physical blow: the whistle shrilling, the door of the van flinging open and men in plain clothes, half a dozen of them, jumping to the ground.

" Save yourself, Jacques," Dany shouted. " Don't mind me." And as she spoke and the men came at them in a spaced, dangerous line, she turned and ran. Without hesitation, Moulines dived into a side-street, his long legs eating up the distance. He saw a startled cat fleeing, and a dustbin rocked and crashed aside in his path. Rotting cabbage leaves, wadded newspaper and coffee-grounds cascaded across the cobbles.

Down the rue Valette Dany was running for her life. She was a tall girl running fleetly, but once as she rounded a corner, she skidded and almost fell; her high heels were betraying her.

Behind her the background music of the hunt bayed into life:
the frantic clattering of feet, the shouting, the wailing crescendo
of the whistle. Run as if all your life depended on it, because
it does, it does. Another corner now, the nightmare closing in.
Ahead of her the street slept in September sunshine: shutters
drawn back, the pastel shades of washing strung on roof-top
lines, no one in sight. Fear shapes the wits beyond analysis,
or why, of all the shops in that street, did she choose a dry-
cleaners? She never knew, but she dived in.

The shop was empty, a bell jingling faintly in the back
region, and then, somewhere in the plunging panic of her mind,
the old ingenuity was resurgent. Stripping off her coat and
turban she tossed them over the counter. Outside on the
cobbles the hard thunder of feet sounded. God grant, she
thought, that the owner doesn't come. She lifted the barrier,
passing behind the counter. Again the bell jingled: a man
hatless and sweating, dangerously flushed, his breath coming in
painful bursts.

Trim in blouse and skirt, Dany smiled inquiringly.

" Mademoiselle, have you seen a young woman in a green
coat and red turban? "

Try to look unconcerned now. " *Mais non, monsieur*—no
one at all." The door crashed to with his departure, and then
the colour flooded to her cheeks as the back door of the shop
opened. A hunched elderly woman was watching her in silent
inquiry.

Dany said quickly: " I'm so sorry—forgive my clumsiness.
I dropped my hat and coat over the counter and I came round
to pick them up."

She thought the woman eyed her curiously before saying:
" *Ce n'est pas trop grave, mademoiselle*—but cleaning nowadays
takes six weeks."

" Any time," Dany said. " Any time at all." And it was
all she could do to stop herself from shaking.

Leaving the shop, she turned away at right angles, back
into the anonymous bustle of the Boul' Mich'. By devious
means she made her way back to the rue Claude-Bernard, this
time approaching from the east. Once in the street she realised

that unless Girard and the others had read a swift warning from Moulines's absence it was too late. A black Citroën with German police markings was parked outside No. 29. So the Gestapo *had* seen Moulines leave the building. They had found the house.

From a doorway farther down she watched, too numb to feel the grief that she knew would follow. The few people who passed took one look at the car, then hurried on, heads bent, as if ashamed that they were powerless to help. An hour dragged by, but the Gestapo did not emerge, and as evening drew closer Dany shivered. At last five men came out, got brusquely into the car and drove off. God be praised, there were no prisoners; the concierge had kept silent. If they had found the right apartment they would at least have taken Madame Wastel. She felt sick with reaction and incredulous joy.

She rang the three-in-one apartment from a café to find Girard in a good humour. All had gone well. Scared by Moulines's sudden absence they had vacated the flat in a hurry, and while Dany and Moulines had played their dangerous game of hide-and-seek, Girard and the others had continued the meeting safely beneath the trees of the Luxembourg Gardens. Moulines, too, had lost his pursuers after a helter-skelter chase.

The three-in-one flat itself seemed safe. The concierge, who was reliable, had seen no suspicious strangers loitering nearby. But thereafter Girard never returned home without first phoning Dany to check that the coast was clear.

So far, so good, but Girard saw the need for decentralisation as more urgent than ever, and on the morning of 10th September he and Dany travelled by train to Le Mans. Saussaye, the tall scholarly head of the Le Mans sector of Century, had given him the name of a contact there who he thought might be useful in starting a Secret Army cell: an ex-Army Intelligence officer named Colonel Becker, who had agreed to a rendezvous in a café near the station.

After the first twenty minutes' discussion, Girard felt his heart sink. Even in Le Mans you could feel the miasma of fear and suspicion, and from the frosty reserve with which he greeted them it was plain that Colonel Becker distrusted them on sight. A forceful, strongly-built man with iron-grey hair, he cut short Girard's arguments, saying: " I know nothing about you, Monsieur, nothing at all. And you can offer no satisfactory proof of your identity. I shall need something more than that to convince me that you're not working for the Gestapo."

And yet, Girard thought, it was only his own attitude of empiricism recoiling on him. " Make up a simple sentence," he told the Colonel. " Anything you like. For example, ' The sky is blue.' " Becker thought and said finally, " The snow is melting fast."

Girard said: " Right. In forty-eight hours listen to the 9 p.m. news bulletin by the B.B.C. from London. Afterwards the announcer will read a list of personal messages for the French. Yours will be amongst them."

The sentence was relayed without delay and the day afterwards, 12th September, Becker joined the Secret Army. Now his first task was to build up an organisation akin to Meslin's in Caen, and under the cover name of " Baron " he set inquiries on foot through the Underground. The search presented one unforeseen problem. Nine days later, when Girard returned to Le Mans, impatient for results, Becker was bewildered

" It's much harder than I'd thought," he complained. " I made half a dozen discreet inquiries—all to people who only know me as ' Baron '—and they promised to scout around and find me a good deputy. Now all of them have come back and told me the best man to get in touch with is some fellow called Colonel Becker."

Despite such setbacks, Girard's reorganisation went on. He shuttled between Paris and Le Mans and Caen, busier than ever, adding fully-staffed auxiliary cells in Rennes and Angers under the leadership of an ex-regular officer, General Audibert. A military adviser, General Robert Marasse, covername " Surlaut," was appointed to keep Secret Army plans in step with the strategy of Allied invasion headquarters. Lamoureux de la Saussaye was given the job of co-ordinating all their activities on a civilian level. The primary responsibility of all these men was organising Secret Army troops for D-Day in Normandy and Brittany, but due to their efforts, details on troop movements, factory output and munition depots eighty miles inland from the Wall were steadily pipe-lined to London.

Girard held conferences with each of them as often as he could, exhorting, encouraging, pressing for more information. The head of his Argentan cell, a cheerful electricity board inspector named Robert Aubin, recalls: " Because he had to be everywhere at once, you didn't see Girard often, but he only had to visit occasionally to make you feel that he was always there backing you up. It was as if he passed on to you something of his strength and his sense of humour and helped the job to go along more smoothly."

And the meticulous Jacquemin, in Le Havre: " I'd been waiting a long time to get into the Resistance, but I'd made up my mind that when I *did* get in, it would be under a chief I could rely on. When Pierre Faure approached me at the end of '42, the first thing I asked was, who ran the network. ' Girard,' he said. ' I'll tell you more about it. . . .' But I said, ' That's good enough for me, I'm in.' When you'd known Girard as long as I had, you knew you could give him your trust. "

Everyone felt this quality of leadership, though none could pin it down more precisely. Part of the clue, perhaps, lay in the simple fact that although Girard travelled almost everywhere in a rumpled sports coat and flannel trousers he saw himself always as a soldier in uniform, under orders. Outwardly he scoffed at himself as a " mothball soldier," but secretly, perhaps, he found comfort in being a link in a chain of command, and sometimes to Dany and Moulines he talked wistfully of the glories of being a Commando. " Stepping ashore in a battle with a hail of fire all round you. . . . What a war that would be." Because he, who led the secret Resistance of 7,000 men, hated the secrecy. He, who in business broke through the tangled skein of verbiage and got results, hated the slowness, the uncertainty—" never seeing the end of the work I was doing."

If he drove others hard, he drove himself harder, sleeping

uneasily, often, when money was short, making do with little food. As he saw it, the way to a planned Resistance capable of administering a stunning shock-punch on the day of reckoning was to live as a soldier, single-minded, ascetic, with the Atlantic Wall as your own front line—an almost Teutonic view and that was part of his secret, too. But if he was quick to blame, he was quick to praise, and a brusque word was soon forgotten. The one thing he stamped on utterly was when an agent began nourishing fancies about the romance or gallantry of his job. To one such he boomed furiously: " You see some men down the road putting up a blockhouse and then come and tell me about it. What is supposed to be difficult or romantic about those simple facts? "

The transmitting facilities, too, came under his eagle eye. With " Operation Grand-Duke " focussed on Paris and arrests swelling weekly, Dewavrin's former conception had outlived its usefulness. There was now little point in concentrating the transmitters in the Paris suburbs when it was Century-cum-Secret Army units receiving arms drops or observing troop and shipping movements along the Wall who needed the sets on the spot. If they could radio London that a drop was " on " or that a battalion had moved within a few hours, that gave the Allies time to act on the information whenever necessary.

That autumn he appointed a new transmission chief for the region, Jean Chibeau, and the stock of transmitters along the Wall began to build up. Four in the Caen area alone—on Arsène's roof; in the cellar of Schulz, the radio merchant; in the house of one of Duchez's workmen, and in the hayloft of a farmer called Roger Savard, seven miles out at Anisy. Westwards towards Cherbourg other transmitters were housed, at Bayeux, Grandcamp and Ste. Mère-Église, in the attics or cellars of Mercader the bicycle merchant, Farine the café proprietor and Maury the electrician. Only Gresselin, in Cherbourg, was without transmitters: the neck of the Cotentin peninsula was too narrow, an easy target for detectors, and the ever-present radar created an insuperable barrage of static.

For Girard's men the tension did not slacken. There were

small incidents, unimportant at the time, which seen in retrospect were like the first faint twinges of pain that betray the fatal sickness.

There was the incident of the Typewriter, when the Germans almost stripped aside the protective camouflage of security which Meslin's work as Government engineer gave the Caen cell. As usual, Jeanne Verinaud was typing the dispatches whenever she could sandwich the job into office hours. Drawn blinds, a light glowing late, only built up suspicion. One afternoon, when Meslin was away, she was alone working on a dispatch which Gresselin had sent through from Cherbourg a week earlier. Her fingers raced over the keys of the Underwood.

" Electricity Supply, Cherbourg Arsenal.

> Following an inspection by a German Admiral, the French engineer in charge of supply has been warned that it would be fatal for this post to run short of coal. It is the only one to furnish distilled water to five Atlantic submarine bases. . . ."

The door opened and Karl Hoëfa walked in.

The girl went on typing almost by instinct, knowing that the worst thing was to betray either fear or surprise. With any luck, seeing that Meslin was absent, the Port Commandant would only pass the time of day before leaving. But Hoëfa didn't. He sat down in a chair facing her, a little to her right, and lit a cigarette. She did not think he could see the paper in her machine. But she wasn't sitting where he was, so she couldn't be sure.

She did her best to seem polite and helpful. M. Meslin was in Honfleur. (Thank God Gresselin's scribbled notes were on the desk to the right of her machine.) Was there no chance he would be back? She made a dubious secretary's face. " Well, I'm very doubtful. . . . He didn't seem to think . . ." She had almost eased the paper from the roller when the tall blond young man craned forward. " But Mademoiselle——"

" Yes, Commandant." Her heart was beating so fast that it hurt her.

Dr. Jacques Sustendal outside his office

Eugène Meslin, government engineer at Caen

Janine Boitard, now
Madame Gille

Jeanne Verinaud at the machine which typed Century's
despatches. In the filing
cabinet were kept Meslin's
secret papers

"I am disturbing your work. Please, please go on with your typing."

Jeanne Verinaud thought, "I can't say I've finished it, even from there he can see the sheet is only half-filled. . . ." Reluctantly she ratcheted the paper into the machine. Would he notice it was a different make? Or ask her what she was typing? In either case she would not know what to say. She could only keep typing and hope.

Smoking and chatting Hoëfa sat on. Apparently he was intent on nothing more than enjoying the society of a pretty girl and a chance to relax. He was not, she knew, a very ardent Nazi; before the war he had been National Skating Champion of Germany, Meslin always said you could talk to him like a human being, but that afternoon, conscious that he was a German and a patriot, she did not seem able to talk to him at all.

He would not go. He talked and smoked and would not go.

She began to hate the sound of her own voice, absurdly stumbling and faltering. Supposing he got up and looked over her shoulder? Sometimes in the past he had done that, but only when she had been typing office minutes.

He lit another cigarette. He would not go.

She had to type twenty-nine lines that afternoon. It seemed like ten times the number. Towards four o'clock Hoëfa got up, bowed slightly, pressed her hand in farewell, then turned and went out. She sat there for some time before she could go on working. She knew that it was all right. Nothing was going to happen; they were safe. But it had been close—very close.

There was the incident of the Transmitter at Ste. Mère-Église. In that village Madame Maury, the charming, self-possessed wife of the electrician, had always felt safer than the wives of some Resistants. She had a Gestapo man billeted in her house. (After he had gone to bed each night, Georges, her small son, made a solemn ceremony of spitting in his boots.) But his presence was comforting, because it seemed to afford protection from neighbours' gossip. The man went to bed early, too early to witness the stealthy midnight arrivals of Moulines on his old bicycle, and he was away from the house all day. He was unaware of Maury's twice-weekly transmissions on the training programmes and daily doings of the 2nd Battalion of 191st Artillery Regiment. Or so they had thought.

Madame Maury was the schoolmistress in the nearby village of St. Marcouf. One day that autumn, during mid-morning break, she saw the children huddled on the low wall of the playground watching something across the road. There was a wagon drawn up and peasants were being hustled brutally from their cottages; German troops and French *milice* were making a house-to-house search. The Sergeant of the *Milice* often exchanged jokes with the children and she called to him:
" What's the trouble, Sergeant? "

" No trouble, Madame." He came trotting importantly over the road. " Tell the little ones not to worry." He tugged his big cavalry moustaches, strong and protective, a devil of a fellow. " Confidentially, Madame, there are terrorists in the neighbourhood, but do not fear. We shall soon have them."

" Terrorists? " The quaver was not entirely assumed.

" Indeed, yes—terrorists who have somehow gained possession of a wireless transmitter. The devils are cunning —it's almost impossible to find them on a house-to-house search. But don't worry—in a few days' time they are sending one of the R.D.F. vans from Cherbourg and then "—he cracked his knuckles triumphantly—" we shall have them."

Suddenly the sergeant and the children and all of them trembled in a wave of nausea, but with an effort she pulled herself together. Two hours from now Maury would be climbing the wooden stairs to the attic above the workshop for the midday transmission. She imagined the panic glazed on his face if the soldiers suddenly crashed in, tearing him from the set and trampling it, setting on him with their boots and clubbed fists. . . . But she could not leave the school before twelve-thirty. To disappear suddenly, when the children had heard the conversation, would set village tongues wagging. At her desk all the rest of the morning there was only a cold coiled lump of sickness where her stomach had been. She was obsessed with the thought: Is it our turn now?

Nothing had happened when she reached home and that same afternoon Monsieur Laurence, the Mayor, accepted temporary responsibility for the transmitter. It would have to be shifted after each emission now. They had just gained a breathing space.

Now the first yellow leaves shivered from the trees, and at night a wet opaque bandage of mist hung above the waters of the Orne. In the orchards the mistletoe berries glowed white among the apple branches, a promise of Christmas. Workmen with good contacts drank a hot grog in their favourite café of a morning to guard against the pinching frosts. At home in the evening men thumbed surreptitiously through calendars and tide-books and argued and discussed endlessly. How could they glean yet more information? How could they throw off the German yoke? And when would the longed-for invaders come?

All of them felt it could not be long.

There was the incident of the First Arrests, which were so nearly the worst.

The reason for them was rooted in the visit that a priest, named the Abbé Luc, paid to the Thomas household in the last week of September, 1943. His was a routine request: an R.A.F. flyer, sheltering under his roof, needed identity papers. Like most others in the network, the Thomases held a stock of papers, not only for agents entering the zone, but for aviators and young men escaping to the Maquis. They gave the priest the papers he needed, but this time, when he left their house, the Abbé was followed by Helmut Bernard's Gestapo agents, arrested and searched.

The second day of October began like any other Saturday morning. Robert had gone early to work at the potato controller's office. The soignée, vivacious Marthe was at her desk in the Caen Prefecture and Jeanne was busy in Meslin's department. Both Papa Louis and Madeleine, the tallest and most outspoken of the daughters, had the morning off. At No. 22 rue Montaigu, breakfast was over. The old man roamed placidly round the living-room. Madeleine and Mama Thomas were busy in the kitchen.

At 10 a.m. came the thundering at the door. " *Aufmachen!* " (Open up!)

No one moved. Papa Louis stood rooted to the ground. In the kitchen, Madeleine and her mother consulted in frantic whispers. At last Madeleine went slowly to answer the door. She was half-way across the living-room to the hallway when Mama Thomas saw the maps.

They were lying on the scrubbed wood of the kitchen table, about half a dozen of them—copies of those that had already passed to Meslin's office for collection by the courier. Mama took in the situation at a frantic glance. Robert must have tossed them down when he left for work, having no time to burrow beneath the soiled linen in the laundry hamper and store them in the two attaché-cases that served as " box files." Bernard would give the Thomas family no quarter if the Gestapo found them. They would reveal the rambling old house for what it was: the branch office of an espionage service whose willing agents were numbered in thousands.

The old lady moved faster than she had ever done in her life. Madeleine was in the hallway now. The Gestapo was still pounding at the door. Trembling with emotion, she seized a box of kitchen matches. A yellow blade of flame sprang into life, but with anguish she saw that the tough cartographic paper only buckled at the edges, turning brown. The footsteps of the Gestapo were in the hallway. No good, no good. . . .

She grabbed the maps and ran to the coal range. A vegetable soup was bubbling gently in a big copper saucepan. Lifting the lid she plunged the maps into the pulp of cabbage and turnips, mashing them down with the ladle. For a moment the maps floated obstinately on the surface. Then they bubbled and sank from sight.

She stood trembling inwardly but very unbending and dignified, in the manner of the French matriach whose privacy has been violated, while Gestapo men in raincoats trampled through kitchen and living-room, spilling the contents of drawers on the carpet. Probing, rending and sorting. They looked briefly at the wicker hamper, then, with a gesture of distaste, turned away. They found bundles of identity cards and several stamps, including the stamp of the Chief of Police at Trouville. But no maps.

The senior Gestapo man said stiffly to old Papa Louis: " You and your daughter will come with us to the rue des Jacobins. Where are your other daughters and your son? " The old man lied that they were out for the morning, shopping in the town. It was obvious that a blanket order had gone out to arrest *la famille Thomas*, but as yet the thugs had not checked up on where the children worked. In any case, they would be found and brought to headquarters before the day was out.

To Mama Thomas the agent said: " Your presence is not required, madame. You will stay here and not attempt to leave the district."

Mama Thomas knew, of course, what the Gestapo intended. They were counting on the fact that human nature would rule out prudence and that, as soon as she thought the coast was clear, she would leave the house to warn others in the network. Bernard gauged correctly that few people are braver than the women of France. His mind failed to grasp that it is sometimes braver to do nothing at all.

It worked out a little differently.

Someone from the rue Montaigu—a woman neighbour, whose name they had never known—had already set off to alert Marthe Thomas at the Prefecture. When she heard the news the plump self-possessed Marthe lost no time. Leaving her outraged boss gasping, she ran through the city to Meslin's office by the Pont de la Fonderie. There she warned Jeanne, her sister. Jeanne went on to the potato controller's office to warn Robert.

But to persuade Robert that he would benefit neither the network nor do his duty as a son by giving himself up—that was a harder job. All morning Marthe and Jeanne sat miserably in a little café trying to reason with him. " You know so many people in the network," Marthe argued, " supposing they made you talk ? We hardly know anyone important, and even the few we do know are helping the airmen, not the maps. I'm sure it's because they think we're helping airmen that all this has happened."

But Thomas sat there, pale and determined, disputing it. All his instincts revolted at the idea of leaving his family in the lurch. All right, he said at last, he'd go, but first he had to get those maps out of the house. It took them another half-hour to talk him out of that. Somebody else must get them, Jeanne said. It would be suicide for him to go near the house again.

As it turned out, Jeanne was right. At the rue des Jacobins just then, the Gestapo were opening a dossier on the Thomas family and in the dossier, still extant, one sentence stands out clearly: " *It would appear that these people have been manufacturing false papers on an extensive scale, possibly with the complicity of the man Paul Berthelot.*" The Café des Touristes was also suspect, though Paul was never questioned; better to wait and watch, Bernard thought, and then to pounce. The Gestapo chief knew that he was dealing with amateurs but it never occurred to him that amateurs were other than clumsy.

" This," demanded a Gestapo official when Madeleine Thomas was led in for questioning. " Where did you get *this*? " Looking down, Madeleine saw the rubber stamp that she had stolen from her boss at Trouville. Without hesitation she lied: " I made it." The man tossed it contemptuously aside. " Just as I thought . . . and a clumsy forgery at that."

As for Robert, he had a lot to do and little enough time to do it in. Early that afternoon he rapped cautiously at the door of the small fisherman's cottage that Girard, who had given up the rue St. Jean apartment, now rented near the river, and Girard, by a stroke of luck, was there to let him in. His face was very grave when Thomas finished; he started to say, " *Mon petit*, I don't know what to say. . . ." And that was true, because for once in his life Girard didn't. Thomas had never seen the tough practical Girard so strangely moved, and when the big man just stood there with his face working, patting him rather absently on the shoulder, he didn't know what to say, either.

For the first time he had the strange thought that he loved Girard like his own father, and Girard, too, had a soft spot for Thomas. The cartographic service would go on, but it was Thomas who had nurtured it and improved on it and sapped his strength in its service. Now the boy looked sallow and ill and without the force to fight any further because in eighteen months he had drawn or collaborated on and supervised close to 4,000 maps—almost fifty a week!

After a spell Girard blew his nose violently, then said with his old energy: " But you've done enough, you know, Robert. I don't know how many maps you've done, but you've done marvels. But you won't be safe now, you know, wherever you go, and it worries me. I think you'd better go to England— I can arrange in Paris for a Lysander pick-up."

But on all counts Thomas rejected this violently. He said stubbornly: " I won't have that, chief. I'll go anywhere here you want me to but not England. I started my war in France and I'm going to finish it here." It was a brave and oddly moving little speech. Soon Thomas left and Girard urged him to quit Caen before nightfall.

Half an hour later Thomas was knocking on Arsène's door in the narrow working-class rue d'Auge. Arsène listened with glinting eye, because this promised action. " You stay here until after dark," he said. " I'll look after you, but first I'll look after your maps." Then, leaving his camionet parked outside the door, he walked out of the house.

For ten minutes he trudged steadily uphill, past the great grey cupola of St. Michel-de-Vaucelles, until he reached the rue Montaigu. The afternoon was still, with the sullen smell of rain in the air. The street looked grey and sombre, paint peeling from the shutters, few people about. The door of the Thomas's house stood half-ajar and Arsène hardly paused to see if anyone was watching. He walked in, through the hallway, through the deserted parlour until he reached the kitchen. Sunk in her private grief Mama Thomas heard a sound and swung round to see him standing there. His finger was at his lips, enjoining silence, and the cry of surprise choked in her throat.

Neither said a word. Quietly, grinning to himself, Arsène opened up the laundry hamper, burrowing beneath until he located the two attaché-cases. His one eye winked farewell, then with his beret set at a jaunty angle, he swung away down the rue de la Porte. Reaching the Cemetery of Vaucelles, he walked cheerfully with his attaché-cases among the white crosses and the rank grass of the graveyard until he came to the door of the crypt. Inside an empty tomb he found a safe repository for 400 of Century's maps.

It was then approximately 3 p.m. but the Thomas family saga was not quite complete. As Frenchwomen, Marthe and Jeanne had decided that they must surrender looking their best. After leaving Robert they went home to change into their smartest outfits, paying particular attention to cosmetics and hair style. Then, as gaily as if they were setting off to a dance, they waved to the gawping neighbours, strolled unhurriedly down to the rue des Jacobins and gave themselves up. All the Thomas family save Mama and Robert were now held in custody for further questioning.

That night, after dark, Arsène got out his camionet and drove fast between steeply wooded ravines to the village of Bretteville-sur-Laize, nine miles away. There he delivered Robert to the care of André Masseron, the big, phlegmatic pork butcher, whose plump pink face and relaxed air were so welcome on all the local airfields.

Masseron agreed to hide the young draughtsman in an upper room, and Arsène drove home again without incident. It had been quite a day.

A month passed. The men and women of Century had almost permitted themselves the luxury of forgetting to be afraid. Then came the incident of the Telephone Call.

Some time in the mid-afternoon of 3rd November the phone rang in Girard's Paris apartment and he answered it. Dany understood that Harivel was talking from Caen, but she could not gather much from what Girard was saying. He said: " I see . . . I see. . . . Yes, I see. . . . Thank you for letting me know." When he hung up he was very quiet, but after a minute, he said: " Harivel. Odette Duchez has been taken to hospital."

That was the cover-phrase the Underground used when they talked about a Gestapo arrest.

Chapter Sixteen

STORM IN THE WEST

How it happened is on record. Why will always be debatable. Some said the Gestapo's monitor service at the Central Telephone Exchange intercepted some injudicious calls made to Duchez by one of his agents. Others charged that " Third Fool " incautiously put his own name and address to a message concerning " seven pots of paint " he had delivered—meaning seven American airmen who had recently passed through the escape chain. Or perhaps the Gestapo kept a check on the movements of a " French-Canadian airman " who was picked up and sheltered by Duchez's spotter service until the R.A.F. radioed that the man's service and squadron numbers were false.

Shortly afterward the " airman " had left for Paris on a one-way ride.

Whatever his reasons, Helmut Bernard decided, early on 3rd November, that the most pressing item on the morning's agenda was an interview with Duchez. That was the worst day of Duchez's life; it brought the hardest decision he ever had to make.

Harivel had called at the house that morning; the calm dependable insurance agent was then acting as liaison officer between Colonel Corbasson's Troisième Bureau, which was carefully screening local targets for sabotage, and Duchez's Deuxième Bureau, which controlled the part-time agents. The children were spending a few days with Odette's brother-in-law, and it was easier to talk freely. But at last Duchez finished his coffee and clapped his beret on his bony head, telling Harivel, " *Allons, mon enfant, au travail.*" Then the knocking exploded into the silence.

Odette felt her heart like ice, void of anything but terror. So this was what it was like. For eighteen months, day and night, the fearful wonder had never left her, and now she knew. It was she who opened the door finally. As the Gestapo men shouldered past her, neither Harivel nor Duchez moved a muscle.

But the painter's brain was working overtime that morning, and in a swift look Duchez had sized them up. New men. He hadn't seen them in Caen before, so the chances were they had not seen him. (And the Gestapo did not carry dossiers or descriptions to the scene of their arrest: that was plain enough from the Thomases' experience.)

These thoughts lanced through his mind as the eyes turned to him, and suddenly, raising his beret formally to Odette, he said:

" Very well, Madame Duchez—since you have visitors, please tell your husband to communicate with me as soon as he returns."

The senior agent swung on him, a tall man with spectacles and a lisp. " Who are you? "

Suddenly " Third Fool " was all outraged probity. " I am Monsieur Dupont, of Dupont and Durand." He indicated the frozen Harivel. " My partner, Monsieur Durand. We have called to see Monsieur Duchez, but as you see, he is not in."

For one instant the man wavered and Duchez knew that he had him. But he asked suspiciously: " What's your business with Duchez? "

" We have come to complain about his work. Only two months ago he painted our offices and already the paintwork is peeling. The man is a charlatan and we shall sue him, monsieur, you will see. . . ." But the Gestapo man, losing patience caught him heavily by the shoulder. " *Raus! Schnell!* " Too dazed to fully comprehend that the ruse had worked Duchez and Harivel were hustled down the steps and into the street.

Once, as they walked, Harivel tried to say something but Duchez, shaking all over, cut him short: " Don't say anything . . . not now." At the corner of the street they separated.

Duchez made blindly for the café on the corner and flung open the frame door. Breasting the *zinc* he ordered a calvados from the *patron*, gulping the fiery liquor so fast that the tears were pricking his eyes. Then he saw two men standing farther up the bar, one of them eyeing him disapprovingly: Arsène, the plumber, whose views on alcohol were well known, who drank only coffee, lukewarm, because of digestive trouble, a tense fidgety man who could not sleep.

Duchez moved over to him. " Look, Auguste," he said, using Arsène's cover-name. " I'm in trouble . . . the Boches are in my house."

Arsène said sharply: " And Odette? "

" Odette's there." Duchez looked closer to a breakdown then than his comrades had ever seen him. " I left her—I had to. . . ." Arsène wasted no time asking questions. He swallowed his coffee and picked up his heavy bag of plumber's tools. " Stay there," he said. " Above all, show no fear." And he pantomimed a man shivering with funk. " You must be calm and smiling." He pictured a man being calm and smiling. " Drink your calvados like a man with nothing on his conscience and then go to my house and wait till I come." He took long innocent sips of an imaginary liquid, nodded once or twice to himself, then loped out of the café.

Outside the painter's house the police car was still drawn up, but Arsène did not hesitate. A man in plain clothes checked him at the door, but Arsène mumbled something about being expected, so the man gestured sourly and let him through. He got far enough to see the ugly chaos that had hit the Duchez's little parlour: blank identity cards stacked in untidy heaps, bureau drawers wrenched open, the portable radio receiver from the basement (thank God it hadn't been a transmitter!) and Odette hunched in a chair weeping bitterly.

Arsène started to explain about the central heating, but the man with the lisp ran at him, caught his shoulder and catapulted him down the short flight of stairs. Bruised and shaken he limped back to the café to find Duchez gone.

Just about then André Masseron, the pork butcher, drove in from Bretteville-sur-Laize and halted his camionet near the station. Ahead of him stretched a busy morning delivering smoked pork to the Germans, but he also had routine information on Carpiquet airfield to pass to Duchez. It would save him time to go to the house, surely just once couldn't hurt, despite what " Third Fool " had said . . . then, with the engine ticking over, some instinct that he couldn't pin down warned him against it. Masseron saved his own life by driving to the Café des Touristes, waiting in vain, and entrusting a message to the boiler.

Meantime Arsène had arrived home to find Duchez in his living-room. " They've found the receiver," he reported, " and the identity cards." Duchez sat there looking very white and after a moment he asked dully: " Odette? " Arsène reported that she had been crying, and Duchez nodded reluctantly. " That's good. She's carrying out our plan."

" Plan? "

" We've always planned that if they came and I wasn't there, she was to blame it all on me. Say that she didn't know what I was up to, that I'd never tell her anything about it. Then she was to start weeping. It unnerves them if a woman weeps."

Arsène looked at him for a moment, but Duchez only sat there with all the fight seeming to have gone out of him. After a moment he burrowed in his pocket and lit his pipe. " What are you going to do? " Arsène asked.

Duchez slumped in the chair. " I've got to work on my part of the plan," was all he would say.

To Arsène it seemed that the painter was in a condition approaching shock; he did not pause to try and extract sense from him just then. Towards midday he approached Duchez's house again and the empty silence told him that the Gestapo had gone and Odette with them. They might return later for a further search, but in the meantime Arsène had work to do. Duchez had confided where he kept papers concerning the Deuxième Bureau.

Outraged squawking and a flurry of feathers greeted the plumber's entry to the chicken run, but after a few minutes he had located the control maps, tucked carefully under the reeking straw. Before leaving he burned them, grinding the charred flakes to powder under his boot. That evening, when he returned home, the painter had gone.

Duchez was spending the night with Paul, in an upper room of the Café des Touristes, not wanting to compromise anyone by resting long under one roof. The painter was tasting the ashes of defeat. He had loved Odette deeply, being more dependent on her than many people knew, and in arresting her the Gestapo had brought home to him the savage misery of war as nothing else could have done. " *C'est le sang-froid* "—like a brave and mischievous schoolboy he had gloried in outsmarting the Germans, but the boyish improvident nature found it hard to come to terms with a reality as stark as this.

He could not even do what instinct prompted and pursue his war with even grimmer purpose. If his escape that morning was to have any meaning or value, his Resistance must end as of now. He must get away from Caen, and he must not be taken alive.

The whole audacious hoax had hinged on one probability —that the Gestapo would not link Odette with an espionage network. With him they would have been more suspicious. They would have brought out their best line in tortures, and if he had not cracked they would have tried other methods. Like bringing in Odette and torturing her in front of him—no wild fancy that, it was part of their technique. That could have succeeded where nothing else had. And Duchez knew or had indirect contact with almost 1,500 people, few agents knew more: what they looked like, where they hid out, their responsibilities. Brossolette, Girard, Meslin, Moulines—none would have escaped.

War is a time of bitter decisions, but in putting his comrades and his country above his wife, Duchez tasted a decision more bitter than aloes, and proved himself a brave man. On the night of the 3rd, Paul remembers, he was hating himself as only a brave man can.

Even now it is not clear what plan Duchez had in mind. But on one thing everyone was agreed: without Odette he was a man demented. Next morning the grapevine brought news that Odette had been taken to the rue des Jacobins for questioning, but that was all, and on 4th November Duchez slipped away from the café and sought shelter with Henri Caillet and his wife. Caillet, too, in his diffident way, was a brave man, brave enough to admit that Duchez's presence in his house over the whole week-end scared him stiff, but shelter with the Caillets had two advantages which other houses lacked. As officials of the *Mairie*, they enjoyed, to some extent, the trust of the Germans, and their house was a useful factor. It was an old house with a garden, circled by high walls, sited on the Impasse Bagatelle in the respectable middle-class quarters near the Botanical Gardens.

No doubting that the network was going to miss Duchez. True, there were factors in his personality that had been unsettling, those madcap pranks, the tuneless humming, like a swarm of gnats—but when you remembered how the bold blue eyes had twinkled at you and the full lips pouting in a mischievous grin—" *C'est le sang-froid, mon ami* "—you had to confess that you missed him.

That week-end it seemed that the Germans were missing him too. On the Saturday afternoon, women holding mops and dusters leaned from upper windows to watch the troops of armed soldiers in field-grey tramping among the gardens, probing in pigsties and outhouses. One of them even invaded the Caillets' garden and there was a nerve-pricking moment as his eyes, glaring across the trim lawn, sighted a full packet of Gauloise cigarettes on a desk inside the french windows. (Duchez who was hiding behind a door, had abandoned them hastily on hearing the garden gate.) Suspicious, the soldier came tramping across the flower-beds, shouting, gesturing with the barrel of his gun. Alice Caillet, a gallant and courageous Frenchwoman saw the association of ideas at once—cigarettes, a man hiding?—but pretended to misunderstand.

As he stormed through the french windows, she pushed them towards him shouting, " Well, take them, thief! Do you expect me to make you a present of them? " He stalked off, grumbling, his suspicions lulled.

About 8th November, unobtrusively, Duchez left the Caillets. It was the time to seek shelter outside Caen. Mingling with the shabby hordes of factory workers as they trooped home through the dusk, he got as far as Arsène's house. There was a brief weighing up of the risks, but Arsène thought they stood a chance. Later that evening he drove out of Caen, Duchez perched warily in the back of the camionet, screened by the tarpaulin hood. According to the false identity card he carried he was now Raoul Jules Denaud, a forty-four-year-old labourer hailing from St. Nazaire, who resided at No. 5 rue Georges Clemenceau, Caen.

Towards nine the van drew up in the tiny cobbled square of Bretteville-sur-Laize and Arsène rapped surreptitiously on Masseron's shutter. The pork butcher led Duchez into a white well-scrubbed room with a roaring fire, trying to calm his nerves with calvados before leading him upstairs to share the attic room where Robert Thomas lay hidden. Thomas swung off his camp-bed to greet Duchez with rather less cordiality. Being cooped up beneath the draughty eaves with no news of his father or sisters was bad enough without Duchez's horse-play. (Only later did he learn they were in the gaol at Lisieux, where they stayed till the liberation.)

But " Third Fool " was in no mood for horse-play. The old fun and the old fire had left him. " He seemed to talk of nothing but Odette," Masseron said later, " and the plan he had evolved to rescue her." Most of the day he spent lying on his bed drinking or smoking, but more often just staring into space. Loyalty to his wife forbade him discussing it, but he knew that a score of people in Caen and Paris were holding their breath whenever they thought of Odette. Did the Gestapo suspect Odette of espionage—and would they find a means to make her talk?

The later evidence suggested that Duchez had guessed right. All Bernard's instincts led him to attach most importance to those bundles of identity papers. On the other hand, there was the portable receiver, which suggested regular instructions from London, and put together, the two hinted at a well-knit organisation, with connections that might lead almost any-where.

When Odette was first led in to see Bernard the tall effeminate man with the high-pitched voice and the narrow shaven head must have decided that she would not crack easily under pressure. He began with blandishments and a talk on the advantage of collaboration, ordering a steak for himself in the meantime. As he sat at the desk and ate it, a radio played soft bitter-sweet music. The questions followed the established pattern, soothing, almost sympathetic.

" Where is your husband? From whom does he take his orders? To whom do you supply your identity cards? Why not be sensible—tell us where your husband is? "

Odette's appearance was deceptive. To look at she was a plump, fresh-complexioned housewife, placid and easy going. You would picture her most easily at a copper washtub or ordering a pound of frying steak from her butcher's. But Odette was a Frenchwoman, and a Norman, and this amiable exterior cloaked an iron will. To all Bernard's questions she offered one toneless reply: " I don't know."

Bernard listened and nodded, finished his steak, then leant forward and slapped her face. Then he sent her back to the jail. For a few hours she was confined in a damp narrow cell without food.

Later in the day Bernard resorted to more recognisable Gestapo tactics. For some moments after Odette was ushered in he affected not to notice her, then, without warning, he rose and smashed his fist into her face. Such shock tactics were believed to have a sound psychological effect in dazing and humiliating the victim before they had even collected their thoughts.

" Now, then," he said, sitting down again, and on his desk she noted there were a pile of white paper and several freshly-sharpened pencils. Evidently he had determined to deliver Odette's confession before the day was out. He said: " We will talk about you and your husband. Where is he, by the way? "

Odette said flatly, " I don't know."

Bernard looked at his wrist watch and began to polish his nails. " You have five minutes," he said. The minutes passed in ticking silence, broken only by the muted crooning of the radio in the background. At the end of it Bernard looked at his watch and said matter-of-factly, " Open the top drawer of the filing-cabinet." She hesitated and then did so, recoiling for a moment as she saw the ox-gut whip stiffened inside with a steel rod and crusted with dried blood.

" Now, then," Bernard said, " sit down facing the desk and put your elbows on it." Then he began to thrash her: for how long she did not know because mercifully she fainted.

That evening, there was another summons. Again the preliminary drubbing with the fists and the questions:
" Where is your husband? Who is your organiser? To whom did you give the cards? "

Then the whip came slashing down, searing and tearing and worrying the flesh until the mind could bear no more and she dropped downwards in a black void. Next day she was transferred to the prison at Alençon, where Gestapo men from Rouen continued the treatment, but Odette did not weaken and she did not talk. Girard, Meslin, and all of them were safe.

Despite her courage it seemed that Century's work in Caen was done and that even the Secret Army cells Girard had created in Le Mans and other towns would be hard put to it to carry on. " Operation Grand-Duke " was giving them no rest. Between the day of Odette's transfer and the 17th November, a succession of chopping blows severed the chain linking Girard's units with the B.C.R.A. in London.

Again it was the Paris Underground that bore the brunt. A random raid by one of Colonel Relling's *Abwehr* squads, commanded by the Belgian traitor, Georges Henri Masuy, surprised the head of C.N.D.'s operations branch, Robert Bacque, in the middle of a transmission. Under torture Bacque gave names and within a fortnight forty C.N.D. men were swept into Masuy's net. One of them revealed an address in the rue de Maine where archives were stored, and from these, when decoded, the rôle of French Resistance in the wider strategy of the invasion began to emerge: the location of arms dumps, the fast-growing railway resistance, the vital link with Post Office headquarters. Masuy exulted later: " In one morning we accomplished a year's work."

In London the pattern of treachery was not at once plain. On Masuy's instructions Bacque kept up daily radio contact with B.C.R.A. in the hope of uncovering yet more Resistance plans. Only after ten days, as small discrepancies in the messages mounted, did the full implication hit Dewavrin. Three years almost to the week that Renault had sent that first famous dispatch, the whole of his Confrérie Notre Dame had been wiped out.

On 16th November at 9.15 p.m. Dewavrin signalled to all his networks via the B.B.C. the four-word alarm call to take cover: STORM IN THE WEST.

That gentle man, Eugène Meslin, who loved the port and the city of Caen almost like human beings, did his best to stop the rot. But the facts were painfully plain. With the C.N.D. wiped out, Paris was a perilous bottleneck where dispatches would pile up uncollected. Right from the first Girard's units had relied on the C.N.D. to route their dispatches by air or sea, and now the transmission agency was no more. Prouvost, the Post Office chief, was on the run. The gruff warm-hearted Alex Tanguy had been machine-gunned to death in a Gestapo ambush. All links with the Post Office and with the *Deux Anges* were snapped clean.

None the less, Meslin did his best. Roger Deschambres, the melancholy red-haired plumber, had developed stomach ulcers, but just the same he was an ex-artillery officer, who knew guns, and Meslin made him take over Duchez's job. Jourdan, Jouvel and Menguy were carrying on the mapping work where Thomas had left off. But Deschambres and the others had to move carefully now. The fear of the Gestapo was like an acid eating into the heart and mind of the Resistance, and then disaster of a kind overtook Meslin, too.

Leaving his office by the canal, one night in the blackout, he misjudged the distance to his car and tripped head first into the icy waters of the Bassin St. Pierre. He managed to haul himself out after a minute, drenched and shudder-ing, but next morning he was running a high fever. The doctor diagnosed pneumonia. The Caen cell was without its leader.

The occasion had its lighter side. One afternoon Meslin awoke from a drugged sleep, burning-dry with fever, to find that Moulines had materialised beside his bed. He managed to croak: " What are you doing here? "

The young aristocrat beamed gently. " I've come to take you away, Monsieur Meslin. Girard thinks—we all think you've had enough. Things are breaking up here, Monsieur Meslin. I'm going to take you somewhere you can rest."

Meslin smiled painfully. " In this condition? You were always very impetuous, Jacques. How? "

" I've brought an ambulance down from Paris," Moulines said calmly. " I got it from one of my contacts."

(An ambulance! Meslin wouldn't have been surprised at that moment if he'd brought half a dozen transmitters in it too!)

But moistening his scabbed lips, he said: " Look, Jacques, I can't. With the pressure that's coming through from London now I've got to stay—unless the whole organisation along the Wall is going to break down. And look how suspicious it would seem." Meslin was a good man, close to death at that moment, but as usual his first thoughts were for others. He pointed out: " The Thomases arrested, young Robert on the run, now poor Odette taken—that's the worst thing that's happened yet. My job is to get better and run things as long as I can. I believe we'll pull through somehow."

In the end Moulines, who had a lot of the St. George in his make-up, took the ambulance sadly back to Paris, rather disappointed that there was no really exciting rescue in the offing. From the long-term view Meslin was right, though he should have known better. The real danger had not yet begun.

At Bretteville-sur-Laize, Masseron and Robert Thomas were having trouble with Duchez. Unable to keep under cover for long, the painter had taken to prowling round the house at all hours, and, once when Thomas had hurried down to fetch him upstairs, Masseron nearly had heart failure because the local Sergeant of *Milice*, who knew Duchez by sight, chose that moment to call and cadge a free drink.

Thomas and " Third Fool " passed a grim half-hour fighting back sneezes in the dusty broom cupboard under the stairs, while Masseron coaxed the sergeant's mind from war with a little smoked ham and a lot of ferocious old calvados.

Masseron was uneasy on two counts: because of the fugitives and because the sergeant became tipsily curious as to how Masseron smoked his ham. The butcher worked manfully to talk him out of a demonstration, because there were grenades, plastic explosives and a machine-gun snugly cached at the base of the smoke-stack in the yard.

And thereby hangs a tale. Masseron was a doubly fortunate agent: first because he had thought better of visiting Duchez on the morning of Odette's arrest and secondly because Léonard Gille, the advocate, Meslin's military deputy, had brought him those arms. By December there had been six major drops in the Caen region—more than three tons of arms lying hidden ready for use by the men of the Secret Army. They had been staked out in seven dumps, the attics or cellars of other agents chosen by Emmanuel Robineau, the rather foolhardy young man who had charge of all dropping-liaison. Robineau knew all those dumps, except Masseron's—and Robineau was reckoned " contagious." Both he and Comby, the coal merchant, had been warned away from Caen by Meslin in September, when the Gestapo uncovered the Falaise and Lisieux dumps and started watching the offices of Normandy Peat-Cutters Inc.

Comby took the hint and vanished but two months later Robineau came back to Caen. The youngster had a fixation that one of the Caen Gestapo's auxiliaries was more dangerous to the Resistance than Helmut Bernard or any German, and he was tragically right.

The Caen Gestapo, like every other, worked with a detachment of the *Milice*, the 250,000-strong army scoured from the

gutters and prisons of France by Joseph Darnand, the Nice
brothel proprietor. Lucien Brière, the Caen chief, was, like
Darnand, a Frenchman; he was also a dangerously clever one,
an ex-faith healer who had known Caen all his life. He was a
pale almost bald man, with a Louis Napoleon beard and the
burning ice-blue eyes of a fakir. With a deeper insight into
French psychology and methods than Bernard and his thugs,
he was already keeping a close watch on so far unsuspected
Century agents like Arsène and Madame Caillet. Sensing
Brière was dangerous, Robineau did the worst thing possible.
He started shadowing him through the winding streets of the
city.

Nothing happened for about a fortnight, but one day,
rounding a corner, Robineau found Brière waiting for him.
The *Milice* chief snapped out: " You're following me, aren't
you, boy? Why? " Robineau was a very young man, barely
of age; in a way, like young Paul Mauger, who had nearly
taken Duchez's plan for Renault on the *Deux Anges*, he was
too young for the job they had given him, but unlike Mauger,
he was a kind of daredevil weakling, who took risks to quieten
his own self-doubt. When Brière spoke to him he coloured
and mumbled and then slouched away.

After that Robineau stopped his shadowing—apparently
without suspicion that Brière was now shadowing him. On
15th December, a little before midday, he was again in Caen,
crossing the Place Saint-Sauveur when Brière and a small
group of *Milice* closed in and took him.

Robineau could not help what happened to him after that;
he was a brave, if quixotic, boy, acting as he thought for the
best, and no blame should be attached to him for his in-
experience. Brière and Bernard were savage and determined
men, and in their zeal to smash the networks they habitually
did the kind of dreadful things that a man hopes not to dream
about. In a small back room at the rue des Jacobins, Robineau
was strapped to a chair, and an iron band placed round his
head and the lobes of his ears and slowly contracted. By
nightfall he was screaming convulsively, like an animal caught
in a trap, and after much too long a time the Gestapo chiefs

had what they wanted—the names and addresses of 120 of Girard's agents.

Jean Chateau had sent positive word to the delicatessen at Bretteville that Odette had been transferred to the prison at Alençon as far back as 4th November. This spark of news kindled all the old fire of recklessness in Duchez and he could talk of only one thing. " We'll stage a prison break," he exulted. " We'll free Odette from those *canaille* yet."

Chateau was normally a placid and objective man, and it says much for Duchez's inner fire that he should not only have coaxed Chateau into discussing it but into helping him carry it out. The chances of two men staging a rescue from a heavily-guarded prison with one machine-gun as armament, loaned by Masseron, seemed slight, to say the least.

But at 3 a.m. one December morning they set off in Chateau's camionet. Duchez's heart was as high as a child's awaiting the coming of Christmas. Soon Odette would be free. She had to be free, for was he not Duchez?

Masseron knew better. " It was the only way of setting Duchez's mind at rest," he said later; " but I knew it was hopeless from the first." And events proved him right. Odette had stayed only a few days in the gaol at Alençon before they moved her to a cell-block in an S.S. barracks on the edge of the town. (In the next cell, which communicated by a tiny grille, was Robert Aubin, head of Century-Argentan, who had been arrested the same day, and he and Odette held gloomily-whispered discussions on the fate of Century.) Local contacts had told Duchez and Chateau where Odette was being held, but after one look at the massive stone walls and iron-barred windows their hopes sank to zero. Duchez did try for a job as a labourer on a new extension they were building, hoping to establish some contact, but there were no vacancies, and after that he knew he was only torturing himself by staying there.

Both Odette and Aubin were caged in their tiny cells until mid-1944, and the Allies had already landed when they were transferred to Mauthausen, " the camp of no return." Both were to return to France in the autumn of 1945, but the gay and feckless " Third Fool " did not know that. He had to go back to Bretteville, summoning up the kind of courage that can accept defeat without losing faith, but it was not easy. The sharpest pain was in visiting Odette's brother-in-law, the schoolmaster at Fleury, where the children were staying, but he tried to put a brave face on it. " Well," he said gaily, as the children came to greet him, " here I am." Young Jacques, aged twelve, bit his lip and said nothing, but Monique looked at her father with big blue accusing eyes. " *Et Maman?* " she asked. For the first time in years Duchez broke down and cried.

He arrived in Bretteville to find the whole structure of the network crumbling. On the morning of 16th December the Gestapo cars were squealing to a halt in side streets all over the city. Professor de Briard of the Caen Faculty; Fouques, the Post Office engineer; Annette Quenardel, liaison agent; that good and upright man, Colonel Corbasson; Henri Rebiard, the electrician; Schultz, surprised in his radio shop in the rue Vaucelles in the midst of a transmission; Pierre Bouchard, Caen's Chief Registrar—all were taken without warning.

The net spread out fast and surely like a web spun by a spider. Thirty miles along the coast, at Port-en-Bessein, they took the cousins Joseph and Arthur Poitevin and the fisherman Georges Thomine. At Luc-sur-Mer a *Feldwebel*, alerted by the Gestapo, called at Dr. Sustendal's surgery to arrest him, but found him out. It was plain that the Germans would return next morning and Sustendal had nowhere to flee, but in the one night of grace granted him, the doctor took his control maps and burned them to a cinder in his grate. Next morning they confronted him with Robineau, shaken and bleeding, who swayed on his feet and said pathetically, " I couldn't take any more, Doctor. I've told them where the arms are hidden."

Sustendal just grunted, " Well, if you have, you have," and led the Gestapo to the cellar of a deserted house in the village of La Délivrande, where he and Robineau had stored the arms. By the end of the day, only Masseron's meagre supply and a minor dump at Condé-sur-Noireau remained undiscovered.

The Gestapo had evidence in plenty now of the " Action " programme of Girard's units—a planned armed uprising organised, as a propaganda release had it, by " the infamous terrorist Colonel Passy, who is a Jewish-Communist agitator." But not one general survey map had they found. Those who still possessed them in quantity—Meslin, Arsène, Deschambres, Harivel, and the three cartographers—had so far escaped the net. Thomas's maps were resting in peace in the tomb where Arsène had interred them, and Kaskoreff, Colonel Corbasson's aide, had fled from Caen, taking his wife and sister with him to seek safety in Paris.

The Caen headquarters were still intact and—incredibly— there was no evidence that for eighteen months thousands of men had been painstakingly piecing together a new blue-print of the Atlantic Wall.

Now a curious thing happened, and because of it, for three weeks, the lives of all Dewavrin's remaining agents along the Wall hung in the balance. One of the men arrested, under torture, revealed a name—the name of a Century agent in Rouen, an ironmonger by profession, named Gilles. He was no connection of Léonard Gille, Meslin's military deputy, but the man in the torture-chamber was too far gone to give any details. Further inquiries showed that there was indeed a Gille in Caen. Bernard ordered that he should be brought in.

At first the Gestapo drew a blank. They did not know that for seven months Gille had been hiding at No. 21 rue de Place, in the house of Janine Boitard, the attractive young sophisticate who was the most dedicated member of Duchez's escape route service. They searched for him all the morning of the 16th, but none of them had any clue how valuable the arrest of Gille would be.

A man to remember, was Léonard Gille. Handsome, in a dark clever way, with what actors call " a presence " and the easy charm of a man used to getting results. Born of wealthy parents, Gille had no necessity to work, or to qualify as an advocate, but he *had* worked and for much the same reason as he resisted—to still the churning demon of dissatisfaction in that restless probing brain. Perhaps because much of his life had been easy, he enjoyed tackling the difficult jobs in war;

once he escorted seven airmen, none of whom knew French, from Caen to Paris, steering them through crowds at railway stations by hoisting a pair of skis on his shoulder as a landmark.

The day the Gestapo began looking for him he had just completed one of the trickiest jobs of all.

It had originated weeks earlier in a brief message from Century's Falaise agent, deposited in the letter-box at the Café des Touristes. Addressed to Gille by his code-name, " Marie," it read: " Marie—1 kilometre from here, before Langannerie, 1200 German pioneers are at work. Subterranean galleries are being constructed. The pioneers work from 8 to 16 hours a day without stopping."

The information went to London as it stood, but Dewavrin's experts did not let it rest there. They wanted further details. What about a sketch map of the galleries? What kind of munitions would be stored, and so on? Meslin signalled back that the Falaise area was heavily policed, an almost impenetrable zone, but the answer, in effect, was: " Send results, not excuses."

Gille, by dint of perseverance, finally coaxed a rough sketch map from the agent. On the morning of 16th December, with Meslin still away sick, he took the map to Harivel, in the insurance office on the Place St. Sauveur.

At three-thirty that afternoon the edges of the sky had the burned black colour of charred paper. From his office on the second floor Harivel watched the early darkness close in on the steep-pitched roofs. Time to make ready. Taking Gille's plan of the subterranean munitions depots, he added it to other dispatches that had arrived, among them the co-ordinates of the batteries at Octeville, a heavily-defended strong point south-west of Cherbourg. He slid them neatly into a thick manila envelope and sealed it. Harivel was on tenterhooks because of the morning's arrests but he knew that much of this information was priority. Century's dispatches must go off as usual.

At the same time, in his small motor-cycle repair shop on

the Avenue de Creully, Maurice Himbert, the courier, was wiping the grease from his hands with a wad of cotton-waste and preparing to leave for home. Himbert, a typical mechanic, a small leathery man with pale-blue impassive eyes and a thatch of dark hair, was not thinking much about the journey, which he had made many times before. His main preoccupation was the curfew in Paris. Usually the train ran late and there was barely time to make it to one of the hotels behind the Gare St. Lazare. Himbert chose comfortable old-fashioned hotels, like the Hotel de Liège in the rue de Liège, because they had no central heating. He slept better if Century's dispatches were lodged safely up a chimney before he snapped off the light.

By four o'clock, when Harivel walked in with the envelope in his breast pocket, Himbert was ready to leave. The two exchanged a few words, but with that morning's news neither of them felt like saying much. Trudging back to his house on the rue du Moulin, Himbert's one consolation was that none of those arrested had known him personally. He was not anticipating difficulties.

Once indoors he washed hastily, changed his suit and packed Century's dispatches into a battered brown brief-case along with a handful of *casse-croutes* and a bottle of cheap red wine. Then, packing a small overnight bag, he kissed his wife and set off on foot for the Gare Centrale, a mile and a half away. On the way he picked up another agent, a girl called Jeanne-Marie, whose job was to cover him until he had boarded the train. As they walked, Jeanne-Marie relieved him of the brief-case, and Himbert carried the overnight bag. It was now quite dark, with frost in the air, and a chapping wind drove across the black gulf of the Orne.

Half an hour earlier the hunt for Gille had taken a new turn. That afternoon a *Milice* agent named Albert Hervé had inquired for him at the Café des Touristes, but Paul's wife feigned ignorance of his movements. Then somebody at Gestapo headquarters remembered that one of Gille's closest associates was Maurice Himbert, the motor-cycle mechanic.

At the garage Hervé, who knew Himbert by sight, learned

251

he had left for Paris. He got into his car and drove hard for the station.

It was now five forty-five. With the wind battering at them, Himbert and Jeanne-Marie were toiling up the incline to the station. As they reached the heavy swing doors that open on the main booking office the air-raid siren whined over the city. The dimly-lit hall was swarming with travellers: German soldiers in coal-scuttle helmets, ragged boys hoping to earn a few sous with their orange-box baggage carts, old women struggling with bundles.

At the guichet Himbert bought a third-class return to Paris, St. Lazare, and tucked it in the strap of his brief-case. Jeanne-Marie, following suit, bought a third return to Flers, where she had a daughter. Shouldering through more swing doors on to the platform, they turned right. Himbert was still carrying the overnight bag in his right hand. Jeanne-Marie held the brief-case in her left.

Ten minutes to six. Just time to descend the flight of stone steps, pass through the subway and gain Quay Three for the Paris express. As they started down the steps, two men loomed from the blackness in front of them. The leader, Hervé, was a young slightly-built man with fair curly hair, wearing a sports coat and flannel trousers. He said, " Monsieur Himbert. Gestapo. Follow us."

It was the next sixty seconds that counted.

Automatically, Himbert and Jeanne-Marie fell back. Hervé and his aide continued past them, not passing through the swing doors to the booking-office but turning right along the platform, beckoning Himbert and the girl to follow. Himbert saw the reason: about 120 yards along the platform, passing a few offices, the left-luggage counter, the office of the German Chef de Gare and the buffet, they would reach the exit to the car park. A thought floated into Himbert's mind idly: How odd to be arrested before you even had time to reply.

Then suddenly the panic broke through, shooting in his brain like an abscess: *Get rid of the brief-case! Get rid of it!*

He glanced furtively at Jeanne-Marie walking level, composed and tight-lipped. Eyes riveted on the men ahead, he swung the overnight bag across, transferring it from right hand to left. In the darkness his right hand stole out to meet Jeanne-Marie's left, fingers wound tight round the brief-case. Fleetingly as he tugged he felt them resist, then the brief-case was in his hand. They couldn't have had time to make a mental inventory of his baggage, it was too dark. . . .

Get rid of the case. Get rid of it!

On the concrete their footfalls were hollow, and the Gestapo men were only grey smudges in the blackness ahead. But they would hear the noise of the case as it dropped.

Get rid of it—but how, how?

From the darkness they came level with the German stationmaster's office, and two things happened. The bright white rays of the electric globe above the door struck at them, and by reflex they recoiled, squinting at the light. Near at hand the ack-ack batteries covering the railway spotted a raider, and all the guns opened up at once: heavy pummelling blows you could feel in the stomach.

Himbert let the brief-case slip from his fingers then. It fell to the platform in the pitch darkness beyond the blinding pool of light, and the pounding of the guns along the river swallowed all sound.

Chapter Seventeen

NETWORK IN SHADOWS

THE DAYS that followed were wrapped in mystery. On the Friday at 10 a.m. Himbert had been due to contact Rivalin, the young medical student, in their new meeting-place, a bench under the trees in the Orangerie in the south-west corner of the Jardin des Tuileries, Paris. Security precautions were stringent now: meetings took place in the open air and it was understood that neither party waited more than ten minutes if the other was late. Just before ten-fifteen Rivalin went disconsolately home across the Seine to the Ministry of War suite on the Boulevard St. Germain. Himbert was rated as dependable as an eight-day clock. It was unlike him not to have sent word that the dispatches weren't coming.

Madame Himbert had no anxieties until the Sunday night, but when her husband did not return, she rang Harivel. Harivel had no news but knowing the contents of the briefcase he was shattered. By Monday the 20th it was plain that the Gestapo must have Himbert and that if they did they also had one of the most dangerous dispatches that Century had ever routed to Paris.

A curious position, Himbert's. On that week-end, as on any other, he had no inkling of what was in the envelope he carried. He had the kind of faith that Dewavrin demanded, knowing only that it meant death if he was caught. When the B.B.C. announced, a fortnight after each journey to Paris: " The three cabin boys lunched well in Dieppe," Himbert did not know that Dewavrin was announcing the arrival of the Caen dispatches in London. But if he was tortured he knew enough. He knew the headquarters of Century-Caen and he knew both Girard and Meslin.

The week before Christmas was an anguished silent week of waiting, and as always it was the suspense that hurt most. They lacked news from Dr. Sustendal, Colonel Corbasson, Schultz (all later deported to Mauthausen) and, above all, from Himbert. If only some news would come. . . .

No word would be coming from Robineau. He was dead.

But when news of Himbert did come it was more bewildering than ever. On the afternoon of Christmas Eve, Janine Boitard answered the phone to find a shaken but free Jeanne-Marie warning her that " Monsieur Legrand " (little Himbert's cover-name) was " in hospital." Janine said cautiously, " Did he have time to deliver the parcel? " Jeanne-Marie said No. He had dropped the parcel, which was regrettable.

That was much worse. Ultimately the brief-case would be found and Himbert's name was stamped inside it. On Christmas Day, three agents spent most of the morning and afternoon scouring the platform, the buffet and the left-luggage office at Caen. Not a clue. With Meslin still sick, the main burden of the search now fell on Janine and on Léonard Gille, but even Gille, with one of the sharpest brains in the Caen cell, found himself foxed by two problems.

If the Gestapo didn't have the brief-case, who did? And if they weren't holding Himbert on suspicion of espionage why hold him at all? Jeanne-Marie could throw light only on point two. For eight days they had kept her in gaol, summoning her daily to the rue des Jacobins and the burden of all their questions had been her relationship with Himbert. And did she by any chance know Gille? (Even this was enough to make Gille leave Caen on Boxing Day.) Finding that she had no startling disclosures, they let her go.

In the gaol at Caen, crammed with two stool-pigeons into a cell nine feet long by six feet wide, Himbert was painfully aware of what they wanted. It came home forcibly each time he was driven across town to Gestapo headquarters for sessions with Hervé that lasted three hours. With his wrist chained to the radiator, soft music playing, he parried the questions: " Where is Gille? What does he do? What does he look like? "

And Himbert answered doggedly: " Monsieur, he is only

a casual acquaintance of mine. It's true we were at school together, but I don't know what he does for a living or where he lives. Perhaps we've had a drink together six times in as many years. And he looks like anybody else—not very dark, not very fair, neither tall nor short."

His private diary came under the microscope, but luckily the addresses listed were business connections and he could prove it. Baulked, Hervé tried another track. " Aren't you worried about what your wife's doing while you're locked up? " he insinuated. " They say in Caen that she runs around with other men."

Himbert shrugged. " When a man's wife is unfaithful to him in France, monsieur," he said with lonely pride, " *he* is the last person to be told."

But they did not torture him and it was plain that never at any time did the Gestapo realise that in Himbert, the humble courier, they had the key to the whole complex structure of Girard's war against the Wall. Nor did they know that the dispatches of the most highly-organised Intelligence network along the coastline had been within reaching distance. They were holding Himbert solely because he knew a man called Gille—and a different Gille, at that, from the man they were after.

Playing for time, Himbert returned to his hard plank bed, to nourish his hopes on sour beetroot soup and do some thinking. In other cells along the same corridor were Colonel Corbasson and Schultz, the radio shop proprietor. Having found the arms depots, the Gestapo had not tortured the Colonel, but the big Alsatian, who had been caught transmitting, had been beaten terribly. Himbert thought there *must* be a way out without endangering himself or the network—*but what had happened to the brief-case?*

And that was one of the strangest stories in Century's unorthodox saga. About two minutes after Himbert dropped the case the German Chef de Gare, Herr Lutz, had left his office and stumbled over it in the gloom. The ticket in the handle-strap showed that it was the property of a third-class passenger en route to Paris. Lutz, like many German officials,

Léon Dumis, Léonard Gille and René Duchez

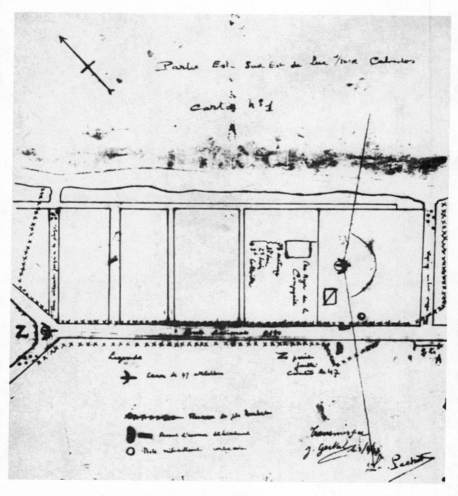

The underground tunnel at Luc-sur-Mer—the bird's eye view of the sea-front as Dr. Sustendal saw it, with the hidden gasoline dump on the right, just within the perimeter of the barbed wire

was scrupulously honest if unimaginative. Hurrying through the subway to Quay Three, he handed it to the guard of the Paris express.

No one claimed it at St. Lazare, so for a month it gathered dust on a shelf in the left-luggage until on 16th January the clerks grew tired of looking at it and sent it back to Caen. This time it was passed to Jean Augé, the bald, smiling little stationmaster, himself a Century agent, and one glance at Himbert's name and the thick manila envelope told him enough. He deposited it with Caen left-luggage office and rang Madame Himbert.

Next day Janine Boitard called to collect it (paying ninety-three francs lost property charge) and took it home. The envelope she later took to Paris herself, but it was when she and Madame Himbert first opened the case that they were faced with perhaps the oddest problem of all. Outwardly, there was no sign that the brief-case had been opened. Himbert's business papers were intact. The seal on the big envelope was unbroken.

But the bread and the wine had gone. To some anonymous citizen, hunger had allowed no choice.

In the third week of January Himbert saw his way clear. Hervé had sent for him several times and told him that the one way to get free was to hand over a photo of his close friend Gille. He dropped the same hint to Madame Himbert, and even gave permission for her to visit her husband in gaol. Once she had told Himbert that " they found the parcel you lost on the way to Paris," he knew the time was ripe. " I can't hold out any longer," he told her loudly, for the benefit of any concealed microphones, " You'd better take the picture of Gille out of the family album and give it to them."

Twenty-four hours later Hervé was the proud possessor of a photograph of Gille—or rather a smudged snapshot of a short dark man wearing a dinner-jacket. Though it may have borne a faint resemblance to Gille, it was actually a photo of Himbert's cousin at a wedding reception, but Hervé was delighted. On Sunday, 30th January, after a last bowl of beetroot soup, Himbert became a free man. Century was safe again.

Hervé never found the cousin, but this was no reflection on his skill as a Gestapo agent because Himbert hadn't seen him for twenty years either.

Girard took fresh precautions after that alarm. His first step was to treble the couriers—diminishing the risks of dispatches not getting through by increasing the odds. Himbert was out of the running now, so the solid reliable Gilbert Michel brought one lot of dispatches from Caen (travelling with brief-case in one compartment and himself in the next) to the Ministry of War, with another courier, Henri Lemoine, taking the rest to Aimé Jean Jean, the Prefect of the Ardèche who worked for Century in the immunity of the Chamber of Deputies with a German sentry guarding his door. Many other dispatches came through the forceful Colonel Becker in Le Mans, although with the *Deux Anges* out of commission it often took weeks to arrange a Lysander pick-up or a boat from some out-of-the-way port. Then, early in February, by the kind of luck which seemed to favour Century, instructions came that in future typed dispatches and maps must be reduced to the minimum.

Dewavrin, it seemed, now had all the maps he needed, and troop movements and modifications of defences could more easily be signalled by radio from the countryside. Thomas's sector maps would still come in useful for the agents to work out the grid references.

Back in the previous November, after the Teheran Conference, the Allies had been fully committed to mount " Operation Overlord " in May, 1944. Under Eisenhower, the pieces were being assembled now for the mightiest jigsaw puzzle in military history and every fact that Century had supplied was checked and double checked and checked again. Every day for months Mosquitoes had climbed above the Wall, first at 40,000 feet, then, concentrating on verticals and obliques, more riskily: first at wave-top height, 3 to 4 miles out, then at zero feet, 1500 yards from the shelving bluffs, then 1500 yards inland at a heart-stopping

2,000 feet, rocketing along the Wall at 400 miles an hour. From these prints and the agents' findings the Navy alone made use of 120,000,000 maps.

Deep in the Duke of York's Barracks, Chelsea, a secret team of 12 men worked on enormous mock-ups of the invasion area, corrugated cardboard covered with cheesecloth and sprayed with green and brown paint. Even Ouistreham lighthouse was there, made to scale out of linoleum, though security was strict enough to leave the team as much in the dark as Century. (Caen was " Poland " and the Orne was the " River Prague.") Planning teams worked on beach folders that listed not only each blockhouse but each foot of pebbly shore. The work of years was bearing fruit.

On the other side of the Channel, *Generalfeldmarschall* Erwin Rommel, who had become Commander of Army Group B in late November, was a great deal less than happy. Early in December he had taken his first view of the much-vaunted Wall and what he saw staggered him.

It came home to the famed desert tactician that Hitler was a victim of his own propaganda. The Wall was not a Wall at all. Only at a dozen points had the Navy and the Todt Organisation come anywhere near creating the impenetrable fortress that Goebbels had sold so long and so loudly. (Only one of these, Cherbourg, was in the Allied invasion zone.) To some extent the batteries did form a continuous cross-fire, but while the naval guns, like a battery Gresselin had reported from Crisbecq, were in steel cupolas, the army artillery, to ensure greater freedom for their field of fire, was only dug in.

Even the few strong points under concrete had head cover only sixty centimetres thick, and between the Orne and the Vire, Century's main hunting ground, there were few enough of these. In all essentials it was still the same wall that had unrolled in blueprint two years before across Duchez's map.

Vague echoes of Rommel's disquiet reached Girard in Paris: nothing too positive, the muttered gossip of orderlies and clerks, sifting through bistros and duly remarked by Century's men. After inspecting the fortifications at Deauville (or elsewhere) Rommel had seemed *très inquiet*. But Rommel faced more setbacks than any commander should be called upon to overcome in six months. The scarcity of steel made it impossible to obtain the gun turrets he needed. The bulk of the Todt Organisation was in Germany, clearing up bomb damage. And who, in the end, was going to defend the Wall? Hitler had reckoned, two years back, that it needed ten to twelve extra divisions to establish a solid front along its length, but the three-front war had steadily siphoned off the cream of the troops and most of the transport. The Wall must be a rampart, Hitler and von Rundstedt had said, capable either of smashing an attack on the beaches or holding it until the massed armour counter-attacked.

But how to use massed armour to effect when the Allies had the mastery of the air? The lesson of North Africa had shown Rommel the futility of that.

No, the only hope, as Rommel saw it, was the Wall itself. It would have to be strengthened, the battle waged from natural positions, as the one means of counteracting Allied mass and mobility. Time and again Rommel stressed, " *We have got to stop the enemy at the water's edge, and within forty-eight hours of his landing.*" Now he was forced to depend on the Wall in a way that von Rundstedt and Hitler had never dreamed, and with time, labour and materials denied him, field-type defences stretching three to four miles inland seemed the only hope.

In February, when he set to work, Century was watching. They had suffered crippling blows, but there were still hundreds left. " Third Fool " was hiding on a windy hilltop above Falaise, whence Masseron had spirited him, with the men of the Maquis St. Clair; Thomas and Gille were with Maquis groups in the Haute Savoie, but many had survived along the Wall and together with the shock troops of the Secret Army they would carry on.

It was soon plain to them what Rommel was trying to do. His aim was to cover every possible landing-beach between high and low water marks with obstacles that would leave no free channel for even a flat-bottomed boat to reach shore. Belgian gates, mined steel stakes slanting seawards, triangles of crossed angle-irons called " hedgehogs," steel pyramid-shaped tetra-hedra, nutcracker mines and above all, " Elements C "—two and a half tons of steel massed in the shape of a picket fence, ten feet high and ten feet broad, on a base measuring ten by fourteen feet.

Some of the new defences came home to Century with the impact of personal suffering. There was the afternoon late in January when a bustling little welfare worker named Made-moiselle Madeleine Verly was taking time off to spend the week-end with her mother and sister at the small family estate near La Délivrande. Around two on the Saturday afternoon a truck load of Labour Corps troops rolled up, and a *Truppführer* with small furtive eyes and an insinuating smile came to the door. With one gesture of his arm he indicated the shadow-grey ranks of the ash plantation stretching west of their home.

" All down," he said, pointing to the troops unloading their sharp-bladed axes. " *Befehl ist befehl.*" Then the bitter protests began and his face grew crafty.

" You like your trees, eh? You do not wish that we shall chop them down? " And when they nodded, hopeful of reprieve: " Very well, madame. I am not a bad chap at heart, you know—you be nice to me, eh, and make me a present of that good old calvados that I bet you've got in your cellar and I'll take my boys somewhere else. How will that do? "

Some might have snatched at the chance, but not the Verlys, mother and daughters. Their lips set tight. Old calvados they had in plenty, but a Frenchwoman's pride would not let her stoop to begging favours of the invader. But as the blades flashed that afternoon, *chock-chock* in the winter sun, and 400 trees came splintering down, they wept as if their hearts would break.

The vandalism had a purpose. To complete his hedgehog fortress, Rommel was planting sharply pointed stakes, mined and slanting skywards, in every open space he could, placing them close enough together to forestall possible glider landings. The French, with wry humour, christened them " Rommel's asparagus," and when even civilians were set to work in compulsory labour teams to plant them, Girard's agents worked among them. One was Mademoiselle Verly, who reported, with satisfied hate, that the obstacles were five feet high, set twenty yards apart.

Even here Rommel found time and transport against him. One of the St. Lô cell, a lean, ebullient callisthenics instructor named Jean-Leopold Étienne, reported a typical setback. In the Forêt de Cerisy, north of St. Lô, the German 352nd Division was cutting these stakes by hand, hauling the wood to the beaches twelve miles away by horse and cart, and driving the stakes, again by hand, into the tidal flats. A sore-handed German in one of the teams, Étienne said, was billeted on his mother.

All over France now the bloodshed and the purges and the tortures mounted but each act of repression brought only new recruits to the Underground. Between Bayeux and Omaha Beach Mercader, the bicycle merchant, had 300 agents, both Century and Secret Army men, feeding information to the hungry transmitter in his wine cellar. Gresselin, the grocer, had another 1,200 in the north of the Cotentin, around Cherbourg. As the S.T.O. conscripted more and more civilian labour, men who had spent two years reporting on the Wall now became the part-time slaves labouring to add the feverish last-minute touches. Chateau, calling on the big blond ex-trawler captain, Léon Cardron in Port-en-Bessein, found him about to flee to the Maquis to escape this indignity.

" You'll do no such thing," Chateau told him firmly. " Don't you realise that you can do more for the network in among the trenches than crouching in some damp wood with a gun on the off chance of ambushing a convoy? "

Most had suffered too much and too long to relish the idea of waging a sit-down war: they hungered for direct and bloody action. It says much for the teamwork Girard had instilled that Century and Secret Army men did what they were told and dug trenches with the rest.

It was not a job that called for daring or foolhardiness. Sweating on the tableland above the cliffs, with the grey-blue waters of the Channel 200 feet below and the white waves creaming on the sand, you needed not only muscle for the job but infinite patience and the power to observe. As late as the first week of February, Mercader had sent off a map, scale 1-10,000 of the whole coast between Grandcamp and Bayeux. Now the pattern was changing; supplementary details were needed. Cardron, St. Denis, the ironmonger, Bouvier, the insurance agent at St. Lô—they were a few of the " amateurs " who reported in advance on Rommel's ingenious mining pattern. With few mines available he was using old shells instead, spreading them over the surface of the ground round every weapon-slit and dugout.

At Point du Hoe the " undisciplined " Farine observed different tactics: shells hung on ropes, like long strings of explosive onions, trailing down the cliffs below the guns.

Information trickled through in devious ways but it did not stop coming. At St. Laurent, Rommel mined all the land between the cliffs and the Port-en-Bessein road, and indignant farmers besieged the land-tax office complaining to the *Percepteur des Contributions* that the old assessments were now out of date. Would the Government assess them, then, on the land which the accursed Boche had stolen? From an agent in touch with developments, Mercader could calculate that the Germans had mined almost 200 acres of land.

Then there were the beach exits—the " doors " which had given Girard food for thought. East of Grandcamp, the minefields stretched for two and a half miles through sand and couchgrass, but in Farine's café dog-tired workers told how they were split by many " doors " at least 600 yards wide. Five " doors " cut the scrub-covered bluffs towering above the crescent of Omaha Beach, though over the months Farine had reported a mighty concentration of almost 300 strongpoints—batteries, pill-boxes, rocket pits, gun-posts—sited to defend them.

Rommel, too, knew that the " doors " were vital, but once the Allies knew where their defences lay, they began planning heavy fire support to knock them out as the infantry stormed ashore.

When reports like that came in, the checkers sometimes asked Girard if he thought the Wall *would* be impregnable in the end. The big man growled like a lion with a thorn in his paw before replying: " That's a hell of a question to ask a cement manufacturer . . . but *we* had a Monsieur Maginot, remember! "

In the wake of success came tragedy—in a way the most fearful thing that had ever touched them. For five months the dark dynamic Pierre Brossolette had been under cover in France, working to smooth out the organisation problems of the Secret Army. It took long heart-breaking weeks to reconcile the differences between the various political elements, but at last he achieved it. As Dewavrin's deputy he was returning to England at the end of January with the finalised plan for the whole mass rising. In Paris, Girard and the others knew vaguely that he was in Brittany, planning to leave for England by sea.

The next news came on 3rd February. Brossolette's fishing boat, the tragically named *Jouet des Flots*, had hit a fierce gale and capsized in the smoking breakers off the Brittany coast. Jettisoning his papers, Brossolette had struggled ashore, with Monsieur Émile Bollaert, an elderly Colonial administrator who was de Gaulle's political representative, and set off in search of a transmitter to warn London. On the way their car had been stopped and checked. They had been sent to the gaol at Rennes for entering the coastal zone without a pass.

The same day Colonel Touny called an emergency session in the " Red Cross " office. The meeting was one of the grimmest on record, and the only reassuring news was that so far the Germans had not penetrated Brossolette's disguise. With the white streak in his hair dyed out, he was posing as Monsieur Pierre Boutet, a traveller in scientific text books. In the smoky room where Girard and " Colonel Nobody " and the other O.C.M. heads were gathered, the arguments raged back and forth, until suddenly Pastaud, the head of Century's Orleans branch cut in: " Messieurs, all this is so much waste of time. Remember Brossolette holds our lives in his hands. He knows the entire organisation along the Atlantic Wall and it is only a question of time before the Gestapo discover that he *is* Brossolette.

"The only way to rescue him and save our whole organisation is to stage a mass attack on the prison."

All of them looked at one another, then at Touny, not daring to voice their thoughts. Century had done some strange things in its time—but could they stage a gaol break and get away with it?

Chapter Eighteen

THE LOST LEADERS

RATHER FLUSHED, Girard cut in, " Excuse me, *mon Colonel*, but I don't agree. Even if such a thing were possible, using as many Secret Army men in Brittany as would be necessary, aren't we forgetting the chance of reprisals? If we fought our way in, hundreds of men in the prison might be massacred because of it. The only way, as I see it, is through a ruse."

Touny thought and decided eventually that Girard was right, but as so often happens to a volunteer, Girard for his pains received the job of organising the escape. He talked it over the same day with Dany and Moulines, in the three-in-one flat, and it was arranged that Moulines and two agents should travel to Rennes and prospect the territory.

This was the worst time of all, and Girard was hard put to it to retain, beneath the taut nerves, the bouncing confidence that his agents expected to see. At bottom, agents were only people, human and scared by the knowledge that arrest and torture was a bigger certainty than it had been even a year back. The tall and lovely Dany was worried sick by the strain of it and could not eat. Girard kept a tight rein on himself, summoning up all the toughness of which he was capable.

On some days—25th February, for example—it was harder.

At 8 a.m. that morning a knock came at the door of Colonel Touny's elegant flat in the rue du Général Langlois. Madame Touny, stirring uneasily in bed, wondered who it could be and the Colonel wondered too, but he slipped on a cashmere dressing-gown and went to see. When he returned to the bedroom, a minute later, he was manacled, with an escort of four Germans. Against the Colonel's unshakable suavity, they seemed ill at ease. One of them told him to get dressed, and the Colonel raised a well-bred eyebrow. " Manacled? That won't be too easy." But while his wife was helping him, they discovered 700,000 francs worth of notes in a suit-case and the Colonel must have known then that it was all up.

Girard heard the news, and his grief was terrible. Brossolette he had known and respected, but Touny he had loved as one can only love a man who has shared the same dangers and ideals passionately for almost two years. Rescue he knew was out of the question; the Underground reported that Touny had been taken for questioning to the Gestapo post at 84 Avenue Foch. That was the last they saw of him. Only later was his body identified in a mass grave at Arras and reburied at Mount Valerien, a national shrine, and whether he was betrayed or the unlucky victim of a routine check up was never known.

A shred of comfort came from Moulines. In Rennes he had succeeded, as only he could, in charming the gaoler's daughter and was now able to visit the prison at any hour he pleased. He reported that the guardroom of the prison was connected by telephone with an S.S. barracks 600 yards away. The prisoners were in good health and so far unmolested. Bollaert in particular had been cheered by a note which mysteriously floated to the surface of his soup, reading " Help is at hand. Jacques Moulines."

The rescue plan was taking shape, with Dewavrin in London lending all the support he could. A few days after Touny's arrest, the cheerful and fearless Wing-Commander Yeo-Thomas, who had so often worked with Brossolette in the field, parachuted back into France and took charge of rescue operations. Working through his new *inamorata*, Moulines was to bribe the gaoler to leave certain doors unlocked at the right moment. The second part of the plan, Yeo-Thomas's, involved a bogus Black Maria, filled with Resistance men in German uniform, driving up to the prison gates. At the same time the telephone wires connecting the two guardrooms were to be cut. Three Resistance men, in *Sicherheitsdienst* uniform, speaking fluent German, were to present forged credentials to the guardroom for the transfer of Brossolette and Bollaert to Paris. As they entered the gaol, a second car, a black saloon, was to drive in behind the Black Maria and stall its engine to prevent the sentry shutting the gate. Bollaert and Brossolette were to be rushed to the waiting saloon and driven round the corner to a second saloon. The first car would make for the open country. The second car would head south to act as a powerful red herring in the chase that followed.

Then, at the last moment, there was a criminal act of carelessness. An overzealous agent in Paris, sending a document for transmission through Spain, added the sentence: " Brossolette and Bollaert in Rennes prison since 3rd February." In his hurry to transmit the report, he forgot to code it, and it was seized by the Germans at St. Jean-de-Luz on the Spanish frontier.

Not so many prisoners had been admitted on 3rd February that the Gestapo could not single out which were Bollaert and Brossolette. On 7th March Brossolette and Bollaert were transferred to Fresnes Prison, south of Paris, for Gestapo interrogation. Yeo-Thomas had been betrayed and arrested a week before*.

The news came to Girard but he was too numb to realise the full implications. He knew that he himself was in hourly peril. A raid on a Gestapo post by a Resistance group in Bayonne had revealed that two men figured high on the list of those wanted by " Operation Grand-Duke." One was named " Moreau " and the other " Malherbe," both leaders of the Organisation Civile et Militaire who functioned in Paris and Caen. It was only a matter of time before they realised that both were Girard.

He avoided the Metro now; there were too many checking points. To help ease his mind he stuck to his bicycle, no joke for either rider or machine when the rider turns the scales at more than 200 lb. But at least it spelt a modicum of safety in the grey police-ridden streets. A shadower on foot has to run to keep pace with a bicycle; a car has to crawl. In city traffic a bicycle made it easier to get rid of both.

* Told in Bruce Marshall's brilliant book, " The White Rabbit."

He knew the Gestapo were getting closer, and he sought an assurance that there was something in life more than fear and sickness of the soul. The fear was upon him, and Dany and the resilient Moulines saw it and were sad. What Touny had been to him, so was he to them—their leader, the fearless and incorruptible one, a man who could truly be called great. Each new day brought new setbacks, the tension and frustration mounting until the screaming nerves could scarcely stand more. Like the time they spent the entire afternoon ringing a " letter-box " at a *crémerie* on the Left Bank. Each time an unfamiliar voice answered with deceptive friendliness: " Hallo, where are you speaking from? " Girard and Dany hung up, not saying anything, to ring again from different cafés and each time there was the friendly voice, loaded with treachery. One more useless " letter-box." One step nearer betrayal.

Once they nearly laid hands on him through Kaskoreff's sister, Suzanne, a quiet studious woman in her forties, more like a university teacher than the secret agent of fiction. On her way from her brother to Girard's three-in-one apartment, carrying a sheaf of reports, she was caught in a surprise check-up on the Metro. As they lined up on the platform she found herself next to an entrance marked " Interdite " and slipped up it. Footsteps scraped in pursuit a moment later but instead of faltering she ran until her lungs were bursting, tumbling on to another platform and into a train. The burly man in the trench-coat just made the next compartment and she could see him glowering through the glass as she sat plainly in view through two more stations, before trying the oldest trick in the world.

At the République Metro, just as the pneumatic doors were wheezing shut, she flung herself on to the platform, bruising her knees, but triumphant. The Gestapo man's reflexes were in slacker shape. As the train thundered out he was beating angrily at the compartment door.

News came on 10th March that all their efforts regarding Brossolette had been sorely wasted. At the Gestapo post on the Avenue Foch he had been tortured three times—he knew quite clearly at the last that he would have to tell them all he knew, and his cyanide pill had been taken from him, so there was no escape that way. After ten hours of it they took him alive and yearning for the peace of death to a small room on the fifth floor. At nine that night he was due for another interview. His only guard, a Roumanian in a German uniform, left him for a few moments to fetch food.

All his life Brossolette had prided himself on his realism, and even in the throes of his calvary, he was clear-headed, without self-pity. He knew—and the messages he smuggled out survive as testimony—that only one fundamental problem remained: to leave the world as expeditiously as once he had entered it. It had to end this way if thousands along the Wall were not to face the same agony: the only problem had been how. But here was a window, and no guard, so at the last there was no problem at all.

In the grey spring light he ran at the window, and as the guard turned the handle of the door he was through. Two floors down he struck a balcony, and for a moment hung poised, awfully, shock and agony pounding his broken body, before squeezing all his will into one swooning gesture and toppling head downwards. He hit the concrete courtyard sixty feet below and did not regain consciousness.

Then the Gestapo struck again. At Girard.

There are conflicting versions of what happened after that, but all are at least agreed that the first warning came in the second week of March, 1944. A meeting was being held in Berthelot's office in the Place Madeleine, and all the Paris heads were there: Berthelot, Girard, Colonel Nobody, Moulines, Kaskoreff. Others, Secret Army and Century chiefs, had been summoned urgently to Paris to discuss a new and troubling problem.

" Operation Grand-Duke " had switched suddenly and bloodily to the districts of Rennes, Angers and Le Mans. It was too early yet to total the arrests (only later did they find that 800 had been swept into the net) but in recent weeks many operations like parachutages had gone appallingly wrong, with the Gestapo catching many teams red-handed right on the dropping-ground. Everything pointed to a high-level leak.

At this meeting it was noticeable that two men failed to appear. One was General Audibert, the head of the Secret Army cells in Rennes and Angers. The other was Lamoureux de la Saussaye, the gaunt scholarly head of the Sarthe section of Century, who had been sent to meet the General at the Gare Montparnasse. Their absence made everyone tense and edgy, and the only light relief came when Girard in passing congratulated Moulines on his audacious attempt to rescue Brossolette. The young aristocrat's face puckered as if he had bitten on a persimmon, and he begged: " Don't mention it, *patron*, please . . . it's something I'd rather forget."

" Being so close to them in that stinking gaol? " Girard was all sympathy. " It must have been hard."

But Moulines, in a voice trembling with disgust, was explaining, " Not the gaol, chief—the gaoler's daughter. My God, she was ugly . . . and having to butter her up every day like that . . ." He ended brokenly, " It wasn't war, at all, it was a sacrifice."

The rich belly-chuckles were suddenly tempered by the realisation that there was still no news of Saussaye or General Audibert. Hastily Berthelot broke up the meeting, and as they went severally and surreptitiously out on to the Place Madeleine, a messenger was already on his way to Saussaye's apartment.

Again it became a time of waiting, with Girard chafing uneasily in the three-in-one flat, too restless now to savour the peace of green buds thrusting above the Ile de la Cité. Each fragment of news was ominous in its brevity. Later that day Berthelot telephoned to say that the messenger had not dared enter Saussaye's apartment. Across the street a man in a rain-coat had been very busy reading a newspaper. Coincidence perhaps—if you discounted the second man farther down the street, equally absorbed in that day's news.

Next the messenger had gone to the apartment of one of Saussaye's assistants, whom we shall call " Lanfranc." Here the concierge was chatty but unhelpful. " Lanfranc " had gone. He had left his furnished apartments that midday carrying a heavy suit-case. Another uneasy coincidence. " Lanfranc," more than anyone else, had been in closest touch with the areas where the arrests had taken place, and had also held a watching brief over the reception teams assembled for parachutage.

The one shred of comfort was that " Lanfranc," if a traitor, could do only limited damage. To the Paris heads he had been an almost unknown quantity, one of many regional organisers; in Paris he knew only a few pseudonyms and fewer addresses. His main contacts had been among the 800 arrested men. There was safety too, in the knowledge of the quiet gentle Saussaye's loyalty to Century's cause. His sense of security, for instance, would have been good enough for him not to inform " Lanfranc " that he was meeting General Audibert at the station.

Next day the news was worse. Word came from General Audibert that Saussaye had not met him; not knowing the rendezvous he had been unable to attend the meeting. Then, from Fresnes prison, where Brossolette had been held so recently, came other news. During the night Saussaye had been brought in, soaked in blood, his face almost unrecognisably puffy. It seemed logical now that the treason could be laid at " Lanfranc's " door. Who else could have forewarned the Gestapo that Saussaye always carried a cyanide pill on him in case of arrest?

For forty-eight hours Girard stayed put. Now he hardly knew what to do for the best, and each time the telephone rang, bringing the latest whispered bulletin from Berthelot, his heart was like a block of ice in his chest. Saussaye was being questioned daily now in the Gestapo post on the Avenue Foch. So far they had not broken him down.

Some days later, around 12th March, Dany was climbing the long cobbled hill of the rue Cardinal Lemoine, past the Co-operatives and the little dark bars, and the École St. Genevieve on the corner, where the clapper of the cracked bell clamoured above the shrieks of the children at play. Walking up the long alley towards the concierge's lodge to check that all was clear her pulse was fluttering in her throat, and when, without warning, the concierge came out of her lodge and gripped her arm it was all she could do not to cry out.

" Don't go up, Mademoiselle. Run, now, as fast as you can, and warn Monsieur Girard. The Gestapo are in his first apartment."

Her voice shaken with the horror of it, the concierge explained how the Gestapo had arrived in a black Citroën, leading a tall emaciated man whose knees gave way so often that his guides had to prop him upright. His clothes were rent and bloodstained but it was his eyes that had most shocked the concierge: glaring tormented eyes that seemed to focus on nothing before they lit vacantly on the apartment building. Then the man had pointed weakly, like an imbecile, and led them upstairs.

Hard enough to bear, but for Dany the worst part was the going back. Back to where Girard was waiting, as always, in the quiet back room of a café on the rue Mouffetard, her brain racing with the appalling knowledge but still compelled by some animal instinct to observe elementary precautions. Three times round the block to check any possible shadowers. Into big department stores like Monoprix and then out at the back entrance.

But she found him at last, sitting patient and prosaic, over an empty coffee cup. She had to sit down and tell him about it, her voice faltering over the description that made the identity plain—tall, emaciated, with deepset grey eyes and strongly-marked eyebrows. Saussaye.

Only with a supreme effort could she recount the other details which demanded compassion for this treason: the bloody stumps of the fingers, where the nails had been torn from the living flesh, the elbows charred black by lighted matches. Talking, she saw the hurt gathering in Girard's face, puckering like a child's as his mind and heart cried out for his friend, before the brown eyes went sightless with passion, and his fist smashed down like a hammer on the café table:

" The filthy degenerate swine! If it costs me everything I have I'll make them pay for this." And blended with the agony

273

for the sickening futile cruelty was (perhaps) anger that the Germans had pierced his own tough armour and shown him as vulnerable to compassion as all the rest.

Dany groped for words of comfort, finding few. The Gestapo didn't know about the two rear apartments, according to the concierge. How could they have done, for poor Saussaye had visited Girard only in the first apartment? The news was welcome in a way, cushioning the intolerable grief with the need for action. Girard knew that it was the second apartment that counted, where papers vital to Century's organisation were stuffed down the padding of the window-seat, the seat, where, long ago, " Third Fool's " plan had found temporary sanctuary.

" I'll go up and get them." Dany had already risen from the table, but Girard, almost maliciously, forced a smile. " Do you know where they are? "

" Well, somewhere in the second apartment, but——"

" And that's all you're going to be told," Girard said. " You're not risking your life for papers that I should never have left there. No one is going up there but me."

All they could do then was wait. And wait. The hands of the clock on the wall seemed paralysed, but at last, after two hours, Dany got up, walking briskly back through the late afternoon. This time the concierge had more cheering news. The Gestapo had gone, their arms loaded with papers and personal souvenirs—all harmless—though leaving behind a grim reminder of their visit. Two men were now posted on the roof with a machine-gun, the barrel pointing through the sky-light directly at the door of the first apartment. Dany listened with a sinking heart. It had been common Gestapo practice for some months, a new refinement of " Operation Grand-Duke."

She returned to the café and told Girard, adding: " You remember the picture of you on the wall in the first apartment? The concierge says they cut it out of the frame and took it with them."

Girard began chuckling mirthlessly; it was typical that in a moment like this his mind demanded some outlet, however small, for a flash of cynical humour. " If the photograph of a young sub-lieutenant in World War I, carrying a great deal less stomach, will help, good luck to them," he said. " Now, if they've gone, I'll go up and take a look around."

Dany cried out, " But you can't, not now! There's the machine-gun. . . ." Then she realised she was talking to the panels of the door that had slammed behind him.

Chapter Nineteen

WILD JUSTICE

Dusk was falling as Girard left the café, walking with the brisk rolling sailor's gait through that quarter of Paris that he loved above all others. As he reached the corner near the apartment building, the light seemed to die in the street; at the crest of the hill, below the Place Contrescarpe, the houses leaned almost together, shutting out the sky, and he sensed rather than saw the velos labouring past him up the long incline from the river.

He nodded to the concierge, walking too quickly to pause and gossip, and began to climb the stairs. There was no electric light to guide him and in the grey almost liquid light that filtered from alcove windows his feet seemed to sound very loudly. Would the steps carry to the waiting gunners somewhere above so that they tensed above the trigger? Girard didn't know, but " it always took everything you'd got to climb those stairs, never quite knowing what was at the top." That evening, perhaps, it took more.

He reached the sixth floor, knowing that whatever he did now he must not pause. One hint of uncertainty in his step and the gunners might shoot without waiting to ask questions. For the same reason he must not pause or even falter near the door of the first apartment. Keep walking, briskly and confidently, a man with nothing on his conscience. Keep walking and don't look up.

He was in the hallway with the last light of the day streaming through the wide windows, and in a lifetime of seconds, all Paris was at his feet: the brown motionless river and the chestnuts budding by Notre Dame; very far away, above the jungle of roofs, the shining basilica of Sacré-Coeur that Utrillo had loved and painted. Beloved shadows, all fading with the dusk.

He could never know whether he saw the machine-gun barrel blurring the skylight. Walking steadily, he was keeping his eyes on the ground. Somewhere above the gunners crouched motionless, making no sound, but a shadow swung with the dappled light as he walked: the machine-gun barrel was keeping pace. Then he had passed it, not glancing at the closed silent door of the first apartment, and on past the second. Unlocking the door of the third apartment, he seemed to feel, not seeing, the gun jabbing at the small of his back above the kidneys. The sound of the turning key grated all over the house.

His body was bathed in sweat now, and after he had stopped, locking the door behind him, he paused and mopped his face. He bent, squinting through the keyhole, but he could see and hear nothing. The hall was dark and empty and in all the apartment building there was no sound.

There was a connecting door between the second and third apartments, used for emergencies like this. He unlocked that and passed through. Moving to the banquette by the window he began to work fast, stuffing papers into his pockets as quickly as he could. Ten long minutes crept by as he waited in the darkness. Then back to the third apartment, open the door, lock it again from the outside. He was halfway down the hallway when he realised his mistake.

He thought, I must be getting too old for the job. Why bring the papers out, at the mercy of any snap-check in the streets or in the Metro? Once Renault had said: " A bicycle and a flush-toilet are an agent's best friends." He should have put them down the toilet.

Too late now. He was under the gun again, and from above, as he walked, there came the slightest rustling sound, like a faint exhalation of breath. But nothing more. He went down the stairs automatically, like a man who had been drugged, and into the darkening street to rejoin Dany.

After that, understandably, his own rôle, like Renault's and " Third Fool's " was more or less played out, though at first his brisk dogmatism rejected any such notion. With Berthelot's help he took a combined bed-sitter-cum-office on the mezzanine floor of the old Palais Royal, which in 400 years had offered hospitality to kings, League of Nations dwellers and private apartment holders before yielding its upper floors, in 1940, to the Economic Planning Division of the Wehrmacht. Girard found the camouflage of field-grey that loomed large on the stairs and in the lobby useful, and he kept in touch with Century and Secret Army activities along the Wall as best he could. The room was the scene of several hit-and-run meetings and others were held in Kaskoreff's apartment near the Gare d'Austerlitz or at a room Harivel had rented on the elegant rue de Rivoli.

On 15th March twenty agents of Century-St. Lô, including the burly schoolmaster, Franck, their chief, were seized by the Gestapo, and it was known that the Germans had set a heavy price on Moulines's head. Two more leaders lost to the cause.

As far as Girard could remember it was on Friday, 31st March, that things came to a head finally, towards three o'clock in the afternoon. Only he, Dany and Kaskoreff were present and afterwards they could not even recall what they were discussing, only that it was something demanding an urgent phone call to someone else in the network. Girard uncradled the phone and once again he had that indescribable feeling. It was as if Dany and Kaskoreff had become frozen in the moment of speaking and all sound and motion had receded, like a film slowing down. They were staring at him, he knew, and the operator's voice came, shrill and mechanical, " *J'écoute.*" But just the same he put the phone down and a second later, before they could say anything, it rang.

It was as if he had been willing all life to halt, waiting for this to happen. He grabbed it and heard the concierge of the Palais Royal panting: " Monsieur! Gestapo! They're taking the lift." He smashed back the phone, growling " Gestapo " and they were out of the door almost as one, running for the stairs. They heard the long whine of the lift ascending as they took them two at a time. In the foyer, doubling for the street,

they heard the lift-gates clash above, and Girard said afterwards
that only thirty seconds had saved them.

The same day Touny's successor, General de Jussieu, known
to the Underground as Pontcarral, ordered Girard to leave
Paris. In some ways the big leonine man who had directed the
war against the Wall for so long could not regret it: no man
can continue to give of his best when he is hunted like an
animal night and day. He went to the country, ostensibly as
a business man on holiday in the little riverside village of
Chatelet, not far from Fontainebleau. The first day there the
head of the local Maquis, a garage man named Aubin (no kin
to Century's Argentan chief), introduced him to two pork
butchers, an ordinary butcher and a friendly grocer, and for
the first time in months Girard began to eat and sleep well.

That was 1st April, two years to the day since he had met
Renault in that middle-class apartment, and it had all begun.
It did not occur to him, being Girard, and he would have
thought that Fate was being ridiculously melodramatic if it
had.

That was about the afternoon when a Very Senior French
Officer in London, studying the casualty reports of the
Resistance, decided that if something were not done about the
wave of repressions organised by the *Milice* there would be no
Century agents or Secret Army—they were the French Forces
of the Interior, or F.F.I. now—left to watch or to fight.
Accordingly he issued high-level instructions and all that April,
like a succession of small shock-waves, outraged Vichy head-
lines were screaming: " Local *Milice* chief assassinated by
terrorists."

In Caen, not unnaturally, the job fell to the Century and
F.F.I. men grouped under Meslin. Because of Lucien Brière
the bearded *Milice* Chief, many of Century's agents were lying
low and many more were dead. Even Girard could not return
to Caen to lead his men on D-Day. At a conservative count
Brière had been personally responsible for 140 arrests and was
rumoured to have received 100,000 francs in Gestapo bonuses.

One of the few agents not lying low was Arsène, the one-eyed plumber, and probably he had escaped only because Brière nourished the hope of catching him red-handed. One day, in the last week of April, Brière ran full tilt into Arsène in the street. "You haven't long to go, Arsène," he said quietly. Arsène looked at him steadily. "When we do meet, friend," he said, "you will be the sheep and I the butcher." Maybe this preyed on Brière's mind, for he told a local shopkeeper, "There are some people threatening my life, but I'm safe enough. I wear a bullet-proof waistcoat." This intelligence reached Arsène a day later, at the same time as he received instructions to remove Brière from the face of this earth.

At lunch-time in the Café de la Consigne they plotted the details. To help him Arsène had three other local agents— two men named Carnet and Jean-Marie Vicquot, and Sonsay, the red-headed coal merchant, who was to drive the getaway car. Arsène borrowed this from Roger Savard, the farmer at Anisy, but although Savard was a Century agent, Arsène did not want him raising objections. "One of my kids is sick," he told Savard. "I need it to take him into hospital." Arsène was a scrupulously honest man, perhaps the most unflinchingly upright of any in the network. When he had borrowed the car, an old grey Peugeot, he did drive his small son, who had bad earache, to the hospital. Then he took the car to a friendly garage and changed the number plates.

Arsène planned the job for the night of 30th April. Brière lived on the rue des Fosses du Château with a bodyguard of two S.S. men—a fieldstone house that stood below the grey old castle. The house was divided from its neighbours by a narrow passage, leading to a communal backyard, and Arsène took pains to visit the old lady who lived next door. "If you hear a noise to-night, quite late," he said, "don't be frightened and, above all, *don't* open the door." She was old and feeble-witted but he thought she understood.

He could not have been more wrong.

The plan was to arrive softly at the side entrance of Brière's house and booby-trap the door handle with half a dozen primed grenades. Then they would beat a retreat up the alley to create a disturbance and the sudden eruption of the S.S. men from the side door, which opened inwards, would jerk the pins from the grenades and bring the house down about their ears. But at eleven that same night, stumbling incautiously in the pitch dark, Arsène's foot caught an ashcan and at once the old lady next door set up a piercing cry of " *Au voleur! Au voleur!* " (Thief! Thief!) Brière and the S.S. men came out with drawn guns, but by that time Arsène and the others were pelting for their lives.

They wasted no time. What had failed one day must succeed the next. From observation they knew that Brière usually returned to his house for lunch about midday, leaving again for Gestapo headquarters towards two. That Monday, 1st May, was warm and sunny; as usual on a Monday in France, most shops were shut and there were few people about. Around midday Arsène took up a position in the front window of the house of Madame Tourmont, the coal merchant, which faced Brière's own. Within minutes he saw the bearded Brière come walking alone, straight in the centre of the street, as he always did, arms rigidly to his side, blue burning eyes glaring ahead. Dry-mouthed, but calm, Arsène crouched below the level of the sill, watching.

The others would be moving into position now. A hundred yards down the street, at the intersection of the rue Alain, Vicquot and Carnet would be loitering. A few yards down the rue Alain, Sonsay would have drawn the Peugeot into the right-hand kerb. From one-thirty onwards the engine would be running.

Time dragged. On his knees, peering through Madame Tourmont's lace curtains, Arsène could see the sleeping street. All Caen was at its lunch-hour. A daemonic compulsion gripped him to kill and have done with it; he was a deeply religious man but he felt no qualms of conscience. His God was a stern Old Testament God: " Thou shalt give life for life." Century's agents had died and others were holed up like rats in a barn because this man—a Frenchman—had betrayed them for gold and his own warped ends.

The little gilt clock in the living-room struck one-thirty and almost on the last stroke the door slammed and Brière came out, walking fast down the street. For a moment Arsène gaped; he had not expected things to crystallise so abruptly, then, not waiting to say good-bye to Madame Tourmont, he doubled into the street. Brière was twenty yards ahead now, striding briskly. Arsène began to run, a steady loping gait, his rubber-soled shoes scuff-scuffing over the cobbles. The gun was hard against his thigh, a heavy Luger, primed with enamel bullets one inch long; they were all using revolvers because an automatic weapon would shudder too much, perhaps only spraying the body enveloped by the bullet-proof waistcoat. He palmed the gun, thumbing back the catch.

Four other people saw the gun before Brière, which was nearly the end of it. Moisy, the hire-car proprietor, saw it from the window of his office; he jumped up and ran to the threshhold but Arsène, still running, was making frantic motions with his left hand: " *Keep back, keep away!* " The German sentry guarding the castle entry saw it, then saw too, the ominous loitering figures of Vicquot and Carnet moving in. The rifle clattered on the stones as he turned and ran. An Algerian seaman, coming from a side-street with a child clutching his hand saw it, and wavered irresolute. Arsène slackened his pace, unnerved, a father of three who loved his children deeply. With a child in his line of fire, he was powerless.

Twenty yards ahead, Brière saw the men loitering and slowed up, scenting danger; he backed a pace and his hand strayed above his hip. The Algerian bundled the child to him and dived for a doorway. Brière heard the steady shuffling of the rubber-soled shoes on the road behind. He turned and saw Arsène ten yards back, the Luger in his hand, closing in.

His hand flew for the gun and in the crowded second that he struggled to free it, Arsène saw not this, but opportunity: the pale expanse of flesh above Brière's collar, below his left ear. He stopped short, sighted and shot him and Carnet fired simultaneously at right angles, the echoes volleying from the high walls. Brière jerked violently across the cobbles as if whirled by an invisible wire.

Coming closer, Arsène turned the body over. They had done better than they had known. One bullet had lodged at the base of the skull, and the other, his own, had severed the left carotid artery. The blood was bright and wine clear, pumping all over the stones; never in his life had he seen so much blood, but the worst part of the job still had to be done. From under his denims Vicquot produced a camera and to prove to London that they had done their duty they took a picture before bolting for the car. Sonsay gunned the motor into life and they drove away.

They buried Brière at the Église St. Jean three days later. Only the Mayor of Caen, Monsieur Detolle, who had no option in the matter, followed the coffin, but along the route the pavements were packed five deep, as in other days the people would have queued for the marathon cycling event the *Tour de France*. Whistles, cat-calls and slow hand-clappings followed the hearse on its way. " Revenge," said Francis Bacon once, " is a kind of wild justice "; the justice had been wild, but the score seemed more equal now.

Chapter Twenty

A WALL IS BREACHED

THROUGHOUT MAY, 1944, the Century-Secret Army situation along and behind the Wall was as follows: Girard was in hiding near Fontainebleau, and Dany and Moulines were lying low in Paris. " Third Fool " Duchez remained with the Maquis of St. Clair on the windy hilltop near Falaise. Robert Thomas was in hiding forty miles from Caen and Gille was in Paris. In Caen, Meslin, haggard and greying with strain, was back behind his desk in the highway engineer's department, controlling a fistful of agents in their last-minute survey of the Wall.

Far inland now the heavy bombers were pounding the rail centres and the river bridges, denying troops and supplies to the Wall, and as the flow of cement dwindled to a trickle, Rommel's chances of gaining victory at the water's edge receded to zero. Between Ouistreham and Isigny the strong-points were spread as far as 1,300 yards apart, like tight knots in a frayed length of rope, and north of St. Lô on the coast only fifteen per cent of these were bombproof. Rommel was making a desperate last-minute attempt, but even given a far tougher wall his troops would have had small leeway to manoeuvre. Time had run out on the conquerors.

New agents were coming on the scene in Meslin's sector, and one of them was Duchez's old friend Léon Dumis. Strictly speaking, the little garage proprietor had been a Century agent from the first, but some of his war, after " Third Fool's " theft of the map, had been spent in the Haute Savoie looking after his family and another period had been devoted to political propaganda. But in the spring of 1944 he returned to Caen. In the last week of May the dapper, courteous little Dumis took up temporary headquarters at Ifs, a small village lying four miles south and east of Caen.

The Mayor of Ifs, Monsieur Paul Rosette, had advertised for someone to travel from farm to farm checking the milk-producing capacity of dairy cattle for the benefit of children and old people. Dumis applied for and got the job. Credentials in French and German furnished a passport for his journeyings.

Ifs was farming country, lonely and flat as a billiard board. Trudging from one dung-spattered farmyard to the next, where the shaggy Norman sheep-dogs strained savagely on their chains, Dumis felt as exposed as a small black purposeful fly on a white wall. Sometimes the sun caught a telltale flash from a field position, and he knew that the Germans had grown suspicious and were watching him through binoculars. But all they could see was a dapper dignified little man, almost a caricature of a provincial Frenchman, eternally pacing the pastures and chewing matches. Eventually they must have written him off as harmless.

But Dumis had a system as he went from farm to farm. The whole village of Ifs was ringed with ack-ack batteries: 88s, 105s, 10.5 howitzers, and these in turn were only a part of the chain of ack-ack girdling Caen from the south, stretching from the villages of Etavaux to Le Poirier. It was guns, not butter, that interested Dumis, and with the bitten matches as his guide he was pacing the distance between them.

One whole match meant 100 yards, a half-match 50 yards. A quarter match 25 yards. The sticks that added up to the distance between any two points went into the same pocket. In the evenings, at the old farmhouse where the Mayor had billeted him, Dumis counted chewed match-ends, temporarily incorporating the figures in his milk tabulations. Each morning early he met Gille in Caen to pass on his findings. Gille had returned from Paris and was once again hiding out at Janine Boitard's house in the rue de Place, where a radio transmitter kept Century in touch with the B.C.R.A. in London. Thus the co-ordinates of almost forty batteries passed to the Allies.

Each movement in the overall symphony was now performed to the thundering crescendo of bombs that seemed to tear the earth apart. Century had confirmed that fifty of Rommel's coastal batteries were not yet under concrete, and since the gun emplacements had given the planners more qualms than any other factor of the Wall, these and forty separate links in the radar chain were receiving due attention from the Allied Air Forces.

Security decreed that two targets outside the zone were pounded for every one inside, but the batteries at Pointe du Hoe, St. Martin de Varreville and Ouistreham, and Michel's radar station at La Délivrande, now trembled under the sledgehammer blows. Due to heavy overcast, the bombs exploded more minefields than batteries, though that helped the sappers on D-Day; it was the Naval shells at H-hour that wrought most havoc among Century's prize targets. But the radar bombing was an unqualified success, and on D-Day, with counter-measures adding to the chaos, the " ears " of the Wall were only five per cent effective.

In the last week of May these things happened:

On Wednesday 31st May, Mercader, the bicycle merchant, went from Bayeux to Paris to meet one of Girard's deputies, a man named Delante, in a flat on the rue Lafitte. He was given four code messages and resolved privately that his parents, who lived in Caen, must leave the city by Monday at the latest.

At No. 48 rue de la Bien Faisance, Paris, Gille, on Meslin's behalf, received the same messages.

André Heintz, the young schoolmaster in charge of Girard's teenage section, who would act as scouts and runners in the battle, was giving an English lesson at the Lycée St. Joseph, Caen. The janitor came to announce a woman visitor and downstairs in the hall Heintz found Madame Barjot, wife of one of Girard's deputies. Heintz paced up and down, gabbling the messages to memorise them, while gathering sounds of insurrection floated from the class room upstairs. Racing back, the messages burning in his mind, he ran into the headmaster, but even fast-talking didn't save him from a rocket or the class from an imposition.

On the night of 1st June, at nine-fifteen, the B.B.C. and the

Voice of America broadcast certain personal messages. The first had an ominous note: " THE HOUR OF COMBAT IS AT HAND." Others were more in keeping with spring and a young man's fancy: " THE FLOWERS ARE VERY RED ": " EILEEN IS MARRIED TO JOE."

Two days passed. On Saturday 3rd June, the stocky bespectacled " Colonel Nobody " was in Rouen. He attended a secret meeting in a house on the left bank of the Seine. When night had fallen he crossed, crouching in a barge, to the right bank and gave instructions to a liaison agent. This man cycled seventeen miles through the night to Lisieux and repeated the message to another man in a café. Now the second man hopped on a bicycle and pedalled off. The message passed along the chain: Make ready.

On the Sunday at six o'clock, Meslin had finished a day's catching up on mail. Jeanne Verinaud was easing the cover over her typewriter when he left the room and walked across the yard to the municipal electrician's workshop, where a secret receiver was stored. At six-twenty he returned and said wearily: " I think very soon it'll all be over."

Mercader was with his parents, urging them to leave Caen, without explaining why, but his eloquence left the old people unpersuaded. He never saw them again.

The night of 5th June was hot and airless. Almost everyone was at home behind closed shutters, sensing that something was going to happen, not knowing when. At nine-fifteen, after the news in French, a dry B.B.C. voice from Bush House, London, began reciting a string of personal messages that had a ring of Alice in Wonderland. The burly placid Jean Chateau and his wife were eating an omelette in the kitchen of their house on Route Nationale 13. Rigid with emotion Chateau said: " Why—I think this is it."

" THE DICE ARE ON THE TABLE," said the voice. " Repeat, THE DICE ARE ON THE TABLE." In the darkness along the coast teams of five men armed with charges and detonators went quietly from their houses to carry out the first instalment of " Colonel Passy's " Green Plan. Explosions erupted along the Wall as Gresselin's men dynamited the Paris-Cherbourg

287

line above Carentan and the line between St. Lô and Coutances. Other teams blew the Paris-Granville line near St. Manvieu, the lines between Caen and Bayeux and between Caen and Vire. (Later Gresselin's men had the unspeakable joy of reporting Germans mounted on bicycles moving into battle from Coutances.)

" IT IS HOT IN SUEZ," warned the voice. " IT IS HOT IN SUEZ." In the heathland above Omaha Beach the " undisciplined " Farine split forty men into eight teams of five and they melted into the darkness. Armed with shears and other tools they cut the mighty telephone cable that ran from Cherbourg to Smolensk in eight 2-inch sections. Century's St. Lô chief, the burly ex-schoolmaster Franck, was still in the gaol where the Gestapo had left him to rot, but one of his deputies, a man named Crouzot, led a team through the darkness to cut the vital military telephone line between German 84th Corps H.Q. at St. Lô and the 91st Divisional H.Q. at Valognes. Gresselin's teams demolished the St. Lô-Jersey cable and the long-distance line from Cherbourg to Brest. The sluggishness of German reaction in the Cotentin to the first shock-punch owed much to Girard's men.

Arsène was in his cellar, one ear cocked for the footsteps of a police patrol, one ear for the messages which crackled and whined in the static. Thick and fast the messages came, more than 300 of them, so crowded together that Resistants and Gestapo were hard put to it to distinguish their own group message from the others: " JOHN REMEMBERS RITA . . . THE COMPASS POINTS NORTH. . . ." Eisenhower had decided to create maximum chaos behind the lines by releasing every sabotage signal at once: a brilliant stroke because *Abwehr* stool-pigeons broke twenty-eight of them before deciding that the Allies had only a night exercise in progress. Last of all came the message signalling wholesale action, the words of an old French song, imbued with grim meaning: " THE CHILDREN GET BORED ON SUNDAY."

That meant Get ready, distribute arms, contact your leader, report every move the Germans make, get ready. . . . And Arsène rubbed his hands and chuckled, thirsting for action.

On and on now, every half-hour till dawn, " THE CHILDREN GET BORED ON SUNDAY. Repeat. THE CHILDREN GET BORED ON SUNDAY."

Léon Dumis did not hear the messages. For the last six nights he had not left the batteries at Ifs. The farmhouse where he had been billeted seemed no longer safe and he was sleeping in the open, beneath a hedge, screened from the stars by a clump of elms. Across the road, 150 yards away, was a German battery and he could hear the talk and the sleepy curses as one shift relieved another. (Six weeks later the Allies blew all those batteries to smithereens.) Through the gloom a man loomed up on a bicycle, and whistled softly, and Dumis struggled through the grass to meet him. " They are coming," the man said and then was swallowed up in darkness. Dumis thought: " At last." But he was too tired to know any more complex emotion before falling asleep.

The citizens of Caen slept peacefully, the men and women of Century among them, until 2 a.m. Then for the 1,020th time since war began the air-raid sirens blew over the city. Soon there came the droning of thousands of planes, followed by the high whistling crash of bombs tearing at the eardrums. Fires were started and a wind blew up to fan the heavy orange flicker of the flames. Soon the old dry wood of the medieval houses was flaming like a blow-torch. The massive Torres, Century's security officer, was sleeping peacefully when he heard a snapping crack, like a great sheet of ice breaking, followed by a rumble like a thousand bricks raining on to sheet-iron. Blinking, he emerged to see beyond his sitting-room, the waters of the canal, mirroring the dancing flames. The blast had taken away the front of his house.

Next morning those who had slept at all awoke red-eyed to the steady rumbling of the guns: warships were crashing broadsides deep into the interior beyond the wall, and all the earth seemed to tremble with the sound. The Channel waters were black with the great armada and as the American boats scraped on the beaches east of Cherbourg at 06.30, four years and two days after Dunkirk, dark swollen clouds hung low in the sky, obscuring the targets for the bombers that were pounding the giant guns.

Almost all the targets on which Century had reported faithfully received priority attention. Along Omaha Beach, at Vierville, Les Moulins, St. Laurent and Colleville, the U.S. First Army had achieved a shaky foothold and were pushing inland through four of Farine's " doors "—to the west, the U.S. Rangers scaled the cliffs at Pointe du Hoe to find the earth ripped for hundreds of yards as if by an earthquake but the lethal gun positions were now empty and unmanned. So, too, were the batteries at St. Martin de Varreville, above Utah Beach . . . the Cherbourg garrison were preparing for a bitter last-ditch stand, but Gresselin slipped through the lines to make contact with the U.S. 82nd Airborne Division, feeding them enough dispositions and details to win him the Bronze Star Medal when the great port fell. . . .

. . . Snarling spattering fire raked the beaches at Ouistreham, but No. 4 Commando under the French captain, Philip Kieffer, doubled behind it to capture the garrison manning the cunningly-camouflaged blockhouses . . . all Dr. Sustendal's territory, the villages of Luc-sur-Mer, Langrune and St. Aubin, were taken on the same day . . . their captors, No. 4 Special Service Brigade, went on later to take Gilbert Michel's radar station at La Délivrande. . . .

And in one day's tough fighting, the Wall was breached and the bridgeheads secured. Here and there, as von Rundstedt had predicted, isolated strongpoints held out, but the Allied armour was probing inland to Caen. The Allies held the air. German transport was slow and sluggish; the raw troops exhausted, pitifully short of ammunition. With almost no mobile reserves to counter the break-through, the Wall was seen at last for what it was—a myth in concrete, of two years standing, exploded in as many days.

Century's personnel had a new rôle behind the Wall now: to maintain contact with the Allied forces in each sector, to supply guides and maps and up-to-date Intelligence and to operate as the G-2 branch of the local F.F.I. But in the first chaos that followed the carpet bombing, the flames spread steadily; the fire station was hit and the whole centre of Caen had become a roaring red-hot inferno. All contact between

agent and agent was cut off. Early on the morning of the 6th
Meslin took his car, driving hard for Falaise to bring back
dynamite but on the way a German plane swooped down over
the highway and shot him up. The car overturned and Meslin
scrambled out in the nick of time as it burst into a shaking
yellow curtain of flame. Bruised and shocked, he was cut off
from Caen by the tanks of the 21st Panzer Division, the one
first-rate unit then at Rommel's disposal, surging up to block
the breaches in the Wall.

In St. Lô, Franck escaped from the blazing gaol to find his
two children lying dead in the ruins. But ten days later he
had set up a new Century post with a team of five agents and
established radio contact with the American lines.

All that day the bombing of Caen went on, so that by the
end of it many had neither houses nor food, nor anything but
the clothes they stood up in. (All water had been cut off in
the first bombardment.) But defeat is in the minds of men, and
they were not defeated.

With Meslin cut off, Century's leadership and the command
of F.F.I. cadres passed to that clever, restless advocate, Léonard
Gille. (By military theory they were two distinct bodies, but
with glorious unorthodoxy each man was now both agent and
fighter.) Gille, returning from Paris, had been cut off at
Evreux on D-Day, and since the only way to cover the seventy-
five miles was on foot, Gille walked. On Friday, 9th June, as
he approached Caen, his heels had worn level with the soles of
his shoes and his already sparse weight had dropped by a stone.
No cars were on the road that day, but as he neared the city
fire-engines from Paris went braying past, and the roads leading
east churned with fleeing refugees: ragged children with hurt
puzzled eyes, the wasted yellow faces of very old women cowled
beneath black shawls, a peasant leading a white horse with the
Red Cross of mercy daubed on its forehead, back and rump.

" Go back," they shouted to Gille. " Caen is burning.
Come with us to Lisieux." When Gille shouted back that
Lisieux was almost razed to the ground, some of them sat down
in the dust of the roadside and cried.

Some who knew Gille gave him more positive news. The

house containing the two-way receiver in the rue de Place had toppled in the first raid. More than anything then Gille wanted to push on to Caen, if need be to claw beneath the rubble with his bare hands, for the husky-voiced Janine meant everything to him, and if ever there was any way out of this he had plans to make her his wife. Then duty became a nagging unattractive voice, telling him that for this he had waited four years, that the first thing for a commander to do was to work south of Caen and set up his command. Limping badly, hating the flies and the dust and the milk-sweet smell of dead cattle, the indomitable Gille first plunged north across the apple-orchards and the farms.

At last, working west behind the German lines, Gille reached the village of Le Tourneur. (Bayeux was already in Allied hands, and Century-Bayeux, in the person of Mercader, was entertaining a diffident senior officer named Colonel Renault, who had landed that day and reminisced: " Century? I remember how I founded that network. . . .") There Gille contacted Roger Deschambres, the red-haired plumber who had succeeded Duchez, and took up the threads of the network. Months before the invasion took place, Meslin had organised a chain of couriers on bicycles in every village between Le Tourneur and Argentan, thirty miles south. Down the chain went the message: " Tell René Duchez to report to Commandant Gille at Louvigny."

Gille planned to organise his command post in the village of Louvigny, where a small cache of arms had been stored in the house of Monsieur Larousse, the Mayor. Jean Chateau was already on the spot, awaiting orders.

On 12th June, Dumis, too, arrived at Louvigny, a small stone village two miles south-west of Caen, by the water meadows of the Orne: one crumbling main street and small cottage gardens divided by mortared walls. That day his heart was sad, for he had been thinking of Duchez, whom he had admired above all other men, and of the reckless buccaneering way in which he filched maps and made the Germans dance to *his* tune. He wondered if he would ever see him again.

Entering Louvigny at twilight he stopped short. A familiar

figure had materialised on the road ahead. A shambling incon-
sequent figure, wearing a beret and a heavy topcoat, a familiar
grinning face that had made some peculiar attempt to disguise
itself by growing a bushy beard and wearing not spectacles but
two separate monocles.

His voice shaking with admiration and love, Dumis hailed
this apparition: " You mean to say that *you* have dared to
come back here? "

" *C'est le sang-froid, mon ami,*" chuckled " Third Fool."

For four days Gille's command post worked well. The battle
was too far north to know very plainly what was going on, but
Gille had made contact with trusted veterans like Marigny the
bookseller and Masseron the pork butcher, and set them to
work gathering information on troop movements and the
whereabouts of mobile batteries. In the front room of a small
stone cottage on Louvigny's main street four of them—Gille,
Duchez, Chateau and Dumis—worked and slept, eating less
frequently and washing not at all. They were grimy with sweat
and dirt and they stank impartially and uncaringly—" Third
Fool " most of all because even in the heat he would never
shed the heavy topcoat, concealing a machine-gun slung from
his shoulder.

It was all right until 17th June. That morning it was little
Dumis's turn to trudge along to a restaurant called *Chez Cebilla*
and collect their scanty rations. But in the deserted café he
ran into trouble. Cebilla, himself a Century agent, had disappeared but he found Madame Cebilla, pale and shaken in a
back room, fending off the questions of a Gestapo man. Dumis
pretended that he was a refugee from the bombing looking for
his wife, but he had answered only a few questions before a
small sick fear rose like a bubble to the surface of his mind:
This man is going to kill me. The Gestapo man's hand had
moved to his breast pocket . . . and stayed there.

Panicky thoughts seethed in Dumis's brain; his hand
dithered towards his own breast pocket. To fire—or see if the
other man drew first? Instinct prompted a bluff. After a long
minute he drew out a packet of Gauloise. At last the Gestapo

man drew his hand from *his* pocket and brought out a lighter. Neither said a word as he lit the little man's cigarette.

Presently the man went away, and Dumis hastened back to the command post, a hundred yards distant up the dusty main street. Slipping through the front door he entered a narrow musty corridor. At its farther end another door gave on to the back garden. The door of the front room was on his left and farther up, on the same side, was another room where a refugee woman lived with her mother. As Dumis entered the main room the others looked up crestfallen. " No food? " said Chateau unhappily.

Dumis was saying " There is bad news about Cebilla," when something like a mailed fist beat against the front door. All of them went very quiet; it was as if the news of a death had clouded their sunlit morning, then cautiously Gille and Dumis inched towards the window. Through a chink in the shutters they could glimpse Gestapo men in plain clothes waiting outside. One of them was the man whom Dumis had met in the café not five minutes back.

He had been watching from somewhere then—and now a truck was drawn up across the road and a troop of black-uniformed S.S. men were with him.

Abruptly the tension snapped like a thread. " Out," Gille ordered, and in Indian file they stole quietly up the corridor to the door at the farther end. As Duchez, the last of them, whipped into the back garden, the woman in the back room went slowly down the passage to open the front door. None of them ever saw her again, but in some way she must have managed to stave the Germans off. The Gestapo were still at the door as the four of them doubled amongst the thick hairy grass of an abandoned orchard, ducking under twisted boughs, until they reached the stone boundary wall of a large house standing beyond.

Three of them jumped at once, and little Dumis was astride the wall when he saw that " Third Fool," bowed down by the heavy overcoat and the machine-gun, hadn't made it. As he craned backwards, Duchez was yelling at him: " Never mind me! Jump—jump! " But somehow to Dumis it seemed

more important than anything that the valiant swaggering
" Third Fool " should survive. He leaned and hauled and got
Duchez astride. When they dropped to the ground, he
discovered that the stone of the wall had torn at his wrist,
cutting it almost to the bone.

Probably the waist-high jungle of the orchard saved them.
Over the wall they could hear the S.S. still beating and
shouting among the bushes. They sprinted across a gravelled
drive on to a lawn, crashing amongst cypress bushes, until they
found a gate. Peering up the road they saw that the S.S. had
abandoned the truck: everyone had joined the hunt in the
orchard. Doubling across the road, they crawled under a
barbed wire fence, jog-trotting along a line of osiers flanking
a stream.

A little after that they saw a military telephone line in four
colours—green, red, black and yellow—running alongside a
culvert, and Duchez showed them gleefully how to cut it and
re-splice each wire to a different connection. " You know," he
chortled as they trudged on, " I love the idea of Rommel trying
to get a command post near Ouistreham and getting a field
kitchen at St. Lô instead."

That afternoon, as they approached cautiously from the
west along the river bank, a strange silence lay over Caen:
the silence of death. Death was in the river, where the fast-
flowing brown water sported the swollen bodies of men and
horses; beneath the ruins of the Miséricorde, where eighty
people lay buried, too deep to be dug out; in the warm air,
where the rotting sickish-sweet smell fought for mastery with
the smell of urine and the stink of burnt-out fires. There was
no water in the town, no longer any sanitation. Death had
tastelessly torn the fronts from houses, callous of revealing the
intimate last-minute details: the crumpled bed, the forgotten
stockings, the stains that only a strong man would have
investigated imposed like a surrealist pattern on conventional
flowered wallpaper. In the distance the guns rumbled and
rolled. Armleted search parties trod among the ruins, seeking
rations for the 1,500 people who had sought shelter in the
Church of St. Étienne. The broken glass crackled underfoot

like dry ice. Thick yellow dust, the powdered bones of their city, drifted everywhere, coating the hair and eyelashes, catching in the throat.

Gille split the party up and set to work. At the rue de Place, treading gingerly among the ruins, he recovered maps and papers of Century's archives and later that day he found Janine, who from the ruins of her parents' home had salvaged only a red dress and a pair of strapless sandals that she had laced to her bare feet with string. "Third Fool" went to investigate his own house but found only a stinking smoking crater; at first he blamed the bombs but eye-witnesses testified later that out of revenge the S.S. had fired both his house and the Café des Touristes. That night all of them slept in a laundry facing the church of St. Étienne, and by the next day they had set up a new command post in a deserted vinegar factory on the rue Caponnière.

The messages coming from the agents as they sneaked through the lines each day suggested a desperate stiffening of German resistance, but to Gille it was a confused and muddled picture, and the one factor that emerged plainly was that he and his agents were still needed. All day messages came through intermittently from the British 3rd Division on the Benouville-Periers line and from Captain FitzGerald, the Canadian G-2 near Douvres: "Have you a map of so-and-so? Can you supply guides to such-and-such?" Nothing that clarified the position for him much further.

Though Gille did not know it, the battered city of Caen— *their* city—was the key to the whole Allied advance. Once the centre from which much of the Wall had been constructed, the focal point of all Century's war, it was now virtually the Wall itself. Caen was the hinge of the Normandy gate, the main pivot of the German defence. By holding Caen, the Germans could deny the Allies the good tank and airfield country to the south, in the Falaise gap, and stop the Allied thrust to Paris 130 miles on.

But Gille, Duchez, little Dumis and the rest, knew nothing of this. All Gille knew was that some time early on 19th June a message came through to the vinegar factory: "Can you

supply maps as to enemy intentions north and west of Caen? "
Gille had no such maps, but the rumour locally was that
Feldkommandatur 723, in evacuating its papers from the
Hotel Malherbe, had moved them to the cellars of the Batiment
de la Jeunesse (Youth Centre) on the Avenue Albert Sorel.

The same morning he called Dumis into the office to explain
the position and Dumis, taking with him a young and attractive
blonde agent, whose cover-name was Marraine, set off to
reconnoitre. A first glance suggested it was not going to be easy.
The Youth Centre was a squat three-storey building camouflaged with green and brown stippling, its one main entrance
zealously guarded by a sentry, a sulky fair-haired boy carrying
a Schmeisser machine pistol.

For a time they watched him from the other side of the
street. The Allied advance seemed to be creating a lot of
confusion. Staff cars drew up every few minutes and high-
ranking officers bustled in and out. Under the trees Dumis and
Marraine held a brief whispered consultation before setting
off in different directions. Dumis had seen enough to realise
that the only way into the building was through the *soupirail*,
the air-hole which opened at ground level from the front wall
of the building to ventilate the cellar. The air-hole was about
two and a half feet wide by eighteen inches deep and given
time and luck he thought he could just wriggle through
without the sentry seeing.

A lot of time and a lot of luck. The sentry's beat was
approximately forty paces from the *soupirail*.

Towards midday Dumis approached the building, cuddling
into the niche formed by a projecting buttress at the south-west
corner. The sentry was still there, pacing glumly, and Dumis
kept well out of sight until he heard the light tapping of shoes
on the pavement and saw Marraine, looking very fetching and
armed with a flask of calvados, approaching the sentry. Her
words carried to him quite clearly in his refuge: " Hallo,
Landser—have a drink."

Dumis did not catch the sentry's reply; he had to peep out
before realising that the sentry hadn't offered one. Perhaps he
had been hand-picked because of an immunity to girls like

Marraine. His face sullen, he kept marching. Five paces left and five right, while Marraine stood her ground, ogling.

Dumis peeped again. Was there going to be a chance at all? The sentry had his back to him now. He came from behind the buttress, fully visible, then saw the sentry's body flex in the moment of turning and flung himself back. Again he heard Marraine's voice, honey-sweet: " What's the matter, *Landser*? Don't you like French girls? "

Dumis stayed where he was, breathing hard. The pacing and Marraine's seductive voice went on. In the damp heat of midday he could feel his pistol pressed hard against his right breast and the knife, solid and reassuring against his leg, inhaling, without pleasure, the sour smell of his own body. He had not shaved or bathed for three weeks now. Hearing silence he again tried to run for it and again the sentry almost caught him. Now, for the first time, he heard the sentry's voice.

That was better. Now Marraine's. And the sentry's voice again now. He peered round the buttress. God is very good, the little man thought, she's done it. She was proferring the bottle and the sentry's face had cracked in an unwilling grin. But he had his back to Dumis, facing Marraine, and they were talking. Now or never.

He sneaked round the buttress, stooping low, shaking so much that he thought his knees would never hold him, cocked one last glance, then wriggled through for dear life. The gloom of the cellar blotted out the sunlight and he dropped heavily seven feet to the floor below.

Chapter Twenty-One

THE LAST MAP

THE DARKNESS was so thick at first that Dumis was straining his eyes to see. That grew better after a minute but it was still hard to think coherently: the trampling of feet above his head never stopped, like the sound of barrels rumbling down a chute. For a moment, panicking, he wondered if they were planning to evacuate the building again.

The cellar was perhaps ten feet by fourteen, but it was the contents that set his mild blue eyes blinking. There were maps right enough, and apparently maps of every country in the world, but there was also ton upon ton of coal, in shining, jet-black piles, besides enough firewood to heat a regiment, many dozen bottles of wine and several hundredweight of carrots. Everything heaped higgledy-piggledy, strange for the methodical Germans. Dumis eyed the wine wistfully, because he was thirsty and because he was thinking also of how much better Duchez would have handled all this, helping himself to the wine liberally and probably carrying a bottle or two out of the cellar to make a really good story for the boys. But Duchez, after all, had a panache all his own; he plunged into danger head first, loving it, like a strong swimmer challenging an icy current. Dumis set to work examining the maps.

He thought later there must have been several hundred of them, though he soon lost count. In any case, he was twenty-five minutes on his knees on the stone floor, sorting, tossing the useless maps in disorder on to the coal. But mingling with the pride that he was proving himself worthy of Duchez's friendship was a niggling sense of worry about Marraine. Could she keep that sentry talking for as long as this?

The footfalls went on clumping overhead and once they seemed to be coming closer—to be descending the stairs that led to the cellar. Dumis drew his knife, flattened himself in an angle of the wall and waited, the urge to strike and stab if he was cornered almost transcending fear. But presently the steps went away and Dumis returned to the maps, almost shocked by a violence in himself that he had not known existed.

He was bulging with maps, when he finally straightened up. There were maps not only in his jacket and trousers pockets, but stuffed down inside his belt, under his trousers, and tucked in the turn-ups of his socks. All were combat maps of the north and west of Caen, which showed that the defences were much stronger than the British—or Century—had believed, both in the weight of armour and of troops massing in the region of La Bijude, Epron and the Château de la Londe. Now came the bigger problem—how to get them out.

Three times, taking a running jump, he felt his fingers curling round the bevelled inner edge of the *soupirail*, but each time, as he hoisted himself level, he saw that though the sentry was still chatting with Marraine, he had stopped marching and was now half-facing the air-hole. Dumis let himself tumble back into the cellar, panting. He stood about five feet five in his shoes and the effort of getting himself out was costing him more than getting himself in.

He made it at last, and, by a wonderful stroke of luck, at the split second when the sentry was taking a drink from Marraine's calvados and could not break off in mid-gulp. He had heard the sound but when he turned there was only a small grimy-looking Frenchman approaching, who at the sight of Marraine courteously whipped off his beret to expose that polished bald head.

Then there were handshakes and delighted cries of " *Ça va?* " and any fleeting suspicions the sentry might have had were altogether lulled. Marraine offered Dumis the drink that he had so richly deserved and Dumis raised the bottle, rather ceremoniously offering the toast " *A la victoire!* " All three drank to victory, careful not to specify whose.

Presently, as if it were the most natural thing in the world,

Dumis and Marraine bade farewell to the sentry and walked off arm in arm. Once round the corner, they had to stop because Dumis couldn't go any further. He just stood there shaking and trying to get hold of himself, thinking that Duchez would be proud to know him now, but he was wet all over as if he had been soaking in a bath.

The maps were in the vinegar factory an hour later, and Gille got busy breaking down the formidable array of field-works and defences into a series of grid references. Units of the 22nd Panzer Regiment and the 125th Panzer Grenadiers had been moved in from other sectors and were deployed in all the woods between St. Julien and Epron, due north of Caen. But what hit Gille most forcibly was the realisation that the Germans had withdrawn from the city centre altogether to defend it in the north and west. It was up to Century now to save what was left of their own city. Somehow they must get a detailed verbal picture to the Allies of how only 20,000 helpless citizens, clustered in the St. Étienne quarter, were left to face the ravages of the Allied bombers.

That night, 19th June, the problem was still unsolved and he discussed it with Janine as the naval shells stitched a red vindictive pattern on the darkness to the north. Gille confessed, " So far as I can make out the Allies aren't much farther inland than Douvres, but things are hotting up. Every man I've tried to get through to them to-day has failed."

Janine said slowly, " I think I know a way," and when Gille encouraged her to go on explained that an English-speaking girl of seventeen with experience in this kind of work had volunteered for duty as an agent only that morning. When she added, in the simple way that women have, that the volunteer was a Girl Guide named Marcelle Haricot, Gille had a hard job to bottle down his mirth, but Janine was a girl of great charm and tenacity, and before she had finished Gille had at least agreed to see the girl. Next morning, despite himself, he was impressed. Mademoiselle Haricot was fair-haired and slightly built, but there was a hint of iron will in her speedwell-blue eyes. Several times Gille tried to shake her determination, asking, " You don't *really* think you can get through, do you ? " in his best courtroom manner, but the girl only answered simply, " I know I can, m'sieu. I am a Girl Guide." Finally Gille gave up.

Gille noted down the grid references, both of the defence positions and of the site occupied by the survivors from the raids, in fruit juice on cigarette paper, and Mademoiselle Haricot secured them demurely in a money-belt circling her slim waist. At dusk on the 20th she set out.

Chance decreed that the toughest part of her mission came *after* she reached the Allied lines. Soon after dawn on 21st June she did reach the village of Buron and make contact with the 3rd Expeditionary Corps of the Canadian Army. But the Canadians were understandably suspicious, and held her for some hours in a stable converted into a lock-up before sending her under escort to Captain FitzGerald, G.2 of the Canadian General Staff at Douvres.

FitzGerald decided the story rang true after a bit, but here a snag arose. To winkle the Germans out of the strongholds charted on Dumis's maps the High Command decided to use heavy bombers in the novel rôle of Army co-operation. But the weather, never good, grew worse; along the broken Wall, from Cherbourg to Havre, fog rolled in with the west wind. Precision visual bombing on any scale was impossible until the ceiling lifted.

And that was how it stayed until Saturday, 8th July, when people all over Caen stirred uneasily in cellars, on filthy pallets and heaps of stained straw, awaking to the deep pulsing of engines. The bombers again, this time away to the north, and as they punched at the targets again and again, even solid cellar walls seemed to quiver like jelly. Bomber Command dropped 2,500 tons of bombs on the northern and western positions, and then at 4.30 a.m. in pouring rain three infantry divisions, British and Canadian moved in through grey treacly mud, rifles at the trail, to help the tanks mop up. People coming from their houses at first light saw German tanks, ambulances and heavy transport streaming across the river to the southern bank.

It was less surprising to Gille and his men. They were already there. Guessing that the push would soon come, Gille had crossed to the southern bank ahead of the German retreat and set up a new headquarters at No. 12 rue d'Auge, in the kitchen of a man called Gentil. ("Third Fool" had crossed by waiting until a German tank closed down its shutter, then

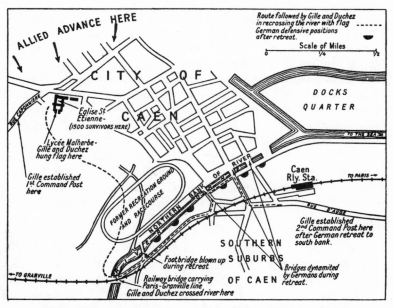

THE ESCAPE-ROUTE OVER THE RIVER ORNE

hitching a ride on the back.) Arsène, who lived a few doors away, had moved his transmitter from his own roof to the kitchen chimney at No. 12. By mingling with the Germans in the guise of A.R.P. wardens, Gille thought he could feed valuable information to the Allies on the new system of defences.

For the next twenty-four hours they worked in the silent gap-toothed ruins to set up a new command post. From time to time explosions echoed in fierce grumbling succession over the city, but Gille and company had no time to investigate their source, which was a pity. As the Germans retreated across the river they were trying to stall the Allies by dynamiting the bridges behind them.

Gille knew nothing of this, but an old vow was echoing in his brain and by early afternoon of next day, 9th July, he could stand it no longer. He said abruptly: " Look, the centre of Caen is free now—and we always swore that when it was we'd raise our flag on the flagstaff above the Lycée Malherbe." There was no sign of the Allies advancing towards the southern bank, and even Gille, well used to the torments of introspection, craved action to ease the pain of suspense. He urged: " Anything would be better than just sitting here waiting. I think it's a vow we ought to keep."

Now the Lycée Malherbe stood *across* the river, next door to the church of St. Étienne. To reach it they would have to cross the river to the northern bank (see sketch-map), braving the worst that the German defenders on the southern bank could do. But as true Frenchmen the drama and the risk of the endeavour tickled them richly. There was an eager chorus of assent.

The flag, of course, was the Cross of Lorraine and for three years they had preserved it tenderly in anticipation of this moment. Sometimes one agent had guarded it, sometimes another; it had been hidden in potting-sheds, in chimneys, under the running-boards of cars, but despite all Century's reverses it was still there intact. As Gille spoke it was under the shirt of one of the group, a willowy lad named Poinlane, wound tightly round his torso.

Towards two, Gille, Poinlane and " Third Fool " set off. Trodden paths ran between the rubble, the piles of stones and the smouldering heaps of rags, but you could no longer see where any roads had been. Small parties of Germans smeared with blood and dirt, passed them at the double, some carrying automatic weapons. Obviously a big push was expected. Far away the guns rolled but when they reached the river there was a curious sunny silence.

For the first time they saw the water boiling white over the fallen bridges.

Duchez spoke first, grinning wolfishly. " No go that way," he said. " We'll have to try farther along," and they ducked through a webwork of side-streets that had escaped the bombing until they came to a footbridge that had linked the two banks farther upstream. That, too, had been blasted, and Gille said then that there was only one chance left, to go via the railway bridge, which carried the Paris-Granville line across the river about a hundred yards farther upstream. He was having to shout now to make himself heard above the bellowing of planes not far overhead, and suddenly once again there was the rending, tearing howl of the falling bombs. They hugged the soft earth, hearing, not seeing, the splitting crack of ruptured stone-work, but as they scrambled to their knees they saw the white core of water rising. A German passed them, head down, running. The railway bridge had gone.

Gille was the first on his feet. " Come on," he yelled. " There may be a chance," and almost before they had risen he was dashing for the embankment. The central arch of the bridge was down, a luminous pile of white stone six feet under the green-brown water, and the sleepers had gone too, but the end arches still held, precariously, one twisted buckled rail. " Let's go," Gille called, and as he scrambled for the embankment he heard Duchez's joyous chuckle. " *Mais bien sûr, mon Commandant—c'est le sang-froid.*" Gille got down, hugging the rail close to his belly, then let himself go, still clutching the rail, until his hands were supporting the full weight of his body. Hand over hand, he began to haul himself across.

The other two followed suit, " Third Fool " grimacing with pain as the combined weight of winter topcoat and machine-gun seared the metal into his palms. Twice a bullet whanged past, chipping sparks from the stonework; snipers on the river bank behind them were trying to pick them off, and as they dropped to the far side and pelted for dear life across the river meadows, the German machine-guns opened up like angry woodpeckers. At the far side, breathless and drenched with sweat, they stopped incredulously, then hugged one another, not speaking. They had made it.

They arrived outside the church of St. Étienne at four o'clock to find the whole city insane with joy. Posters of de Gaulle flapped on every wall still standing, and the Canadians were everywhere, grinning battle-worn men who had brought cigarettes and chocolate and chloride of lime for the dead. It seemed that everyone in the world who had survived had survived for this moment. There was little Dumis, drinking tea out of a Canadian's billy-can, and assuring him that even four years of hell had been worth it for this, and prominent above the crowd outside the Lycée Malherbe were Gille and the beaming stubbly grimed face of "Third Fool."

By now a crowd of many thousands had gathered in the dusty square, filthy and verminous, many in tears. Yellow dust still drifted over the city, but above, like a resurgence of hope, the sky was blue and cloudless. Tears streaming down his face, Gille raised the great shout "Vive Général de Gaulle" and slowly, prompt on four-thirty, fluttering in the slight breeze, the Cross of Lorraine slid towards the summit of the Lycée flagstaff, an undefeated flag raised by an undefeated network. Suddenly at that moment, all that they felt came bursting through, raggedly, at first, after four years servitude:

> *Allons, enfants de la patrie*
> *Le jour de gloire est arrivé . . .*

Then, more powerful than the guns, swelling from twenty thousand throats, the immortal thunder of the *Marseillaise*:

> *Aux armes—citoyens!*
> *Formez—vos battaillons!*
> *Aux armes—aux armes*
> *Pour-la—patrie! . . .*

The fate of the Wall had been the fate of Jericho; their triumph was complete.

And that was very nearly the end, except that three pioneers in the long struggle were still unaccounted for. About a week later, towards dusk on 15th July, hot, dusty and dog-tired, they were dismounting from their bicycles outside a farmhouse about seventy miles west of Paris—Girard, Dany and Moulines.

The farmer's wife, who reluctantly agreed to let them spend the night in the hayloft, warned them a battle was raging to the west: it would be madness to go farther. But Girard knew they must go on.

Early the previous day Colonel Personne, now military head of O.C.M., had summoned Girard from the country to his headquarters in the rue Forge Royale, Paris, and ordered him to cross the lines near St. Lô and establish contact with Renault and Dewavrin and the Civil Government in Bayeux. Girard asked permission to take Moulines and Dany with him, adding wryly that if all three got through, it would be a miracle. The southern suburbs of Caen had not yet fallen and the might of eight German Panzer divisions were now massed to halt the Allied break-through to Paris.

For four days, as the battle raged, they hung about the farm, not talking much, their nerves made raw by the terrifying symphony of the shells. On the fifth morning, Dany awoke in the hay to sunlight and deep silence then glancing down, she started laughing, nudging Moulines into wakefulness. She gurgled: " Look! "

On the first few nights they had all been resting level in the hay and only on the third night had the bulky Girard slid a little to one side. Now he was sunk so far below them in his bower that he might have been curled up in a separate bunk. With some of the old light-heartedness, they slithered down to him. " Hey, wake up, Monsieur Le Mince! Time for your reducing exercises! "

For the next few days there seemed to be a lull in the battle, and they made good going each day, riding through glinting river valleys and tall rustling forests of oak. Some days later, at nightfall, they reached a small stone village somewhere east of Le Mans and a man in blue denims stepped from the shadows with a pistol cocked to challenge them. He turned out to be the local Resistance leader, and ironically the one place he could recommend their spending the night was the cottage of the local collaborator, a woman in her fifties who swore, shifty-eyed, that not a scrap of food or drink remained in the house. The 200,000 francs that Colonel Personne had given them, now housed in Dany's handbag, might have been unnegotiable currency. Then the woman wept noisily on Dany's shoulder, claiming that next morning the Resistants were coming to shave her head, but Dany and the others went to bed racked more by hunger than pity. It wasn't until next morning that they found the café opposite open and were able to break their fast.

When they set out again, the going was tougher. The road was dusty and pot-holed, winding slowly uphill through wooded gorges, and soon the shells were screaming over them again as the great break-through of General Patton's Third Army gathered momentum. Then with a jolting, teeth-gritting jar, Dany's rear tyre went.

Precious minutes passed as she bent to mend the puncture, then they were riding for dear life, Girard's heavy frame streaming with sweat, coiled up until his chin almost nudged the handlebars. Five minutes, ten, with the barbaric wail of shells as background music, then the telltale jarring: Dany's tyre again. She was down in the grit, the sweat matting her hair in the sticky sunlight, and Moulines was shouting, " Ride on the rim, Dany, the fire's coming nearer." Dany went on until the job was done, but fifty yards on they heard from her again—a moan of anguish. " Marcel—my handbag! "

Girard felt his heart lurch. " Well? "

" All our money—I hung it on the back of the chair at breakfast. I must have left it there."

Girard closed his eyes in mute appeal. " This," he said softly, " is the end." Then to his horror, he saw Moulines swing his machine round, crouching low over the handlebars. " Jacques," he bellowed. " Come back." But the only answer was a distant " Don't worry. I'll get it," as Moulines went catapulting away down the hill like a toboggan down the Cresta Run. The earth shuddered with the guns now; a shell burst not 200 yards from where he rode.

Minutes passed and the guns pounded. Dany and Girard crouched miserably in the green underwater light of the trees. The agony of suspense was so strong now that neither of them felt like talking. Then the young count was back, riding cheerfully up the hill as if he did this every day of the week, the bag draped over his handlebars. They hugged him as if they had not seen one another for years.

By mid-afternoon they had headed off into the forests somewhere south and west of Mayenne. Once a band of Germans passed them, doubling through the pools of sunlight that dappled the beech trunks, but they had no time to worry about three grimy French stragglers wheeling bicycles. Suddenly they heard from Dany again: " Marcel! "

" What now? " said Girard wearily.

" We are in the Allied lines. Look at the cigarettes! "

" Explain," Girard ground out.

And Dany, with the wisdom of a woman who had known four years of privation, answered: " Only Allied soldiers could afford to throw away cigarettes half-smoked, *mon cher*. Look and see."

Girard bent to examine them and saw that she was right. He picked up a handful and saw that they *were* American cigarettes, all brands, before tossing them down again.

All except one whose trade name suggested that uncanny stroke of luck which Century had so often enjoyed. He lit that one, leaning against a tree in the sunlight, and smoked it to the end.

EPILOGUE

CENTURY NETWORK survives to-day as a memory of old glory and courage. In Caen and a few other towns along the Wall there is still an annual reunion in a café, a group resurrecting old fears and friendships over wine and black tobacco. But each year a few more faces are missing from the board because death or distance or the business of wringing a livelihood from a hard world has removed them from the scene.

Some of the survivors, in any case, live barely a cycle ride from the Wall, and the memories, all the year round, are inescapable.

The long Atlantic Wall is not very much of a Wall in these days. In the American sector, Utah Beach and the tawny crescent of Omaha retain a few, a very few, crumbling concrete structures to testify to Hitler's dream of sealing off Europe from Allied retribution. A few strongpoints likewise remain in the British sector near Ouistreham but the salt water is slowly rotting the last of the " Mulberries " at Arromanches. When the tide goes out at Port-en-Bessein, a few objects once more lethal than rocks lie rusting in the seaweed by the harbour wall —a steel picket, the uprights of a Belgian gate. But that is all. The gulls cry above the shingle and the grass and sand have crept in.

Only history can assess how many British and American lives were saved on D-Day by Century's vigil. A senior officer close to the planning once summed it up to me this way: " The Channel was a gulf and even the best aerial photography couldn't quite bridge it. It involved a bit of " hunching " in the interpretation and it lacked the range and mobility of the living eye. If you couldn't be there on the spot, seeing, the next best thing was to have eyes there doing it for you." So perhaps history's verdict will be that the eyes of Century missed little that was worth seeing. When it was all over, Major-General Walter Bedell Smith, SHAEF Chief of Staff, wrote warmly to de Gaulle's Minister of Information, Jacques Soustelle: " Without the networks of the French Resistance, the invasion would not have been possible." Eisenhower, too, added his tribute: in the field, he said, the work of units like Gille's had been worth fifteen divisions to him.

Glory is a small reward for those who died loving life, though Girard's agents won their full share of that. In the invasion sector alone, the thousand-odd survivors won, between them, more than 2,500 decorations and awards for valour. But their greatest reward has been the chance to live and ply their trades peacefully in the towns where most of them were born. Any visitor to Caen will find Dumis still keeping the principal garage, Arsène still the master plumber, Madame Vauclin among the most respected of the town's good wives. Both Dumis and Arsène, for their exploits, won the Croix de Guerre twice, but few of their neighbours know that.

Madame Vauclin, like big Jean Chateau who died recently, was made a Chevalier of the Legion of Honour, but the most prized of all her possessions is the citation she received from Lord Alanbrooke for the dispatch of twenty-two pigeons. She has framed that, and it occupies a place of honour in her sitting-room.

Meslin is dead. Two years after Caen was liberated, the strain and illness finally broke him, and he never lived to see the port that he loved rebuilt. Little Jeanne Verinaud works for the new Government engineer now, and the old Underwood typewriter that typed so many of Century's dispatches, though honourably retired, remains a treasured souvenir. Often, as she walks home in the evening, she chooses the route along the south bank of the river. It has been re-christened " Quay Eugène Meslin," and the blue enamel plaque is there for all to see.

Duchez, too, is dead, worn out by the rigours of his unforgettable and unorthodox war. He died a few years after Odette's return from Mauthausen in the autumn of 1945. Odette—now a Chevalier of the Legion of Honour—is still in Caen, running her own small business, but sometimes she finds it hard to believe that Duchez has gone. His portrait still grins from the dresser in the parlour, with the old lovable rascality, and for the benefit of his children the tokens of his courage are carefully preserved in a special drawer.

The Poles honoured him, the Americans awarded him the Medal of Freedom, the highest honour a civilian can attain, and the French gave him not only the Medal of the Resistance but the Croix de Guerre. It is the words of this last citation that Odette feels sum it all up best:

René Duchez, Commandant of the Deuxième Bureau of Sub-division M.1. A model of tenacity and Lorraine patriotism. For two years he relentlessly pursued the battle against the enemy, despite the sacrifice of his family and of all his worldly goods.

Thomas was reunited with his family at the war's end. Now married, with a small and lively son, christened Hubert, who shows signs of inheriting Papa's artistic talent, he has become a Government draughtsman, designing blueprints for rather more peaceful ends. Sometimes at week-ends, he sees Girard at the Gare Centrale, travelling back to Paris on Sunday, and, as always Girard slaps him on the back in passing and booms: "Ah! Thomas, *mon petit*, those maps were wonderful—wonderful." And Thomas feels just as bucked as he did in the old days.

Girard, of course, married Dany. They have built a small house on a hill north of Caen, looking out over a new city rising from the ruins, and Girard has installed a bowling alley and a rose garden and a tank of tropical fish, being more addicted to these pursuits, with the aid of a glass of wine, or to fishing with his gargantuan friend Wilfrid Torres, than spiriting top-secret plans from under the noses of the Gestapo. Ask him if he'd do it all again and he scowls broodingly at you

for a moment, before relaxing with a wink, and answering,
" Well, I *am* on the Reserve."

Sometimes, but not often, he sees Gille, for the advocate's
social life is busier than Girard can face up to these days. Gille
married Janine and entered politics, being now President of the
Council-General of Calvados, and were you to attend one of
his discreetly memorable dinner parties you would hardly
believe that your host once scaled a stone wall with the S.S.
baying at his heels or that your hostess was decorated for saving
the lives, under penalty of death, of sixty-two aviators.

Such thoughts would not really spring to mind on meeting
anyone in the Century saga. Certainly not if you saw Dr.
Sustendal on his way to visit a patient along the sea front at
Luc-sur-Mer, or met Maury or Farine or Mercader, business-
men all, or saw Cardron returning from the day's fishing at
Port-en-Bessein. With Moulines, perhaps, for although he is
happily married and a proud father, his old restless tempera-
ment has sent him crop-dusting in, of all places, Morocco. But
not with Colonel Personne (Monsieur Piette), one of the
wittiest speakers in the Chamber of Deputies, or with Renault,
that good and gentle man, who lives with his family in a little
villa high above the Mediterranean at Lisbon and has became
a successful writer on his own account.

And Dewavrin? It was he, after all, who began it, and with
him you are less sure. Now a banker, he has given up the
Army, though he still answers readily to the title " Colonel
Passy." As ever, he seems deceptively mild and scholarly, but
now and again, when controversy is in the air, the lips set in a
taut line, the blue eyes blaze, and all the old obstinacy shows
through, just as in the days when he fought to establish the
network in Normandy. But on one subject he *is* humble, and
that is when you pay tribute to his courage and vision in setting
in motion one of the greatest intelligence triumphs of the
war.

" No, no," he says, " it was them that you've got to write
about because *they* had the faith—very much like the Bible,
you know, and what Paul said to the Hebrews. He was talking
about Abraham and Noah and the others and he called faith

' the substance of things hoped for, the evidence of things not seen.' And he said this about them, too: ' These all died in faith, not having received the promises, but having seen them afar off, and were persuaded of them, and embraced them, and confessed that they were strangers and pilgrims on the earth.' "

APPENDIX

CAST OF PRINCIPAL CHARACTERS

ARSÈNE, FERNAND (*Auguste*), a Caen plumber, one of Century's earliest agents.

AUBIN, ROBERT (*Jonquet*), an electricity board inspector, head of Century's Argentan cell and chief of the Orne department of Normandy.

AUDIBERT, GENERAL, in charge of Secret Army units at Rennes and Angers.

AUGÉ, JEAN, the stationmaster at Caen, who supplied details of rail traffic.

AUSTIN, JOHN L., peacetime Oxford don who headed the "Martians" (Theatre Intelligence Section, G.H.Q., Home Forces), in London.

BACQUE, ROBERT, who succeeded Oliver Courtaud as chief of C.N.D.'s "Operations" transmissions branch in Paris.

BECKER, COLONEL (*Baron*), ex-Army officer who headed the Secret Army unit for Le Mans.

BERESNIKOFF, ALEX (*Corvisart*), the agent who embarked on a joint secret mission to the Normandy coast in August, 1940.

BERNARD, HELMUT, chief of the Caen Gestapo.

BERTHELOT, MARCEL (*Lavoisier*), ex-diplomat who was head of Century network and deputy to Colonel Touny in the Organisation Civile et Militaire, Paris.

BERTHELOT, PAUL, proprietor of the Café des Touristes, Caen.

BOITARD, JANINE, the wine-merchant's daughter who worked for Century in Caen.

BOLLAERT, ÉMILE, de Gaulle's political adviser in France from 1943.

BRIÈRE, LUCIEN, head of the *Milice* detachment in Caen.

BROSSOLETTE, PIERRE, the journalist who planned the mass uprising in France until his arrest in February, 1944.

CAILLET, HENRI, assistant to the Secretary-General of the *Mairie* at Caen, in charge of identity and ration cards.

CAILLET, ALICE, his wife, who also worked at the *Mairie*.

CARDRON, LÉON, the ex-trawler skipper who worked for Century in Port-en-Bessein.

CHATEAU, JEAN, an electricity board inspector who organised many agents in the Caen area.

CHATEAU, ALBERTINE, his wife, another Century agent.

COMBY, PIERRE, the Caen coal merchant who worked for Century as head of Normandy Peat-Cutters Inc.

CORBASSON, LT.-COLONEL GASTON, head of the 3rd Bureau for Calvados, Normandy, who selected targets for sabotage in the Caen area.

COURTAUD, OLIVIER, radio operator who aided Renault's escape from France in June, 1942, later head of C.N.D.'s " Operations" transmissions in Paris.

DANSEY, SIR CLAUDE, the wartime Deputy Director of M.I.6. in London.

" DANY " (Denise Fernande Geninatti-Banck), secretary and shadow of Marcel Girard and liaison agent between Paris and the provinces.

DE BEAUFORT, ALAIN, Alex Tanguy's deputy at Lorient, Brittany.

DE LA SAUSSAYE, LAMOUREUX, head of the Century-Secret Army units in the Sarthe department of Maine.

DELATTRE, ROBERT, Gilbert Renault's chief personal radio officer until his arrest in May, 1942.

DELESTRAINT, GENERAL (*Vidal*), appointed as first chief of the Secret Army by General de Gaulle.

DE SAINT-DENIS, HENRI, an ironmonger working for Century in Port-en-Bessein.

DESCHAMBRES, ROGER the plumber who succeeded René Duchez as head of part-time agents in the Caen area.

DEWAVRIN, ANDRÉ (*Colonel Passy*), chief of the Free French Intelligence Service in London.

DOUIN, ROBERT, a sculptor working for Century in Caen.

DUCHEZ, RENÉ, the Caen house-painter in charge of all part-time agents for the area.

DUCHEZ, ODETTE, his wife, in charge of Century's false identity paper service.

DUCLOS, MAURICE (*Saint-Jacques*), the ex-stockbroker who, with Alex Beresnikoff, undertook the first secret mission to Normandy in August, 1940, and later headed de Gaulle's " Action " section in London.

DUMIS, LÉON, the ex-garage proprietor who worked for Century-Caen.

FARINE, ANDRÉ, ex-sailor and café proprietor who worked for Century above Omaha Beach.

FAURE, FRANÇOIS, the deputy head of Renault's Confrérie Notre-Dame (C.N.D.) in Paris until his arrest in May, 1942.

FAURE, PIERRE, head of the Premier Bureau for the Caen area.

FRANCK, ADOLPHE, ex-schoolmaster from Lorraine working at the Prefecture, St. Lô, in charge of Century-St. Lô.

GILLE, LÉONARD (*Marie*), peacetime advocate who was military deputy to Eugène Meslin in Caen and became head of Century-Secret Army personnel in Caen after D-Day.

GIRARD, MARCEL (*Moreau, Malherbe*), western regional organiser for Century and Secret Army chief for 14 departments of Normandy, Brittany, Poitou, Anjou and Maine.

GRESSELIN, YVES, the Cherbourg grocer in charge of all Century-Secret Army agents for the area.

HARIVEL, PIERRE, an insurance agent, one of Meslin's deputies and liaison agents for the Caen area.

HERVÉ, ALBERT, one of Brière's *Milice* agents in Caen.

HIMBERT, MAURICE (*Legrand*), the motor-cycle mechanic who acted as Century's courier between Caen and Paris.

HOËFA, KARL, the German Port Commandant for the Caen area.

JACQUEMIN, LUCIEN, a cement executive, in charge of Century-Le Havre.

JOURDAN, ALEXANDER, in charge of the Service Maritime at the Government Engineer's office, Caen, and Robert Thomas's deputy in Century's cartographic service.

JOUVEL, JEAN, a cartographer working with Robert Thomas in Caen.

JULITTE, GUY, chief radio consultant for the Confrérie Notre Dame in Paris until February, 1942.

KASKOREFF, ROBERT (*Gertal*), deputy to Colonel Corbasson in Caen, who later supervised the Secret Army's 3rd Bureau activities in Normandy from Paris.

KELLER, BAULEITER ADALBERT, who succeeded Hugo Schnedderer as Todt Organisation Army liaison officer in Caen.

LEBLOND, ROGER, a police inspector working for Century in Caen.

LE CROM-HUBERT, MADAME, who sheltered Gilbert Renault's family at Baud in Brittany until June, 1942.

LOMENECH, LT. DANIEL, R.N.V.R., the Breton skipper of the British trawler N 51.

MANSION, JACQUES, the first of de Gaulle's agents to found a network in Brittany.

MANUEL, ANDRÉ, deputy chief of the Free French Intelligence Service, London.

MARASSE, GENERAL ROBERT (*Surlaut*), military adviser for Secret Army units in Normandy and Brittany.

MARIGNY, HENRI, a Caen bookseller working as an agent at Ouistreham.

MASSERON, ANDRÉ, the pork butcher of Bretteville-sur-Laize who reported on airfield defences in the Caen area.

MAUGER, PAUL, a young liaison agent of the C.N.D. in Paris, chosen to bring the plan of the Atlantic Wall to London.

MAYORAZ, PIERRE, the Swiss proprietor whose Hotel de Rouen, Caen, was both letter-box and refuge for Century agents.

MENGUY, a cartographer working with Robert Thomas in Caen.

MERCADER, GEORGES, a bicycle merchant, head of Century-Bayeux.

MESLIN, EUGÈNE (*Morvain*), the Government engineer for the Caen area; head of all Secret Army-Century agents between Caen and Cherbourg.

MICHEL, GILBERT, a cement contractor working for Century in Caen and sometimes Cherbourg.

MOULIN, JEAN, de Gaulle's political representative on the National Council of the Resistance in Paris.

" MOULINES, JACQUES " (Jacques Bertin, Comte de la Hautière), Marcel Girard's chief field organiser for the Cherbourg area.

PELLETIER, JEAN, head of the C.N.D.'s micro-film unit in Paris until May, 1942.

PETIT, MAX, Gilbert Renault's deputy, acting head of the C.N.D. in Paris from June to October, 1942.

PIETTE, JACQUES (*Colonel Personne, Colonel Nobody*), an intelligence expert for the Organisation Civile et Militaire in Paris and later O.C.M.'s military head.

POITEVIN, JOSEPH, a ship's carpenter working for Century in Port-en-Bessein.

POITEVIN, ARTHUR, his cousin, a blind music-master working in Port-en-Bessein and Bayeux.

PROUVOST, ERNST, an official of the French postal service who gave undercover facilities to Century's dispatches.

RENAULT, GILBERT (*Colonel Rémy*). Also known as Watteau, Morin, Recordier, Jean-Luc, Raymond and Roulier. The founder and chief of the Confrérie Notre-Dame (C.N.D.), Paris, central transmission agency for all French networks.

RENAULT, EDITH, his wife.

RENAULT, JEAN-CLAUDE, his eleven-year-old son.

RENAULT, CATHERINE and CÉCILE, his daughters.

RENAULT, MICHEL, his youngest son, aged eighteen months.

RENAULT, MAISIE AND ISABELLE, Gilbert's sisters, occupying their brother's old apartment in the Avenue de la Motte Picquet, Paris.

RIVALIN, RICHARD, former medical student working as an O.C.M. Intelligence expert in Paris.

ROBINEAU, EMMANUEL, head of Marcel Girard's 4th Bureau, organising reception teams and arms dumps in the Caen area.

SCHNEDDERER, BAULEITER HUGO, Army liaison officer for the Todt Organisation, Caen.

SCHULTZ, ALOYSE, the Alsatian radio store proprietor of Caen.

SUBSOL, chief radio operator for the Paris C.N.D. during March, 1942.

SUSTENDAL, DR. JACQUES, the country doctor of Luc-sur-Mer, Calvados, who worked for Century along the Atlantic Wall.

TANGUY, ALEX, Gilbert Renault's chief agent in Lorient, Brittany.

THOMAS, ROBERT, an ex-garage mechanic who ran Century's cartographic service in Caen.

THOMAS, LOUIS (*Papa*), Robert's father, who worked for Eugène Meslin in the Dept. of Roads and Bridges, Caen.

THOMAS, LOUISE (*Mama*), mother of Robert Thomas.

THOMAS, MADELEINE, Robert's sister who worked for the Chief of Police at Trouville.

THOMAS, MARTHE, Robert's sister, who worked in the Prefecture at Caen.

THOMAS, JEANNE, Robert's youngest sister, who worked in Eugène Meslin's office at Caen.

THOMINE, GEORGES, a fisherman working for Century in Port-en-Bessein.

TILLIER, JEAN, Gilbert Renault's chief assistant in Paris from October, 1942; later head of C.N.D.'s " Intelligence " transmissions branch.

TORRES, WILFRID, harbour works contractor, Century's security officer in Caen.

TOUNY, COL. ALFRED, head of the Organisation Civile et Militaire (O.C.M.) in Paris.

VAUCLIN, RENÉ, a tiler working for Century in Caen.

VAUCLIN, OLGVIE (*Madame Marthe*), his wife.

VERINAUD, JEANNE, secretary to Eugène Meslin in Caen.

YEO-THOMAS, WING-COMMANDER F. F. E., G.C. (*The White Rabbit, Shelley*), a British agent of Special Operations Executive (" F " Section) working with Pierre Brossolette to organise the Secret Army in France.

YEQUEL, LOUIS, the skipper of the *Deux Anges* on her voyages from Pont-Aven.